Bowling with a Crystal Ball

To Maya, Shira, and Anat,
Who make it all worthwhile

Bowling with a Crystal Ball

How to predict technology trends, create disruptive implementations and navigate them through industry

Yoram Solomon

2007

Bowling with a Crystal Ball

Table of Contents

Acknowledgements

I owe a debt of gratitude to many people. I did not write **Bowling with a Crystal Ball** in a vacuum. Quite a few friends helped me in the process, but beyond that, the experience I will convey through these pages has the fingerprints of many people I am privileged to know and would like to thank. Throughout my professional life, I learned from my successes, I learned from my mistakes, but mostly I learned from *people*.

In 1998, I moved from Israel to the Silicon Valley in California. I did not have the experience required for an executive position in the high-tech industry. Two people I am honored to call friends mentored me through the process, tolerating my inexperience, offering me advice, and patiently waiting for me to absorb and implement. The first is Ray Shook, the founder and chief executive of Voyager, a small Silicon Valley wireless engineering company, who believed in me enough to hire me for my first US position as vice president of marketing. Ray has a very rich executive experience that began with a position as a senior Navy officer and continued through several executive-level positions in public companies, until he finally started his own company, Voyager. Only now can I appreciate the trust he had in me in turning Voyager around from an engineering company to a product company, eventually selling it to PCTEL in early 2000.

My second mentor was Mark Wilson. PCTEL hired Mark as the vice president of marketing. He became my boss and—more importantly—my mentor there. Mark taught me the basics of *leadership through influence*, cross-functional teams, pragmatic marketing, and becoming a credible member of the executive leadership team. Mark was patient, too, through my growth in PCTEL, and remained a close friend after my departure from PCTEL.

Having a good technology or product is not enough. You need to navigate it through the industry, as you will read in this book. I joined Texas Instruments' (TI) wireless LAN group in beautiful Santa Rosa, California, owning some political skills required to drive products through the standards-based industry. In Santa Rosa, I learned from one of the best industry "politicians"—Bill Carney. Our industry strategy discussions helped me move to a new level in my ability to influence industries. At times, we wished we would end up on opposite sides of an industry conflict, and for some time after Bill left TI, we did.

There are many ways to project technology trends. Numerous articles are available, and market research firms publish periodic projections. Nothing contributes to the understanding of a fast-growing industry like the interviews I was so fortunate to have with the evangelists, pioneers, and revolutionaries of those industries. The technology industry is not very old. The modern semiconductor industry started in 1960. The hard disk drive industry started in the late 1950s. The Internet was launched in 1969. Many of the people who were there then are still around as authoritative driving forces. I had unique opportunities to interview some of them. Bob Doering is a *senior fellow* at Texas Instruments and one of two US representatives to the International Roadmap Committee, the governing body of the International Technology Roadmap for Semiconductors (ITRS) organization. He offered me his insights into the semiconductor roadmap and confirmed my suspicion that the semiconductor roadmap will stay on the trajectory of Moore's law when he started our interview with, "We are not *predicting* the future; we already know what it is. We are simply *making it happen*." Ed Grochowski is the executive director of IDEMA, the International Disk Drive Equipment and Material Association. Formerly with IBM and Hitachi, Ed is one of the most knowledgeable people in the hard disk drive and storage industries. In our interview, he overwhelmed me with his ability to move fifty years back and ten years forward, leaving my head spinning. For the *Digital Signal Processing* section of the book, I met with Gene Frantz, the only *principal fellow* at Texas Instruments, the highest technical ladder rank in the company, and a relentless visionary. The meeting with Gene was among the most amazing ones of my professional life. It helped me understand the deep impact that DSPs have on our everyday life.

I also wish to extend special thanks to TI's marketing communications team. Tracy Wright, Marisa Speziale, and Paul Gaither helped me during their free time to come up with names, but most of all I want to thank Renee Fancher for her continuous support and personal involvement with my initial work that resulted in this book. Writing the book was a humbling experience, especially throughout the editing process. I would like to thank Sarah Southerland, the Editorial Products Manager at BookSurge, and the excellent team of editors: Gail Chadwick, Vivian E. Rogers, and Ronald L. Donaghe, who added so much value to this book and made it a learning process for me.

Many people impacted my work, my experiences, my learnings, and the writing of this book. Every one of those people made a difference in the way I think, and I would like to thank them all. They are Mike Foley, Frank Hanzlik, Deepak Kamlani, Jim Zyren, Michael Stich, Doug Rasor, Paul Struhsaker, Amit Haller, Clark Hise, Bill Krenik, Rick Wietfeldt, Don Shaver, Ted McGehee, Larry Bassuk, Jeff Ravencraft, Bob Koppel, Derek Obata, Gal Hasson, and Carl Panasik. More than all, I have to thank Clayton Christensen, Geoffrey Moore, and Michael McGrath for inspiring me with their ground-breaking work.

Finally, I could not have written this book without the support of my wife Anat and my daughters Maya and Shira, who give me my perspective in life every day. With the same breath, I want to thank Moshe and Margalit Rotman, my in-laws, for their continuing support ever since I became a member of their family. I would also like to thank my mother for inspiring me through her courageous battle with cancer, a battle she lost just as I completed writing this book.

Introduction

When I started writing this book, I had a general idea of what I wanted to write about. I felt very passionately that the fast-moving technology trends were moving at a constant rate and were more predictable than generally believed. I was determined to find out why. I have to admit, I am a great follower of Clayton Christensen's work on disruptive technologies, and that has guided me in my pursuit to understand the impact of those technologies on consumer markets, and specifically the $1.3 trillion electronic product market. It was not until I sat through a lecture by Michael Raynor, Christensen's co-author of *The Innovator's Solution*, that I realized how my book is different.

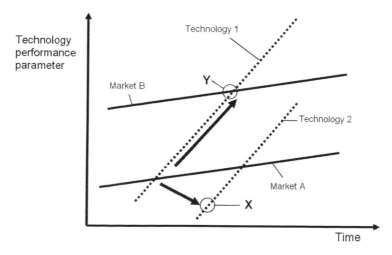

Figure 1—Where to look for disruptions

Christensen (*The Innovator's Dilemma, The Innovator's Solution, Seeing What's Next*) takes a market (Market A), once disrupted or created by a technology (Technology 1), and looks for the next technology (Technology 2) that will disrupt it next by adding a new dimension of value, and therefore will look for the new disruption at Point X.

Bowling with a Crystal Ball focuses on the technologies themselves, which have disrupted and will disrupt markets, and follows them to the point of disrupting another market. As the investment in those technologies continues, regardless of the fact that the improvements in those technologies offer no real value-add to the markets they serve, they look for other markets to disrupt. I follow the technologies, and not the markets they disrupt. I look for the next market (Market B) vulnerable to disruption by the same technology (Technology 1) that disrupted Market A. I will look for new disruptions at Point Y.

There is no right and wrong here. Both disruptions will occur. A new technology will disrupt Market A, while the "old" technology will go on to disrupt Market B.

I proved my theory through interviews of the key innovators in different high-tech industries—those technologies do progress at a constant rate, and there is a reason for that!

I gained an interesting insight through this research. The initial investment in those technologies, be it the semiconductors or the hard disk drives, was fueled by the electronics product market. However, those technologies, or markets, then took on a life of their own and went on to disrupt those same markets that gave birth to them. Those technologies then went on to disrupt other markets.

This book is not about theory. This is a practical book about finding where disruptions are likely to occur, identifying those potential disruptions, creating business opportunities around them, and turning them into reality. This book is a "how to" manual for visionaries.

Market disruptions create opportunities. The $1.3 trillion electronic product market is a hotbed for them. Some can reach billions of dollars, and some "only" hundreds of millions of dollars. One of the key underlying technologies that enable the growth of the electronic products market is the semiconductor component market, a $250 billion market by itself. *Bowling with a Crystal Ball* will help you identify opportunities, big and small, that are close to your line of business, enabling your company or business unit to experience the type of growth possible only when discontinuities are involved.

Is it enough? I have been involved in many industry activities, ranging from participating in standard creation, to billion-dollar company alliances, without which none of those opportunities could turn into revenue and profits. I decided to include all three components in this book: the ability to predict the key technological trends, the ability to find the opportunities for those technologies to disrupt markets, and finally the actions you need to take to turn those opportunities into success stories.

Predicting the future

On April 19, 1965, *Electronics* magazine published a four-page article, written by the director of the Fairchild semiconductor research and development laboratories. The article, "Cramming more components onto integrated circuits," was subtitled "With unit cost falling as the number of components per circuit rises, by 1975 economics may dictate squeezing as many as 65,000 components on a single silicon chip." This article would turn out to be one of the most visionary technology papers ever written. Dr. Gordon E. Moore, the author, left Fairchild in 1968 with Bob Noyce to create the largest semiconductor company in the world today, Intel. In the decades that followed, adherents referred to the futuristic view presented in that article as "Moore's law."

I was born in the same year, 1965, and was three months old when *Electronics* published this article. Of course, at the time, I was not as aware of the importance of that article as I am today. I was busy with other things, more existential and primitive. As I am writing this book in 2006, a 12-inch silicon wafer, manufactured with a 90-nanometer CMOS process, can hold 25.7 billion logical gates and a single $25mm^2$ integrated circuit chip can hold more than three million logical gates. All of a sudden, Moore's predictions seem utterly remote and conservative, but back in 1965, Moore's paper was one of the most visionary ever written.

We need to understand the background for Moore's article. It was only seven years earlier, in 1958, when Jack Kilby of Texas Instruments invented the first integrated circuit. That crude-looking device earned Kilby the Noble Prize in Physics in 2000. In his article, Moore writes, "[A]t present, it [minimum cost] is reached when 50 components are used per circuit." Then he goes on to project that in 1970, the minimum cost would be achieved with 1,000 components, and in 1975, that minimum would be 65,000. He was being somewhat held back by his own imagination when he stated, "I believe that such a large circuit can be built on a single wafer."

Can we really predict the future? The answer is no. And, yes. Nobody (well, at least nobody I know) can predict the future *accurately*. However, you will be surprised how close to reality you can really get if you ask the right questions, and more importantly—if you do not let your imagination be an obstacle. The biggest problem we have is that we limit ourselves with our own "built-in" conservatism and slow rate of adjustment. It is hard for us to envision things that are wildly different from what surrounds us now.

One day in 2004, as part of a project, I focused on predicting the capacity of hard disk drives. Specifically, I was interested in the capacity expected by 2008. To accomplish that, I dug out historical data on capacities of hard disk drives from the 1990s through 2004. I found that the capacity of hard disk drives grows at a rate that is close to 104% every year. With the "sweet spot"[1] being 160 gigabytes of storage in 2004,[2] and with the "sweet spot" being 540 megabytes in 1996—this meant that the "sweet spot" of hard disk drive capacity in 2008 will be 2,750 gigabytes, just short of 3 terabytes. Quite an amazing prediction, is it not?

Then I turned to ask a few of my colleagues what they thought about the number. The common answer, although disappointing, was not surprising. Very consistently, they did not believe it. While understanding the rationale behind the number, they would rather have believed that the hard disk drive capacity curve would "level off" at some point between now and then.[3] It did not matter that the graph was actually consistent since the 1970s, nor did it matter that the hard disk drive companies were continuing in their endless quest to manufacture cheaper, smaller, less power-consuming hard disk drives, always with greater capacity. All they asked, repeatedly, was "Why would anyone need such a big hard disk drive?" To me, the right question to ask would have been, "What can I do with 2.75 terabytes of storage that could never be done with less?" Can you hear the cash register bell ringing already? This book will attempt to instill that discipline in its first part.

Inventing the future

In the late 1990s, the innovators at Apple®[4] Computers conducted a similar analysis. Their analysis showed that in 2001 there would be a hard disk drive that would fit into a device smaller than a cigarette pack, would be capable of holding 1,000 CD-quality, compressed songs,[5] and would be able to run off a small battery for more than eight hours. They invented the iPod®[6], which was launched in October 2001. During the forth quarter of 2003, Apple had sold over 200,000 iPods. By December 16, 2004, Apple had sold 10 million iPods. In the second quarter of 2006 alone Apple reported selling over 8.5 million iPods. With a retail price between $200 and $300, Apple successfully created a market that generated over $6 billion in annual revenue for themselves in less than three years.

The conclusion is that limiting our imagination will limit our ability to predict the future and, more importantly, to act and capitalize on it. What would you say if I asked you how thick a piece of paper would be when folded fifty times? Most people I asked thought it would be as thick as a telephone book. The real answer is that a piece of regular printer paper, folded fifty times, would be as thick as almost the distance between the earth and the sun.[7] Finding it hard to believe? Well, it's true.

We enjoy hearing market-disruption success stories but we associate them with pure luck when, in reality, they are based on a somewhat predictable future. More than everything, they rely on believing that technological trends will continue at the same rates. Perhaps *Inventing the Future* will help change the way we think about those future trends. Instead of challenging their validity, we need to assume they will continue as they have in the past and seek the opportunities that they create. Instead of asking, "*Will* this really happen?" we need to ask, "What can I do *when* it happens?" When I adopted that way of thinking, I came up with many innovative and disruptive ideas. Some of them are still unfolding while others have already unfolded and I discuss them here in detail.

The value of the ability to predict the future and act on it, delivering products to the market ahead of one's competitors, has significant Return on Investment (ROI) implications, due to an advantageous market share position gained by being first to market.

Influencing the future

So does the ability to predict the future rely solely on the ability to draw technology trend lines? If that were the case, there would be a lot more hi-tech billionaires. It's not as simple as that. We must combine our ability to predict a future based on those technological trend curves with the understanding of the forces affecting the market into which a new product is about to enter and our ability to carefully design a plan that capitalizes on those trends.

However, even *that* is not enough. The *predictable* future that we can project using the technology trend lines can propose only a *plausible* future, but not necessarily an *inevitable* one. The predicted future is far from being inevitable. That is the bad news. The good news is that we can actually *influence* the future. The right people need to be in the right place at the right time for technologies to succeed.

It was the existence of a little-known evangelist in Microsoft by the name of Steve Powers who supported the FireWire®[8] connectivity standard and assured that Windows®[9] 98 supported this interface, helping create a market for FireWire components in digital camcorders, personal computers, television sets, and other products. On the other hand, late in 1998, when Intel realized that USB® 1.1[10] was "running out of steam,"[11] they turned to Apple,[12] wishing to adopt FireWire[13] into the PC and peripheral market. Apple, deciding to capitalize on its intellectual property and patent portfolio at the time, asked Intel for steep royalties for such implementation. Needless to say, this discussion did not go anywhere. Intel, in turn, announced the formation of the USB 2.0 promoters group in February of 1999, only four months later. The rate specified for USB 2.0 was 480 Mbps.

In my opinion, that rate was selected not as a 40 times improvement over USB 1.1, but rather as a 20% improvement over FireWire, initiating the demise of FireWire as a connectivity technology. Only two years later, Apple introduced the iPod with two interfaces—USB and FireWire. In 2005, Apple decided to drop FireWire, their own developed interface, and left USB 2.0 as the only interface between the iPod and personal computers, acknowledging the market adoption success of USB and the rejection of FireWire. Many still believe that FireWire is a better connectivity technology than USB. It offers better performance and better quality of service to support high-quality streaming media. FireWire also has a peer-to-peer topology, easily supported by non-PC-centric products.

This is one of the numerous examples used in this book to demonstrate that pure technological (and thus economical) superiority is not enough for a technology or product to win in the marketplace. It will take social interactions, continuous nurturing, plenty of politics, and "the right people in the right place at the right time" to make this happen. The ability to influence the future and make the right decisions down the road is what causes disruptive innovations to succeed. The following simple diagram illustrates the not-so-obvious way to get from the technology trend as predicted to the plausible (and favorable) future sought:

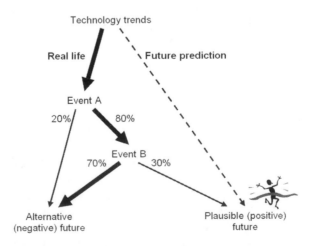

Figure 2—From technology trends to plausible future

The dashed line describes the theoretical path from the technological trend prediction directly to the plausible future. This future reflects "what *can* happen." However, in reality, many events will happen between the starting point and the finish line, some of which can cripple the possibility beyond repair of the plausible future from happening. This diagram illustrates a high-probability path with a wide arrow while a narrow one illustrates a low-probability path. The events A and B can represent many different possible scenarios, such as the infamous call between Intel and Apple, or the existence of Steve Powers in Microsoft's core driver group. In the hypothetical diagram above, event A has an 80% probability of leading in the direction of the favorable future (although not guaranteeing getting there), and only a 20% probability of leading to a future in which the predicted product or technology will fail. Event B, on the other hand, has only a 30% probability for success of the new technology, and a 70% failure from this junction.

Overall, in this diagram, the success of the technology (the plausible future) has a probability of only 24%.[14] In reality, the probability of reaching a plausible future is typically lower than that. A successful path from prediction to the *plausible* future cannot be guaranteed. Navigate this dangerous and treacherous path very carefully. This book will help you identify those events, and show strategies of influencing those junctions to assure that every junction keeps leading to our favorable future and the probability of getting there significantly improves.

Bowling with a crystal ball

Some time ago, I prepared a series of lectures for Texas Instruments' executive education program on strategic marketing topics. It allowed me to convert my passion for topics such as *disruptive technologies, predicting the future, influencing industry and standards,* and others into a series of lectures called "The Competitive Toolkit." Combined with many technological position articles that I wrote on various topics and technologies, it did not take long before I decided to take the next step and write this book. I have written it to help strategists and risk-takers in technology companies understand how to implement the process of predicting the future and the actions required to influence it in a direction that will make their companies or businesses "unfairly" successful. I wrote *Bowling with a Crystal Ball* for people looking for *the next big thing,* people who are looking for opportunities that are four years (or more) out.

In this journey, I included my insights from multiple different technologies that I have witnessed firsthand, and interviewed people who, whether they knew it or not, had a significant impact on the success or failure of those technologies. Some of those achieved dramatic success, and some ended up as miserable failures. I learned from all of them. I also included my experience in facilitating strategic planning processes that allowed companies to predict the future with a degree of accuracy, and to influence the future in a way that helped companies become competitive in the new markets predicted.

Mostly against company beliefs, I was always an industry evangelist. Many times, I managed to influence the direction in which an industry organization was going so that the new direction became more favorable to the company for which I worked. I met with many senior managers in market-making companies to reach "back-door agreements" that led to significant successes. I never overlooked the personal aspect of the industry, and harnessed it to achieve success.

In this book, I will take you through the three steps of creating successful and sustainable disruptive implementations and products: *predicting* the future, *inventing* the future, and *influencing* the future.

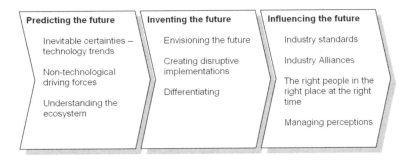

Figure 3—Predicting, inventing and influencing the future

The structure of the book follows these three steps. The first part addresses the process of predicting the future, the second part suggests how to turn those predictions into disruptive and competitive offerings, and the third part shows how to influence the future enabling those competitive offerings to become and remain, well, competitive.

Part 1 discusses techniques to predict the future. Those techniques will be based on understanding technology trends (which I will refer to as "inevitable certainties"), as well as the other underlying driving forces that will affect the technology future, although not as fast as technology. The technology trend predictions offered in Part 1 will be very valuable when you decide to predict your own market's future, and will serve as an excellent tool to understand those inevitable certainties.

Part 2 starts with the process of developing disruptive implementations that will change the marketplace and create new markets where none existed before. Opportunities surface where technological trends intersect with consumption trends. The cellular phone disruption emerged at the intersection of wireless technology and the social trend of mobility in the voice communications market. The iPod disruption materialized at the intersection of hard disk drive technology and the trend of personalization in the music player market. Part 2 includes a discussion of past and present trends that, when not implemented in a market, offer significant disruptive opportunities. Part 2 also addresses the importance of understanding the ecosystem in which the technology will exist.

Technologies and products do not exist in a vacuum, but rather alongside other forces in that ecosystem. Once the future is predicted and a competitive offering is invented (in concept, at least), it is time to create a favorable environment for those products and markets, and this is what Part 3 is about. Those technologies cannot have such an impact by themselves, and they require significant industry support. You must navigate through this minefield called *industry*, and make sure you take every turn in a way that gets you closer to the future you seek. More often than not, you will get only one chance to fix the outcome if you have taken a wrong step. Throughout my career, I managed to influence the development of industries, as well as affect their dynamics.

You need to remember that people, for the most part, determine the success or failure of new and disruptive products. The right people have to be at the right place at the right time, and believe the right things about your products and everything to do with them. This will not happen by itself—you have the ability to influence it. The tools described in Part 3 will include understanding and influencing industry standards, interacting with market-makers, and creating the right perception and atmosphere to make your offering competitive and sustainable.

Bowling with a Crystal Ball focuses on the $1.3 trillion electronic product market. It further focuses on the *consumer electronics, personal computer,* and *cellular phone* markets for products and related services. Those markets are huge in nature, each accounting for annual revenue of hundreds of billions of dollars. However, the concepts in this book are applicable to other markets, technology-related as well as non-technological, consumer-oriented as well as others. When you read this book, have a market in mind, and translate the examples given from the electronic product market into your market of interest.

All the information I provided in this book, including my personal experiences, is available in the public domain. Nothing here is confidential. I might have saved you a lot of time finding this information independently, but you could have reached it yourself. Some examples that would have been perfect to include in this book as proof, from technology prediction to the creation of industry organizations, were not included as they are still in an early, confidential phase.

Finally, I hope that my passion for strategy, disruptive technologies, future prediction, understanding the dynamics of industries, and influencing them will somehow come to live through these pages. Most of all, I hope you will enjoy reading this book as much as I enjoyed writing it.

---

[1] See Chapter 5 for an explanation of the concept of "sweet spot."

[2] A 160GB internal hard drive was offered at a retail price of $250 in 2004.

[3] If you think about it, and given that the trend has not changed since the 1970s, the probability of the trend curve leveling off in the next four years is much lower than the probability that it will stay straight.

[4] Apple is a registered trademark of Apple Inc.

[5] A typical MP3-compressed song requires approximately 4MB of disk storage. The first iPod released had a hard disk drive with over 4GB of capacity.

[6] iPod is a registered trademark of Apple Inc.

[7] Folding a piece of paper 50 times would have 2^{50} times the thickness of a single sheet of paper. The thickness of a piece of paper multiplied by 2^{50} would be over 62 million miles. The distance between the Earth and the sun is 93 million miles. Folding that piece of paper once more (51 times) – makes its thickness more than that distance.

[8] Also known as iLink® or IEEE 1394. FireWire is a registered trademark of Apple Inc. iLink is a registered trademark of Sony.

[9] Windows is a trademark of Microsoft Corporation.

[10] USB stands for Universal Serial Bus, used to connect personal computers and their peripherals. The USB Promoters Group and USB Implementers Forum, mostly driven by Intel, drive it.

[11] The data rate of USB 1.1, also known as "USB Full Speed," was limited to 12Mbps (million bits per second).

[12] Apple was the key patent holder on the FireWire technology.

[13] The specified data rate for IEEE 1394 was 400Mbps, more than 30 times faster than USB 1.1.

[14] An 80% probability of event A times a 30% probability of event B.

Part 1
Predicting The Future

Chapter 1
The Semiconductor Technology Roadmap

This book focuses on turning disruptive implementations into revenue generators. Before we go to the end, though, I wish to discuss the process. *Value* generates revenue. In order for products or service to generate revenue, they have to first generate value to a significant enough customer base on a consistent basis. Sometimes products generate *perceived* value that turns out to be fictitious or irrelevant, but in any case, not sustainable. I am not alluding to companies that try to deceive customers, but rather to companies that *think* the product or service they are offering will actually create value when, in reality, after the initial adoption period, they have not created any meaningful added value.

In the following chapters, I will give a few examples. One of them will be PCTEL's soft *internal* DSL modem. While PCTEL failed to generate revenue with this product, a competing company, namely Texas Instruments, managed to generate some. This revenue stream, however, did not last long, and did not cover the initial development costs. After supplying the initial demand (which was a significant few hundreds of thousands of units), the demand dried up. A similar story appears later in this book about my own start-up company in Israel, Solram Electronics. After I developed an Internet telephony adapter and sold quite a few products (thus generating initial revenue), the demand dried up.

The above are examples of products that while initially causing both suppliers and buyers to perceive value in them, eventually turned out to show there was no real value. Both seemed to have had great potential to be disruptive. For the purpose of the following discussion, I will only focus on identifying opportunities for products and services that create real and sustainable value to the buyers.

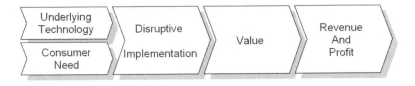

Figure 4—The value-creation chain

In the value-creation chain (not the classical value-chain), one building block is identified as the *disruptive implementation*. Clayton Christensen[15] discusses a somewhat similar term—*disruptive technology*. To me, the underlying technology is predictable (although fast moving). What makes it disruptive is the *implementation* of that technology into consumption areas that did not use it before. Therefore, it is the *implementation* that is disruptive, not the *technology* itself. One of the examples I often use in lectures is the cellular phone. There is nothing *technologically disruptive* in the phone itself. The *wireless* technology used in the cellular phone is a technology that developed linearly over a long period, long before the introduction or conception of the first cellular phone. There is no doubt that this technology has improved dramatically over time, but in no way was there a discontinuity in that development—at least nothing that all of a sudden gave birth to the cellular phone. It is the telephone industry, or the demand for telephony services, that changed and demanded mobility. The wireless technology "spilled over" to a consumer need (telephony), where it never existed before. That *implementation* was the real nature of the disruption. This is why I prefer to discuss *disruptive implementations* rather than *disruptive technologies*.

The one thing certain about the future is that it will be different from the present. The question really is how *much* different. We find it easy to make plans and develop products assuming that the future will be relatively similar to where it is today. Society, politics, government, economics, and nature do move at a relatively slow pace. Some of them do tend to have dramatic "step changes,"[16] but overall, when we average those changes over a long period, we see that the pace of change is relatively slow. Technology, on the other hand, moves quickly and consistently. The opportunities created by advances in technology are tremendous, but our ability to predict them is limited. The major limit is our imagination, restricted by its ability to adapt to a future that is so different from the present. This is exactly why I faced so much skepticism when, in 2004, I indicated that hard disk drives will hold 2.75 terabytes of memory by 2008, only four years later. At the same time, I am sure I would have faced exactly the same skepticism and disbelief if, four years earlier, I had suggested that the average capacity of a hard disk drive in 2004 (four years later) would be 160 gigabytes. But it was.

If the book cover and introduction did not deter you from continuing to read, I am certain you realize the overwhelming value of predicting the future. I am also certain you realize how such prediction can help identify significant market opportunities. Many driving forces will affect the future: governmental, political, social, natural, technological, competitive, global, or local. It is our job to identify which ones will have the greatest impact. The most important driving forces are those that will have the greatest impact on technological and business decisions we make. In this chapter, I focus on one dimension of evaluating those driving forces—the rate of change. As Chapter 4 will show— and this should not surprise anyone—government moves slower than technology. In fact, everything moves slower than technology and, in particular, *high technology* moves faster than anything else does. The rate of change identified by Moore's law is amazing. Anything that can double its performance while reducing its cost by half over a period of twenty-four months has a very high pace of change and, therefore, a significant impact on the future. It might be interesting to learn that, in fact, a few high-technology trends move even faster than Moore's law. One of those is the growth in capacity for hard disk drives, which, in fact, doubles every year. When we attempt to predict the future, we often treat high-technology trends as uncertainties. They move so rapidly, that nobody can tell what they will do four to five years down the road. The high-technology trends are definitely steep, and, therefore, performance changes dramatically over time. However, they are far from being unpredictable. In fact, you will be amazed how predictable they really are.

In 2002, I prepared a *scenario planning*[17] session for the wireless LAN business unit in Texas Instruments. At that time, I wanted Gordon Moore's ability to predict the future in his revolutionary 1965 article to inspire the event participants. I was determined to find the original article online. As I set out to find it, using the term "Moore's law" with the search engines, I came across multiple articles predicting the "end" of Moore's law. This reminded me of when, in 1983, while serving in a technical division of the Israeli Defense Forces, I listened to an instructor from IBM. What sounded to me almost devastating at the time, turned out to be completely *wrong*. The instructor claimed that, while the silicon *process node*[18] in 1983 was 2.5μm and still shrinking, according to Moore's law, the physical limitation will be 1.5μm, and it will not shrink beyond that. I remembered how amazed I was by how close we are to the "bleeding edge of technology" and the end of Moore's law, which served us consistently for the past twenty plus years. It was as if we were finding out that the Earth, after all, is flat and we are about to fall off the edge. In 2006, some twenty-three years later, Texas Instruments has announced its silicon roadmap to deliver 45nm (0.045μm) process, while delivering 65nm (0.065μm) products already. It exceeded the "absolute limit" described in 1983 by an IBM instructor, by a factor of 33 while increasing the number of components on the same silicon area by over a thousand times.

So, why did Moore's law not level off after all? Why did the IBM instructor in 1983 think it would? What has changed? The simple answer is that the challenges and barriers that suggested the absolute limit would be 1.5μm were crossed. When the semiconductor engineering society applied itself to cross those barriers, it did.

To understand why those barriers were crossed, we need to understand what high-tech companies do for a living. High-tech companies focus on a specific differentiator. If they wish to be successful (I would be surprised if they do not, although the strategies of some companies make me wonder), they need to apply themselves to continuously improve along this vector of differentiation[19] and improve their competitive position. That is, if they are good at what they do. What do semiconductor companies do? At the risk of sounding superficial, they find ways to build integrated circuits with *more functionality, smaller size,* and a *lower cost*. That is all they do, and everything else is secondary.

This might be an appropriate time to divide semiconductor companies into three groups: semiconductor companies that own fabs,[20] fabless semiconductor companies, and pure-play foundries. The small number of fab-owning semiconductor companies includes Intel, Texas Instruments, Philips, Freescale, ST Microelectronics, Toshiba, Fujitsu, IBM, and others. Those companies design integrated circuits, and then use their own fabs to manufacture them. There is even a smaller number of pure-play foundries, the major ones being TSMC, UMC (both in Taiwan), and Chartered in Singapore. The pure-play foundries serve as a contract manufacturer to the fabless semiconductor companies. The latter do not own fabs, and they design the integrated circuits in-house, while outsourcing the manufacturing to the pure-play foundries. The cost of building a fab is on the order of $3 billion[21] or even more, and it gets more expensive with every new process node. This represents a dramatic entry cost to the industry. Building a fabless company requires a much smaller investment, as the investment will be limited to the development and marketing of the integrated circuits in which the company will specialize. The number of *people* working in the company drives the investment rather than the billions of dollars required to build a new fab. Fabless companies are not necessarily small companies (although they can be). Fabless companies include Broadcom, Qualcomm, and Marvell, among others. Those can be multibillion-dollar companies. The Fabless Semiconductor industry Association (FSA[22]) claims that in 2004, while the fabless semiconductor industry represented less than 16% of the overall semiconductor industry revenue, its six-year revenue growth outpaced that of the overall semiconductor industry. In fact, when the overall semiconductor market declined 32% during the 2001 recession, the fabless semiconductor industry revenue grew 6%.

For the purpose of the following discussion, I will initially focus on the companies that own fabs, as they represent more than 84% of the overall semiconductor revenue, worldwide. *Integrated* companies that own fabs as well as designing and selling integrated circuits (such as Intel and Texas Instruments) consist of two major internal divisions: the functional business units that design the specific integrated circuits for different end products[23] and the fabrication facilities (the fabs). While the business units compete with the fabless companies, the fabs compete with the pure-play foundries.

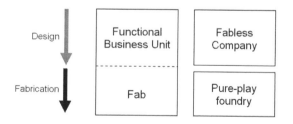

Figure 5—Types of semiconductor companies

You can consider the fabs in those vertically integrated companies and the pure-play foundries as direct competitors in the same market, the market for fabricating semiconductors to specifications.[24] Fabless companies or functional business units within integrated companies that compete over the market for the end products provide those specifications. Furthermore, often you will find that even the companies that own fabrication facilities outsource some of their manufacturing capacity to the same pure-play foundries who service the fabless companies as well.[25]

What do the integrated companies' fabs and the pure-play foundries have in common? They both continue to differentiate along the vector of delivering more functionality in a smaller area and at a lower cost. They drive shrinking the *process node*. A look at the process roadmap plan created by the International Technology Roadmap for Semiconductors[26] (ITRS) will tell us what to expect from the semiconductor industry in the next twelve yeas. ITRS plays a significant role in the understanding of our ability to predict technology trends, even as steep as the semiconductor process roadmap and the consistent continuation of Moore's law. In reality, it seems that ITRS believes that the steepness of the process node shrinking will decline over time. While Moore predicted a 50% area shrinkage every eighteen months, ITRS noted that from 1998 to 2004 that same area shrinkage took twenty-four months, and ITRS further believes that beyond 2004 it will shrink 50% in area every thirty-six months.

2-year cycle				3-year cycle				
1998	2000	2002	2004	2007	2010	2013	2016	2019
250nm	180nm	130nm	90nm	65nm	45nm	32nm	22nm	16nm

Figure 6—ITRS Semiconductor Roadmap

Note that the process node shrinks only 30% every "cycle," which means a shrinkage of 50%.[27]

So was the IBM instructor wrong when he clearly stated in 1983 that physics would prevent the silicon process from shrinking beyond 1.5µm? I will surprise you now: he was *not* wrong. It *was* impossible for the physical limitation of the semiconductor technology used in 1983 to shrink beyond 1.5µm without a dramatic change.

However, the fab and foundry companies could not let that obstacle limit them from continuing to shrink the *process node*. Allowing Moore's law to level off would mean two things. On one hand, it would mean that technology could not develop beyond what it is today. New smaller and more functional electronic products could not enter the market and progress would stop, as the semiconductor technology is most likely the biggest progress catalyst. It is most likely the second reason, though, that drives the semiconductor researches to find ways to overcome those obstacles. If Moore's law ever levels off, the semiconductor industry will commoditize. If no performance (advanced processes that enable new applications) options exist, the only thing that could improve would be price, and that would mean only one thing—commoditization of the semiconductor industry. Beyond the avoidance of the commoditization risk to the semiconductor manufacturing industry, the continuation of Moore's law adds value to the electronic product industry. ITRS has identified several areas of value-add to that industry:

- *Cost*—lower cost of products with given functionality
- *Speed*—higher speed processing
- *Power*—lower power, enabling mobility and portability
- *Compactness*—smaller and lighter products
- *Functionality*—higher level of functionality, more functions, convergence

So the advanced semiconductor technology engineers found a way to overcome the 1983 limitations, but those were not the only obstacles to continue to shrink the *process node*. Later, other obstacles prevented the silicon process node from crossing the 0.5µm barrier and beyond. In 2005, ITRS named the following obstacles to achieving the process nodes they project for future years, and called them "Grand Challenges." Those challenges fall into several categories:

- **The silicon transistor structure**—finding ways to create a smaller transistor that can still perform the required functions. This focuses on the area of the manufacturing process itself.

- **The silicon transistor performance**—improving the performance of the transistor to support higher-frequency wireless functionality, lower power consumption, and other performance parameters. It will also include the ability to have higher-level integration memories.

- **Wireless signal isolation**—with higher-level integration and higher-frequency wireless products, the ability to isolate digital signals from affecting highly sensitive wireless receiver components is crucial.

- **Lithography**—in order to produce silicon chips, we need to be able to create production *masks*, those glass "templates" that will be reflected on the wafer to create the required silicon features. Those features are becoming smaller and smaller, and the ability to accurately reflect them on the wafer gets harder.

- **Interconnect**—with more transistors, logical gates, and memory cells on a chip, connecting them to one another becomes a challenge. Even with a very small component, the overall length of connections increases measurably.

- **Design tools and methodology**—designing components that are so small, have such a high level of functionality, are so diversified (processors, memory, radio transmitters, and receivers all integrated into one), and include such a high number of components in them, poses significant design challenges.

- **Modeling and simulation**—with the high cost of production (even test components), the importance of modeling and simulating components before production increases, and the complexity, small size, and integration level of those components make modeling and simulation challenging too.

- **Testing**—manufactured components need to be tested. The combination of high-frequency radio components with large-capacity memory, high-speed processors, and logic components, not to mention their small size, requires advanced testing equipment and techniques.

- **Assembly and packaging**—those offer new and increased complexity. Addressed are multi-chip modules, system-in-package, and the overall packaging of those miniature dies into packages that the product manufacturers can use at reasonable cost.

- **Factory integration**—all the manufacturing steps have to occur within one factory in a quick, seamless, and efficient way.

- **Yield enhancement**—"yield" is the percentage of good products than can be manufactured out of a silicon wafer. I have yet to see a wafer that produces 100% yield. Getting close to this number will certainly allow lowering the cost of a device, because the whole wafer determines the cost. Yields close to 100% are available today, but as we get closer to "bleeding-edge" processes, the yield tends to be lower than it is for mature processes.

Not a small number of challenges, is it? However, if there is one thing we can count on, it is the fact that the fab and foundry companies will continue to overcome those obstacles and continue improving along their major vector of differentiation—the process node size reduction. Otherwise, they face commoditization. It is as if the collective thinking in those companies projects a trend line that remains constant in its trend, and then they find innovative ways to overcome the obstacles of current technologies and continue along those lines. It is this psychological phenomena within those pure-technology companies that we can so reliably count on when we project technological trends of the future. When projecting technology trends, we should not be limiting ourselves by the known obstacles of the current technologies. We should simply count on the technology companies to continue innovating and stay the course of the trend lines they have so reliably kept in the last years or decades.

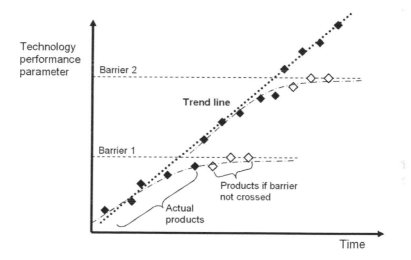

Figure 7—Maintaining consistent technology trends

You can see in Figure 7 the phenomena I described above. A technology has a key performance parameter along which companies focusing on that parameter continue to differentiate and improve. Every now and then, such improvement reaches a technological barrier. In the chart above, the improvement of the technological parameter (silicon *process node*, for example) is potentially leveling off due to a physical (or chemical, or any other) barrier I will call **Barrier 1**. The black diamonds represent actual products (for example, in the semiconductor industry they would represent production silicon *process nodes*), whereas the white diamonds represent products that would have been in production if **Barrier 1** were not crossed. However, the semiconductor fab and foundry companies keep innovating and find a way to cross **Barrier 1**. As a result, we see the second group of black diamonds that, surprisingly, continue along the same psychological original trend line (in the semiconductor industry, you can call it "Moore's law"). Then, the trend line would potentially level off again at a higher performance level due to **Barrier 2**, resulting potentially in the second group of white diamonds, unless the companies mysteriously discover how to cross that second barrier and, once again, continue along the same original trend line. As you will see in the following, there is actually nothing mysterious about those consistent trend lines and barriers that companies conveniently cross to keep those lines consistent.

A few years ago, I attended a lecture by Bob Doering, a colleague of mine at Texas Instruments. Bob is one of two distinguished individuals who represent the United States on the *International Roadmap Committee* of ITRS, which consists of only thirteen members worldwide. The purpose of ITRS, simply put, is to project the silicon process roadmap and identify and address the roadblocks in achieving that roadmap. Years later, as I was preparing a lecture on the topic of "Predicting the Technology Future," I sat in Bob's office to discuss the roadmap in detail, focusing on the barriers. In the first minute of our meeting, Bob confirmed what I suspected. When I told him what the topic of the lecture was, he said, "Oh, no. ITRS does not *project* the silicon roadmap. We already *know* what it is. We are merely identifying the barriers that keep us from getting there!" Bob took me first through the barriers projected in the future of the semiconductor roadmap. Later, we got into the details of barriers already crossed. That was when I learned how the semiconductor industry had overcome the 1.5μm theoretical limit I had heard about more than twenty years before. In fact, a combination of technologies had helped the industry cross that barrier. One of those technologies was the use of Silicide[28] material for silicon transistors. Another technology was the use of *steppers* instead of reduction scanners for semiconductor lithography. Another technological barrier crossed so that the silicon process could be smaller than 1.5μm was silicon modification through a process called *etching*. Etching is the process of removing parts of the silicon material to create the transistors or the logical gates. Until the early 1980s, etching required simply immersing the silicon wafer in the etching liquid. In the early 1980s, however, the industry switched to "dry etching," using plasma. That allowed etching much finer characteristics on the silicon wafer. Finally, the process of adding material to the silicon wafer (called "deposition") changed in the early 1980s to a process called Plasma Chemical Vapor Deposition (or "Plasma CVD").

Seems like a whole lot of trouble just to cross that 1.5μm barrier, doesn't it? How was this industry collectively smart enough to address the limitations of technology to keep the silicon process roadmap continuing along the same trend line? The answer was not technical. It was psychological. Doering explained that the roadmap projected by ITRS simply took the trend line that had existed over the last thirty years or so and projected it into the future, identifying the barriers to achieving the future roadblocks and envisioning ways to cross them. The majority of work done addressed the barriers, as opposed to projecting the future. ITRS created a roadmap that reduced the silicon process node size 30% every twenty-four months. This was almost an arbitrary number, based on history and not on the capabilities of the future, as those are unknown. ITRS used a simple statement to arrive at the number: "The number of transistors will double every twenty-four months." What drives this industry to innovate is finding ways to meet this semiarbitrary roadmap.

Figure 7 above is somewhat overly simplistic. It shows only two barriers to cross to keep the trend line constant. When I had my conversation with Doering, I was very interested in finding out about the technological challenge that hindered breaking through the 1.5μm barrier in the early 1980s. I expected him to name only one barrier, and I expected him to name only one solution to it. In fact, he named several of each.

What was also interesting was to find that this is not an effort by a single company. It is a joint effort by many companies in order to meet the silicon process roadmap. Why are those companies cooperating in finding solutions to the barriers when those solutions should otherwise be their competitive advantage? After all, the semiconductor companies are differentiating almost along a single vector—the ability to achieve a smaller process node faster than their competitors are. Bob used a very interesting phrase, "*pre-competitive research and development*."

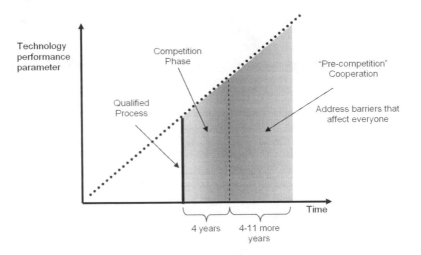

Figure 8—Pre-competition cooperation

Time is a measure of competition. If you have a team inside your company that is investigating, conducting trials, and testing a new silicon process, you are in the *competitive* stage. Semiconductor companies typically conduct internal research and development to address a process that is three to four years away from being qualified[29] for mass production. However, if companies are not yet *internally* investigating a new silicon process, they can cooperate in the "pre-competitive" phase. This phase is characterized by being far out in time enough for the challenges to be equally overwhelming to all companies. The moment one or more companies find a way to solve a challenge, it is no longer a challenge to all, and industry enters the "competitive" phase for that process node. If the industry projects the introduction of the 45nm process in 2010, you would expect companies to cooperate openly in researching the challenges and barriers of that process (in the *pre-competitive* phase) until 2006. In 2006, companies will go into the *competitive* phase and start *internal* research and development, which will be much more practical and much less cooperative. The *pre-competitive* cooperation will then move to 32nm process, which the industry expects to be in mass production in 2013.

Now you can understand why Moore's law never leveled off. Simply by continuing to strive to meet a somewhat arbitrary roadmap, those "leading-edge" researchers are identifying barriers and finding ways to address them in a cooperative way. One of the methods used to solve the barriers is to jointly fund university research and create talented PhDs who will later be able to solve those barriers. The *pre-competitive* research simply will not let the industry fall behind the trend that started more than thirty years ago. This psychological effect also explains why the process roadmap does not outpace the trend line. The researchers are simply not trying to exceed it. They are only identifying the barriers to meeting the trend line, and then finding ways to solve only those barriers. This process leads me to the conclusion envisioned in the beginning of part one of this book: *the technology trend lines will remain constant.* They will not level off, nor will they change their *improvement* rate in a significant manner. Accidental inventions do not drive them. Instead, they respond to intentional inventions made in order to keep the trend lines constant by solving the barriers identified that would otherwise prevent those trend lines from being constant. We can count on those technology trend lines to remain constant. We do not need to understand or challenge the barriers or their solutions. There is just too much intellectual power invested in keeping those trends constant, and there is a tremendous risk of commoditization of the technology companies if their underlying technology trend levels off. There is no incentive as strong as fear.

In this part of the book, I am focusing on projecting trend lines as far as six to seven years out. Without the above context, these will look like somewhat risky predictions. Look at the work done by organizations such as ITRS and IDEMA, projecting the technology trend lines fifteen years out.[30] The best minds in the industry are working to address the barriers to meet that trend line (not more, nor less). Now, you can start getting the sense that projecting the technology six years out is not as risky or inaccurate as you might have thought. The semiconductor industry was the first example.

---

[15] Clayton Christensen, "The Innovator's Dilemma," Harvard Business School Press, June 1997.

[16] A recession is a "step change." Some regulations can create "step changes" and have dramatic impact over industries, impact that requires coping skills. But, once coped with, it stops affecting the industry in a significant way. The events of September 11, 2001, had a dramatic impact on our lives, our society, and the economy, but since then, social and technological reactions have met those changes. The Telecommunications Act of 1996 that the 104th Congress approved changed the face of communications in the US and promoted

competition dramatically. Global warming, on the other hand, is a consistent yet slow change, rather than a "step change."

[17] The process of *scenario planning* involves several steps. First, it involves the identification of driving forces that will affect the market you are interested in. Second, it involves identifying which two driving forces are the most critical to market development, as well as most predictable. Taking the two extremes of how those forces might develop, you then identify four possible future scenarios, and strategize for the possibility of each one of them occurring.

[18] Simply put, process node is the width of a single transistor made of silicon.

[19] The term "vector of differentiation" is defined by Michael E. McGrath in "Product Strategy for High Technology Companies," McGraw Hill, 2000.

[20] Semiconductor fabrication facilities.

[21] In 2003 Texas Instruments publicly estimated investing $3 billion in the fabrication facility they started building in Richardson, Texas. An interesting point to notice is that while manufacturing of almost everything is moving to China, India, Mexico, and other low-labor-cost areas of the world – silicon fabrication is still done in the US. The reason is that capital equipment investment rather than labor and real estate drive the cost of silicon fabrication today.

[22] www.fsa.org.

[23] The term *end product* in this book refers to electronic (mostly) products consumed by consumers.

[24] The typical name for those specifications is GDS-II files, or *tapeouts*.

[25] To augment manufacturing capacity, or to diversify and stabilize it.

[26] http://public.itrs.net.

[27] Shrinkage of 30% in one dimension equals 50% shrinkage in two dimensions, or areas.

[28] A silicide is a compound that has silicon with more electropositive elements.

[29] A silicon process is qualified for production when the manufacture of wafers results in a relatively high yield, which would typically mean that 90% or more of the dies on a wafer would be operational and result in working integrated circuits.

[30] In the ITRS roadmap report published in 2005, the process roadmap until 2013 (eight years out) is referred to as "Near-Term," and the roadmap until 2020 as "Long-Term."

Chapter 2
The Hard Disk Drive Roadmap

If you think that Moore's law and the fast growth in semiconductor technology are impressive, the hard disk drive technology is even more impressive, growing even faster over the last five decades. Starting in the 1950s and well into the twenty-first century, the hard disk drive density grew at a rate close to 100% every single year, compared to the growth of the semiconductor industry that grew at a rate of 100% every two years.

No discussion of fast-growing technologies would be complete without an analysis of the hard disk drive industry. After researching it thoroughly, I found the expert I was looking for. Dr. Ed Grochowski worked for the IBM Almaden Research Center in California where he focused on the evolutionary trends of the hard disk drive and component technologies. He holds nine patents and has authored and presented numerous articles on magnetic disk drives and component technology, and created quite a few storage trend charts. Many regard these charts as industry road maps and cite them widely as references. He is currently the executive director of the California-based IDEMA USA (International Disk Drive Equipment and Materials Association), a non-profit hard disk drive organization serving the storage industry.

I flew to California to meet him. Ed eagerly joins into any discussion about hard disk drive and solid-state memory component trends. I do not know many people who can discuss the history of any technology for the past fifty yeas in such detail as he does, knowing every dimension of those technologies, and in the same breath talk about the future of the technology into the next fifteen years, almost ignoring the point in time we are in. He shared a presentation he was about to present to the IEEE Magnetic Society, showing trend lines starting in the 1950s and continuing until 2020. I noticed only one thing was missing from all his graphs—a "you are here" symbol.

It should not come as a surprise that the hard disk drive industry was doing exactly the same thing that the semiconductor industry was doing—staying on a consistent trend line and solving barriers preventing the industry from remaining on that trend line. In fact, the hard disk drive industry and the semiconductor industry have a lot in common; the industries need to solve some of the same barriers.

The key *performance parameter* of the hard disk drive is the *aerial density* (compared with the key *performance parameter* of the semiconductor industry, the *process node*). Similarly, the key performance parameters of both industries aim to achieve more content in less space (and therefore lower cost for higher functionality). The higher the *aerial density* is, the greater the data storage capacity is on the same disk area, and for the same cost. Ed believes that by the end of the decade we might reach aerial density of 1 terabit per square inch. I could not resist and had to compare that to the memory cell density of semiconductors. Using a 90nm process, one square inch of silicon (assuming that manufacturing a silicon die that size was practical) would host only 240 megabits of random access memory (RAM). With a magnetic density of 1 terabit per square inch, a 0.85" diameter disk drive will be able to hold over 20 gigabytes.

Interestingly enough, the hard disk drive industry has one more degree of freedom than the semiconductor industry. Maybe this is the reason why the capacity density of hard disk drives grew faster than that of solid-state memories. The only way to increase density of memory cells (or digital gates) on silicon is to have smaller geometry ("feature size") cells. That is a two-dimensional progression. Decreasing the feature size by 30% (what the semiconductor roadmap does every two years) to 70% of its previous size, reduces the area by close to 50%. This would be the equivalent of having a magnetic head shrink by 50% in area, and, therefore, have bits 50% smaller recorded on the magnetic surface of the disk. However, there is another way to reduce the magnetic bit size on a hard disk drive surface: get the head closer to the magnetic surface, which will make the magnetic field more concentrated and therefore decrease the size of the bit even further. The hard disk drive industry is addressing this improvement as well and, therefore, progressed faster in increasing the *aerial density*.

Once again, it is interesting to see the barriers that the industry overcame in the history of the hard disk drives. Until 1980, the magnetic material was in the form of ion oxide deposited on a metallic disk (the disk *surface*). The maximum *aerial density* that was achievable (achieved in 1980) was 10 megabits per square inch. By 1980, the magnetic heads evolved in an electromechanical way by wrapping an electrical wire around a ferromagnetic core. In 1980, the magnetic surface transitioned into *thin film media*, which was a lot more homogeneous and granular, allowing the possibility of recording smaller bits on it. The older, electro-mechanical heads could not write such small bits, and a new technology, prompted the development of *thin film heads*. The industry actually *prints* the thin film heads on the head substrate, much like semiconductor fabrication. In fact, they use the same lithography technology for semiconductor fabrication as for hard disk drive magnetic heads.

A brief history of the hard disk drive industry is in order. The first disk drives appeared in the mid-1950s, with the arrival of the first *mainframe* computers. In fact, the hard disk drive industry emerged to *serve* the mainframe computer industry. We will return to this fact later, when we discuss *main* and *derivative* technologies. The first disk drives were 24 inches in diameter, but held only 5MB. They were prone to failures, and those failures were devastating at times.[31] While disk drives had only one initial function, and only one market to serve (the mainframe computer market), they quickly evolved to serve different markets and different applications. Different sizes were required, as well as different parameters. Overall, the disk size shrank, while capacity increased, and *cost-per-capacity* decreased. The diameter shrank from the original 24 inches to 14 inches (which happened just about the time I first encountered mainframe computers and hard disk drives during my service in the Israeli Defense Forces). Then they shrunk to 8 inches and became fixed (there are no longer *mountable* hard disks that can be separated from their drives). They continued to shrink to 5¼", 3½", 2½," and beyond. Since they serve different applications, some of them exist in parallel, having different *sweet spots* (a term that is described in Chapter 5). In 2006, there were five "standard" disk sizes:

- 3½" drives, with the highest *overall capacity*, for *servers*

- 2½" drives, with the best *price-per-capacity* ratio for the cost-sensitive *desktop PC* market

- 1.8" drives, with the best combination of *size and capacity* for the size-constrained *laptop PCs*

- 1" drives for mobile and extra small computing devices

- 0.85" micro-drives for very small portable music players (such as iPod) and possibly for smart cellular phones

Like the semiconductor industry, the hard disk drive industry had to solve many barriers to get to the small size, the capacity, and the capacity-cost of today's versions. Some of the technologies deployed (the *breakthroughs*) over the years were as follows:

- In the 1950s: the use of NRZI coding that allowed more bits to be recorded on the same track length, the use of a hydrostatic air- bearing head, and the use of iron oxide material over an aluminum substrate for the magnetic surfaces.

- In the 1960s: the use of ferrite heads, head suspensions, and hydrodynamic air-bearing sliders, as well as lubricated disks and dedicated servers to move the heads in and out of the surface area.

- In the 1970s: the use of thin film inductive heads instead of electro-mechanical (wire-wrapped) heads, further advanced suspension, rotary actuators to move the heads, as well as further improvements to data coding with Run-Length-Limited codes.

- In the 1980s: magnetic-resistive (MR) heads (one of the biggest improvements), printed like a circuit board, as well as the use of thin field disk material.

- In the 1990s: GMR heads, AFC media, and glass substrates, that replaced the aluminum disks and allowed the head to get much closer to the surface due to the smoothness of the glass surface.

- In the twenty-first century, innovations such as PZT-based secondary actuators, perpendicular recording, fluid bearings, TMR read heads, 4K sectors, and femto sliders allowed further improvement in disk capacity.

I will not go into the details of each one of those improvements, and will settle for stating that much like the semiconductor industry, the hard disk drive industry is working hard at identifying barriers to "staying the course" and delivering a consistently improving roadmap.

As stated before, the main *performance parameter* in the HDD industry is the *aerial density*. This parameter, as its name suggests, describes the number of *bits* that can be stored on a certain area. The first hard disk drive, introduced in 1956, had an aerial density of 20 kilobits per square inch. It took a diameter of 24" to get an overall disk capacity of 5MB. Between the mid-1960s and 1990, the growth rate of the disk aerial density was only 25% annually. It was slightly lagging behind Moore's law of the semiconductor industry, though, which stood at 100% biannually, or 40% annually. With the introduction of the personal computer in the 1980s and the dramatic growth in this market in the 1990s and with the commercial use of the Internet, significant price pressures guided the HDD industry to reach an aerial density growth rate of 60%, growing from 100 megabits/in² in 1991 to 2 gigabits/in² in 1997. It started moving even faster after 1997, and was, in fact, on a growth rate trajectory of 100% annually until 2002. At that point, Grochowski believes that the aerial density growth trend was reduced to 40% annually, the same growth rate as the semiconductor industry experiences (well, it drives it rather than experiences it).

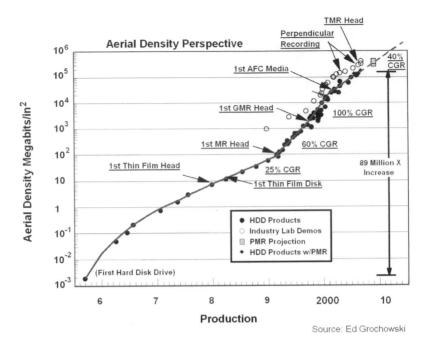

Figure 9—HDD aerial density trend

To me, those different trends are part of a *core* trend. In 2005, the aerial density was 100 gigabits/in². In 1991, it was 100Mb/in². If I drive a trend line between those two points, only fourteen years apart, I will see a growth trend of 64% annually. I would lean toward assuming that this trend line would continue. At the same time, we must be careful. The analysis, thus far, proved that the technology trends remain constant due to psychological reasons, with the technology-driving engineers resolving barriers to remain on a somewhat arbitrary trend line. If the HDD technology engineers believe that the trend line continues at a rate of 40% annually instead of 64% percent, they will solve only those barriers that will keep the HDD aerial density from growing 40% annually, rather than 64%. At the same time, the semiconductor process technology engineers will assure that the process node (50% area reduction due to 30% geometry reduction) happens only every *three* years (as ITRS is plotting) rather than the *two* years by which it has progressed over the past few decades, or even the original *18 months* as Gordon Moore projected in his 1965 article.

What is the impact of the difference between 40% and 64%? In 2006, we saw a 750GB hard disk drive. If we maintain a 40% trend line, that same drive will hold 2.9 terabytes in 2010. If the aerial density had grown by 64% every year, that drive would hold 5.4 Terabytes in 2010— not even double the capacity using a 40% trend line. As our planning time horizon will most likely be four to six years, both numbers will be adequate for our planning. Perhaps even more interesting would be to know that 0.85" microdrives will have a capacity of between 15GB (using a 40% trend line) and 29GB (using a 64% trend line) in 2010, up from 4GB in 2006. What does that mean? Well, suffice it to say that a high-definition movie requires some 25GB to be stored. You do the math.

Another interesting parameter, although a derivative of the aerial density of an HDD, is the data transfer rate. The transfer rate is the rate at which data is transferable to and from the hard disk drive. The *data transfer rate* is in direct ratio to three parameters:

- The *linear density*—the density of bits along a track, which will be close to the square root of the *aerial density*, which is the fastest moving *performance parameter* for hard disk drives;

- The *spin rate (RPM)*—the rate at which the disk spins. This speed, while increasing over time from a few thousands of RPM in the 1950s to 15,000 RPM in 2006, represents a growth rate of less than 5% annually;

- The *disk diameter*—which actually becomes smaller and is the only parameter of the three that acts to *reduce* the data transfer rate rather than increasing it as the overall length of a track that turns in every round is shorter.

From 1990 to 2005, with *aerial density* growth close to 100% annually, the data transfer rate grew 40% annually, affected mostly by the *aerial density* growth (or the square root thereof). In 2005, the data transfer rate of a 3.5" server HDD was close to 150 megabytes per second, and the data transfer rate of a 2.5" mobile HDD was close to 80 megabytes per second, representing the ratio between their diameters and spin speed (a server HDD spins faster than a PC's HDD). We should therefore expect that in 2010, a server HDD will have a data transfer rate of between 350 megabytes/second to 800 megabytes/second. The variability is based on the source of our assumptions, ranging from the data transfer rate growth of 18% annually (based on an aerial density growth of 40% as IDEMA is projecting) to 40% (based on the 40% data rate growth observed between 1990 and 2005). Since we typically discuss *serial* connectivity, we measure connection speeds in *bits-per-second* rather than *bytes-per-second*, which translate into data rates between 2.8Gbps and 6.4Gbps, respectively. I did not factor in any overhead required for data transfer. Now you understand the impact of the increase in data transfer rate, a bi-product of the *aerial density* growth.

Are hard disk drives reliable? A general trend (described in Chapter 7) is to move from mechanical products and technologies to electromechanical ones (combining mechanics and electronics) and to solid-state ones (including electronics only, with no moving parts). A substitute storage technology to hard disk drives is the flash memory (non-volatile memory) technology. Having no moving parts increases the reliability of a product, for obvious reasons. Mechanical parts tend to fail, more so than their electronic counterparts. The hard disk drive has two main electromechanical components: the disk itself with its motor, turning at some 15,000 RPM, and the magnetic head, moving in and out over the magnetic surface. I have to admit that I am very nervous leaving my (HDD-based) digital video recorder (DVR) on all the time, as I am afraid that the HDD will quit at some point. I have had too many disk drives "crash" throughout my professional career. Haven't you? However, the HDD industry has been making great progress in this area. In the late 1980s, the mean time between failures (MTBF, a common term used to denote the average time between system failures) for HDD was a few thousands of hours. With 8,760 hours in a year, there is a high probability of failure if the disk is left running for a year or so. Back than, the question was not *if* the hard drive would ever crash, but rather *when*. In fact, the alternative of turning the disk (and computer) off and on to improve this performance parameter would turn out to have the opposite effect, since the disk suffers "trauma" during the power on-off cycle. In 1997, the HDD MTBF crossed the million-hour mark (which means that, on average, an HDD will work 114 years without failure). The trend seems to be an improvement of 3% annually. While we cannot expect this to be a dramatic disruption source (as it will not change significantly in the next ten years, offering opportunities that do not exist today), we should still remember that applications can assume that an HDD will work twenty-four hours a day, for a period longer that its owner's life expectancy.

A very important trend analysis done by Ed Grochowski is that of the *retail prices of storage.* Just like hard disk drives exist in several different capacities and diameters at any point in time, the competing nonvolatile storage technology, flash memory, also exists in several different form factors (from the smallest *micro-SD®* to the largest *compact flash*) and different capacities.

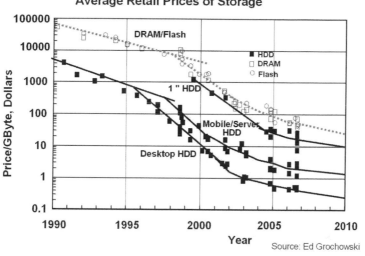

Figure 10—Retail price of storage (HDD/Flash)

Both have a *sweet spot* of pricing (the *sweet spot* concept appears in Chapter 5). You need to remember that a 1" HDD will not be 3.5 times cheaper than a 3.5" HDD (if you consider the diameter as the cost driver), or 12.25 cheaper (if you consider the area ratio). It still needs to have a motor to turn the surface around, an actuator to move the magnetic head in and out over the magnetic surface, the electronics required to read, write, and transfer the data, as well as a package and other parts that will prevent perfect scaling of prices relative to the disk size. The larger-capacity 3.5" HDD will be the most price effective, while the 1" and 0.85" micro-drives will be the least price effective.

In 1995, the average retail price of a hard disk drive was close to $800 per gigabyte. At the same time, flash memory cost closer to $20,000 per gigabyte. Don't try to remember seeing a $20,000 flash card in 1995. A gigabyte flash card did not exist in 1995, but $80 in 1995 would buy you a 4MB card. Given how dearly I paid for my 8MB (state of the art in 1998) memory card when I bought my first 1.8 megapixels digital camera (also state of the art, sold for $995 then), I would say that's just about right.

The price leader, the desktop PC HDD, continued to keep its distance from the flash technology. Around 1997, both storage technologies, most likely driven by demand, moved to more aggressive trend lines, reducing their retail price ten times every three years, equivalent to reducing their price more than 50% every year. In late 2006, an 8GB flash card cost $640 (or $80/GB), while a 500 GB HDD cost $250 (or $0.5/GB), maintaining a ratio close to 150:1 in price/GB between the flash memory and the desktop HDD. However, the 1" hard disk *micro-drives* were much closer to the price/capacity ratio or flash memory products. In 1999, they cost just over $1,000/GB, while flash memory cost $2,000/GB. They continued to maintain a ratio of 2:1, and later in 2006, with flash maintaining $80/GB, the micro-drives maintained $30-40/GB.

If the *aerial density* (and thus the price/GB) of the HDD industry were to move faster than the silicon process density (affecting the flash memory price/GB), we should expect applications currently using flash memory cards (such as digital cameras) to be using microdrives in the future. If, on the other hand, the flash memory density were to shrink faster than HDD, then we should expect the opposite trend; an application currently using micro-HDD would start using flash instead.

However, as it stands, it appears that currently both technologies are moving at a relatively similar pace. For products requiring significant storage capacity, there will be no substitute for the HDD. I do not expect the digital video recorders (DVR)—requiring capacity to record more channels simultaneously and over longer periods, using large-capacity HDD—to transition to the more expensive flash technology. The DVR market did not reach the point at which it "doesn't care" about HDD capacity or price/capacity improvements anymore. When will that happen? Probably not before they can record one hundred TV channels simultaneously for two months. Given the ratio of 150:1 between flash and cost-leading HDD, and with an improvement of 10x in price every three years, we could assume that the flash technology can reach the same price/GB that the mainstream HDD technology has today, in no less than forty-five years. Since the ratio of price/GB between flash and microdrives is only 2:1, we can assume that for the price we pay for an HDD microdrive today, we will get a flash card only a year later, and maybe less. Before I met with Ed Grochowski, I was certain that, with a hard disk drive density growth rate outpacing that of flash memory, we would continue to see smaller and smaller hard disk drives taking over what would otherwise be flash-based applications. Ed, however, convinced me that both technologies should remain generally parallel in their growth, with a 1" HDD almost overlapping the flash memory price/capacity parameter, and a 0.85" HDD overlapping it (see Figure 10). According to Ed, flash will outperform HDD in power consumption, communication speed, size, and mechanical rigidness. There will be no reason to move beyond a 0.85" HDD.

For products such as portable media players (PMP, of which the iPod is one example), we will see the dichotomy of existence of *both* flash and HDD storage, with flash leading the small form factor, music-only devices, and HDD leading the video (and other content-intensive) devices. At this time, Apple's leading iPods are the 8GB flash-based iPod nano for pure music applications, and the 60GB, HDD-based video iPod.

Another parameter to consider is the time it takes to access pieces of stored data. Hard disk drives have *seek time*, the time it takes the magnetic head to move from where it is now to where the needed data is stored (or needs to be stored), measured in milliseconds. While suitable for most applications, it might not be for some. Flash components have different configurations. While in general they allow access to data in a more *random* manner, they still do access blocks of data, and take some time to access specific data. They are much faster than HDD though. The time it takes to access required data stored on a magnetic tape is the longest, as it requires fast forwarding or rewinding of the tape to the right place, measured in *seconds*, and sometimes in *minutes*. Another parameter to consider is the overall physical space that a certain amount of storage takes. How many cubic inches would it take to store one terabyte of storage using the different technologies? I did *not* conduct this specific research, but if you think it is needed, please use the tools provided in Chapter 5.

---

[31] The devastation was a dual one. On one hand, potentially critical data was lost and required additional effort to recover. On the other hand, the physical damage to the disk and the disk *drive* (the two were separate at the time and the disk was "mounted" on the disk drive) was substantial. With the high cost of the disk drives, a disk *crash* was a capital-intensive event.

Chapter 3
Processing Power Trends

Microprocessors

I learned about the term *microprocessor* for the first time in 1976. Focused on telecommunications in high school, I came across a book titled *Microprocessors*. At the time, I was not sure if *Intel* was the name of the author or the publisher of that book. In 1976, I am not sure many other people knew. What fascinated me the most was the ability of this flexible, programmable "machine" to replace functionality that would otherwise require a significant number of logical gates and was limited to only one purpose. Simply by changing software, the microprocessor can behave like a completely different device. There are several different types of processors:

- Data processors
- Microcontrollers
- Digital Signal Processors (DSP)

When I encountered the microprocessor revolution in 1976, the 8008 was capable of performing close to 70,000 instructions per second. In order to emulate logical gates, it had to perform quite a few instructions in a software loop, which meant it would have a signal *latency* on the order of a few tens to hundreds of microseconds. Logical gates were much faster than that, which meant that a microprocessor could not perform these high-speed, time-critical functions. However, when the Pentium®[32] processor was introduced in 1993 with a processing power of 100 million instructions per second (MIPS), that latency shrank to a few tens of nanoseconds, and relatively high-speed, real-time data processing could be achieved.

In 1978, Intel introduced the 8086, the first processor to cross the one million instructions per second (one MIPS) line. In 2002, Intel's processors crossed the 10,000 MIPS line. Over a period of 24 years, processing power went up by a factor of 10,000. This represents a trend line of 47% every year.

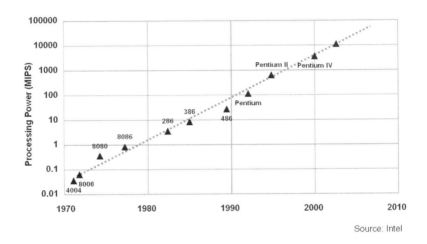

Source: Intel

Figure 11—Microprocessor processing power

The x86 and Pentium family of processors, for example, are known as "Central Processing Unit" (CPU). They typically serve as the core, or brains, of a computing device, such as a PC. They process data—lots of it, and very fast, as you can see in Figure 11.

As the processing power increases, the cost per processing power decreases, allowing two orthogonal trends: more powerful processors for the same price, and less powerful processors for a much lower price. The latter led to the emergence of the *microcontroller* market. Microcontrollers are *Computers on Chip*. They have everything required to operate as a complete computing unit, including the program and data memory, as well as the *input* and *output* interfaces.

A CPU is part of a *centralized* architecture, where there is one CPU[33] surrounded by memory, mass storage, and input and output devices. In contrast, the *microcontroller* is typically part of a highly distributed, decentralized architecture, where each microcontroller is responsible for a specific task. Microcontrollers are not part of dedicated data processing devices (such as a personal computer, PDA, or even a cellular phone). Rather, they are parts of a complex system such as a car. A car today has tens, if not hundreds, of microcontrollers embedded in it. I remember encountering the first microcontroller to go below a price of $1 in 1993. With a program memory of only 512 instructions, and data storage of only 64 Bytes, it could perform some dedicated functions and communicate with other processors, controlling other parts of the complex system.

Digital Signal Processing

Microprocessors process data. As such, you will find one processor in every personal computer. As a consumer, you are very much aware of the presence of such a component, and as a buyer, you are very aware of its performance when you decide to buy a new PC. Digital Signal Processors (DSP), on the other hand, are not getting the same recognition from consumers. Consumers do not *buy* DSPs. They do not even know they exist. Yet, those DSPs are pervasive in our lives. They exist in every walk of life, and lead to many of the electronics and communications disruptions in our lives.

Gene Frantz is the only holder of the highest rank on the *technical ladder* in Texas Instruments, *principal fellow*. He joined TI in 1974 and led the development of the Speak & Spell™ technology. He is a true evangelist, spending a big part of his time in finding new opportunities and reasons to use DSPs. I was so excited about my interview with Gene that I had to wait a few days before my adrenaline level returned to normal and I could write about him.

Without question, 1965 was a good year. Cooley and Tukey, not as well known as Gordon Moore, published an article called "An Algorithm for the Machine Calculation of Complex Fourier Series" in Vol. 19 of the *Mathematics of Computation* magazine. To paraphrase Gene, this "Aha!" moment eventually sparked the development of the DSP. In simple words, the article started the theory of analyzing analog signals by a digital mathematical processing device. It wasn't until the early 1980s that the first devices were introduced, and then put into action. It was the discovery (some say the *rediscovery*) of the Fast Fourier Transform (FFT) as a tool for numerically analyzing signals, leading to the DSP architecture, optimized to perform quickly the *Multiply and Accumulate* (MAC) function in hardware. Performing multiplication by a microprocessor took too long. It was done using many instructions, using the *add* function. When a microprocessor wanted to multiply 258 by 761, it would add 761 to itself 257 times to reach the result. It would take too long. The FFT function requires many multiply functions, and the ability to perform *multiply* in hardware and in a single instruction cycle is what made DSPs what they are today. While microprocessor performance in measured in MIPS (million instructions per second),

DSP performance is measured in MMACs (million multiply and accumulates per second).

Figure 12 shows the DSP processing power improvement trend. With the first production DSP in 1982 capable of 5 MMACs, and the TI C64x+ DSP in 2006 crossing the 10,000 MMACs mark, this *performance parameter* grows at an annual rate of 37%.

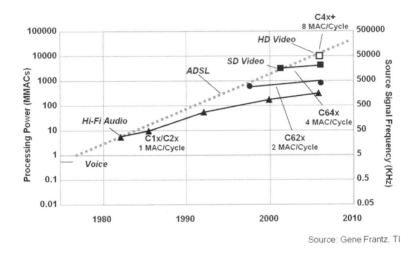

Source: Gene Frantz, TI

Figure 12—DSP processing power

What does it mean, and why do we care? The ability to perform numerical calculations on analog signals allows machines to be smart. It allows electronic products to be flexible and perform multiple different functions. It allows dial-up modems to convert telephone line signals into data and vice versa. It allows DSL modems to do the same at 50 times the speed of dial-up modems. It allows the conversion of high-quality music into digitally stored data on a CD or MP3 player, and then turning that data back into the same high-quality audio without any loss. It allows cellular phones to understand the radio signals transmitted to them and decode the voice from them, as well as many other functions of our daily lives. As I said, DSPs are in every walk of life, and we are unaware of them.

How will this DSP performance improvement affect our lives? One of the basic theories associated with DSPs is the Nyquist-Shannon sampling theorem, that states, *"Exact reconstruction of a continuous-time baseband signal from its samples is possible if the signal is band-limited and the sampling frequency is greater than twice the signal bandwidth."* In simple words, if you need to be able to turn an analog signal into a numerical representation, for calculations by a DSP, you need to sample that signal at twice its highest frequency, at a minimum. This is the *Nyquist rate* for sampling. Voice signals, with telephone-call quality, have a highest frequency of 4KHz, and, therefore, require a sampling rate of 8K samples/second. High-quality audio has a high frequency of 24KHz, and, therefore, a sampling rate of 48K samples/second. Standard-definition (SD) video signal requires 12M samples/second, and a High-definition (HD) one requires 120M samples/second. Gene shared an interesting rule of thumb with me. "If you want to do something, anything, with a DSP, you need to be able to perform at least 100 MACs for each sample you take." Gene called this number the *"performance barrier."* "You cannot begin to do anything with a DSP if you cannot perform at least those 100 MACs per sample," he said. If you have more than 100 MACs per sample—you can do more things.[34]

Gene is left-handed, like me. Left-handedness is typically associated with a preference to process *visual* information, and so during our conversation Gene used many charts and graphs to make his points. One of Gene's charts took the DSP processing power trend (Figure 12), and then divided it by the number of samples required for each of the four media formats described above. In 1982, a 5-MMACs DSP could execute 625 instructions for every single voice sample. Exceeding the *100-instructions-per-sample* rule, there is no surprise, then, that the first applications of DSPs were voice related. In the same year, those DSPs were very close to performing 100 instructions for every high-quality audio sample. It was not until 2002, when DSPs were capable of reaching the 100 instructions-per-sample bar for SD video, that we were led to the introduction of *digital TV.* In 2006, a DSP could perform 100 instructions per sample of a HD video signal. Figure 12 also shows the signals that the different DSPs could process, by dividing the processing power (MMACs) by 100 instructions per sample and 2 samples per Hertz (Nyquist rate). This chart gives us a very interesting view on the capabilities of DSPs, associated with the highest frequency of the application they can handle. You can take any application and find the point in time at which a DSP could handle it, and you have the point in time at which this application will become pervasive. You can see why DSL modems became viable in the late 1990s, for example. You can also project digital processing of a 3GHz radio signal in 2019, the year in which DSPs would be capable of performing 600 billion MACs. Indeed, this could be the year for the magical *software-defined radio (SDR)*[35] concept, a term that has fascinated me ever since I heard a lecture by Dr. Carl Panasik, another key Texas Instruments technical guru.

You must wonder, though, what happens once the DSP processing power exceeds the 100 instructions per sample bar. Here, a phenomenon occurs very similar to that described by Clayton Christensen in *The Innovator's Dilemma*. Once the DSP reaches that "performance barrier," we do not care for performance improvements anymore. The focus shifts to other dimensions of value, creating new applications and disruptions. Gene Frantz describes three dimensions of value, conveniently represented by three P's: *performance, price,* and *power*. It is not until the DSP *performance* reaches the 100 instructions-per-sample line that the use of it becomes viable for the application, but at that point in time, the importance of *performance* diminishes almost immediately. Different applications will then require emphasis on different parameters.

Back in 1992, Gene predicted DSP performance in 2002. In 1982, a DSP was capable of 5 MMACs, consumed power of 250mW per MMACs, and cost $30 per MMACs. In 1992, a DSP performed 40 MMACs, consumed 12.5mW per MMACs, and cost $0.38 per MMACs. He then predicted that in 2002, a DSP would perform 5,000 MMACs, consume 0.1mW per MMACs, and cost $0.02 per MMACs. He was almost exactly right. Predicting forward into 2012, the DSP would be capable of 50,000 MMACs, consume only 0.001mW per MMACs, and cost $0.003 per MMACs.

In 2012, therefore, a DSP will be capable of performing more than 10,000 instructions per sample of hi-fi audio. However, if we do not care for performance beyond 100 instructions per sample, we could optimize the DSP to consume less power or cost less. Handling the hi-fi audio signal at 100 instructions per second will require only 5 MMACs, and using Gene's 2012 predictions means that it will cost only 1.5 cents and consume 0.005mW. An important technology of the future to observe is *power scavenging*, or the ability to produce power from natural sources such as daylight, sun heat, wind, and even body heat. Measured in mW per area, this technology might be able to drive a battery-less, perpetual operation MP3 player. Alternatively, hi-fi audio functionality will be practically free.

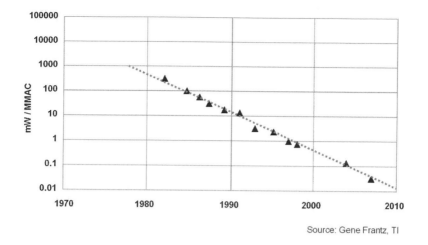

Source: Gene Frantz, TI

Figure 13—DSP power consumption

The DSP processing trends were interesting for another reason. They develop differently than the semiconductor and hard disk drive trends. Unlike those, there is no *pre-competitive cooperation* between companies. Each company develops those for itself. Advanced university research is typically taking place, funded by companies such as TI, but there is no *organizational* cooperation between companies in the pre-competitive phase as there is in the semiconductor and HDD technologies. There could be several reasons for that. Gene, for example, provocatively stated that if we needed to develop the 600 billion MACs DSP needed for 3GHz software-defined radio today, we could. Nothing prevents us from "breaking the trend line." There are no technological barriers like the ones facing the semiconductor and HDD industries. However, the trend line is still psychologically driven. Gene believes that innovators of new applications could not comprehend a DSP performance improvement that is faster than has occurred in the past twenty-five years. This is the reason that when DSP engineers prepare to design the next DSP generation, they keep it on the same trend line. The DSP evolution happens in a cycle of three phases: theory, product, and enablement. First, DSP theories were developed (as in the 1965 Cooley & Tukey article), then products were developed (early DSPs in the 1980s), and then they enabled applications. As the performance improved along different dimensions, new theories were developed and new products were developed, enabling a completely new set of applications. This cycle will continue into the future.

An interesting insight I got from the interview with Gene was that at some point in time, you could not perform faster—not with a single processing core anyway. The technology gets to the point where machine cycles cannot go faster. However, Moore's law still allows us to put more transistors on the same size silicon die, and for a lower cost, and then our only way of improving performance is through parallel processing, or including multiple processing cores within a single processor component. This is what led Intel to jump off the mere processor speed improvements to the dual-core and quad-core processors.

---

[32] Pentium is a registered trademark of Intel Corporation.

[33] Intel released its "Dual Core" architecture, and later its "Quad Core" architecture, where the microprocessor chip has several processing cores, side by side, and, for the first time, increased processing power not by delivering faster processors, but by actually integrating several processors in the same package. The processor, though, is still in a central location, and the different cores share the overall processing burden.

[34] For voice communications, one of the most pervasive uses of DSPs, you will be able to add functions such as echo cancellation, voice compression, and noise cancellation.

[35] Software-defined radio is a term used to describe the ability to sample radio signals, almost directly from the antenna, giving the ultimate flexibility to radio equipment.

Chapter 4
Other Technology roadmaps

Connectivity, communications, wireless

Another underlying technology to observe (and harness to cause disruptions) is communications and connectivity, wired and wireless. Just like other driving technologies, as they progress, they can enable applications. The key *performance parameter* for any type of connectivity or communication is the data speed. We need to be careful when we identify the *signaling* speed versus the *payload data rate*. What we really care about is the latter, as it tells us how long it would take to move *payload* data from Point A to Point B. Unfortunately, when described to us, most of the communication and connectivity technologies measured use their *signaling* speed, and not their true *data rate*, for measurement. USB 2, for example, reportedly has a speed of 480 Mbps. However, in reality, it can move between 240 Mbps and 320Mbps of *payload* data. The Wi-Fi®[36] 802.11g technology reportedly has a speed of 54Mbps (which is what you will find printed on boxes) when, in fact, it will deliver no more than 30Mbps of *payload* data in the most optimized network, and less with a network (or connection) that is less than optimized. The highly optimized synchronous FireWire (IEEE 1394) network is considered one of the most efficient communications technologies, capable of delivering *payload* data at close to 80% of its *signaling rate*. As a rule of thumb, assume that the real *data throughput* functions are anywhere between 50% and 80% of the advertised *signaling* speed. Why such a big difference? Because communication technologies require a lot of overhead to assure reliable and secure transfer of the correct data between the data source and the destination.

I will describe several types of connectivity. They all have different characteristics (other than the main *performance parameter*) and topologies. Even the main *performance parameter* (in this case, the *data rate*) is different between them, and between their *wired* instantiations and their *wireless* ones, just as there are different capacities and price/capacity for hard disk drives in existence in every point in time, due to the different HDD physical sizes and applications for which they are needed.

- **On board connectivity**—not having a specific acronym like the following ones, those technologies connect components of the same electronic board or system. Typically of very short ranges (several inches, up to one foot), they are capable of running extremely high-speed data to allow a system to utilize the speed of its components. Serial ATA is one example of a connectivity technology aimed at connecting hard disk drives and other system components.

- **Body Area Network (BAN)**—preliminary work has begun in the area of networks that connect components mounted on the human body.

- **Controller Area Network (CAN)**—aimed at the automotive industry, there are standards prepared to address the connectivity of the different car sensors, actuators, and microcontrollers.

- **Personal Area Network (PAN)**—a widely used category. The PAN (to be distinguished from the *body area network*) is a network aimed typically at ranges of up to 10 meters (30 feet), that would typically be considered one room, or the work space of a single person. Technologies addressing this level of connectivity are USB, ultra-wideband, Bluetooth®[37], and short-range FireWire (the IEEE 1394a standard). Personal area network will typically connect devices that belong to the same person (such as PC, peripherals, TV, DVR, portable media player, digital camera, camcorder, and the like). While requiring only a relatively short range, it demands very high throughput, as significant amounts of data require transfer (song and video downloads from PC to personal media players, picture and video uploads from digital cameras and camcorders to the PC).

- **Local Area Network (LAN)**—typically associated *multiple* users. The users are typically connected to the "outside world" via a *wide area network* (see following). Therefore, the protocols and topologies will require *LAN* to support multiple users and provide a bridge to that outside world. *LAN* includes the ubiquitous Ethernet (IEEE 802.3) and Wi-Fi (IEEE 802.11) as its wireless complementor.

- **Metropolitan Area Network (MAN)**—mostly associated with wireless technologies. While the infrastructure required for delivery of *wide*-area and *metropolitan*-area *wired* communications is similar, it might be different for *wireless* technologies. Standards such as IEEE 802.16 (WiMAX[38]) target MAN communications, aimed at covering metropolitan areas. Sometimes there is another *tier* of connectivity defined between MAN and LAN—the *campus area network*. It provides coverage to specific campuses (universities, enterprises). Both *metropolitan* and *campus* area networks are "intermediate" technologies, the coverage of which is typically achieved by either LAN (such as the Wi-Fi offering in "hot spots") and WAN (such as the high-speed cellular technologies HSDPA and others). The phrase "MAN technologies" refers to wired broadband technologies (cable and DSL).

- **Wide Area Network (WAN)**—the widest coverage network, aimed at connecting every two points in the world. The most pervasive ones are the *Internet*, the *cellular network*, and the *telephone network*.

There is an interesting behavior difference between connectivity/communication technologies and *stand-alone* technologies such as the semiconductor and hard disk drive technologies. As we have seen in previous chapters, the semiconductor and the HDD technologies develop in gradual steps. Those steps are very rapid, but they *are* gradual. The growth steps are 30% to 50% at a time, but relatively frequent. Within a period of three to six years, we can expect two, three, or even more of those gradual steps to take place. Connectivity speed, on the other hand, while over long stretches of time grows at a slower pace, but does it in bigger steps. Ethernet moved from 10Mbps to 100Mbps, and then to 1,000Mbps (1Gbps), and now it continues to move to 10Gbps. That is a ten-time improvement every time! USB moved from 12Mbps (USB *full speed*) to 480Mbps (USB *high speed*), a 40-times improvement in a single step! Why is that?

The reason lies in the fact that connectivity technologies take time to disseminate through an industry. One does not care that at any point in time there will be different *aerial density* hard disk drives in existence in multiple products, because that *performance parameter* is invisible to the outside world, and has no impact on it. Connectivity, on the other hand, requires two or more devices to connect. It does not matter if one device can connect faster than any other device. The slower device determines the speed of connection. Say your PC supports USB 2 at 480Mbps, but your digital camera supports USB 1 at only 12Mbps. How fast do you think your pictures will upload to the PC? No more than 12Mbps! The true value of a new connectivity technology will appear only once it trickles into *all* the devices that need to be connected.

A second reason is associated with the fact that supporting higher-speed (or different in any way) connectivity requires significant infrastructure modifications that are extremely capital intensive. The migration from 2.5G cellular networks to 3G networks was a very painful one, and involved billions of dollars of investment just to upgrade the infrastructure (not to mention the investment associated with acquiring the required radio spectrum). The migration from 100Mbps Ethernet to 1Gbps Ethernet in an organization requires a lot of equipment changes, as well as cable replacements, as typically 1Gbps Ethernet and 100Mbps Ethernet require different wires.

For both reasons, no one takes lightly the improvements in connectivity technologies, and *big* and *infrequent* changes are required. There is no doubt that the overall trend, over a long period, must be significant. More people need more content delivered. As mentioned, while averaged over a long period, those connectivity speed improvements are significant. However, they should require as few steps as possible.

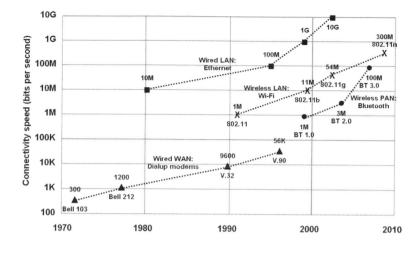

Figure 14—Connectivity speed evolution

Another important characteristic of connectivity technologies is *backward compatibility*. Since connectivity connects to different devices, purchased at different times, they might support different versions or different speeds of connectivity. As described before, the slowest one will dictate the maximum speed at which they can communicate. However, even for that to happen, the device that embeds the faster connectivity version must support previous versions. Otherwise, they will not be able to connect. This *legacy carryover* is sometimes an inhibitor of faster speeds, as the connections might be the same, and limited by the maximum speed they can carry. USB cables that supported signaling at 12Mbps may not have supported 480Mbps. Given that the average consumer will not be able to distinguish between the two types of connectivity—the faster-speed USB had to operate over the cables built to support the slower speed.

The infrastructure built for the voice telephones was not necessarily suitable for higher-speed signaling and posed significant restrictions on the deployment, the distance, and maximum speed of DSL. Dial-up modems, operating at 56Kbps had to be able to support speeds down to 300bps, since there was always the possibility, as remote as it might have been, that the remote modem would be able to support only the 1970s 300bps standards and not work at the higher speeds.

A communications or connectivity technology discussion is not complete without discussing Internet traffic. When the Internet emerged in 1969, the Internet traffic was very limited. Traffic grew until 1982 at a rate of 100% every twenty-one months.[39] After 1982, with the adoption of the ubiquitous TCP/IP protocol, and with the pervasive adoption of the Internet, the traffic started growing 100% every nine months, accelerating to a growth of 100% every six months, or 300% annual growth today.

Typically, communication technologies involve two performance parameters: range and rate. Figure 47 shows a typical performance of a connectivity technology, wired or wireless. They all suffer from *path loss*. The longer the range is, the lower the throughput is. Perhaps the performance parameter to use would be the data rate multiplied by the log2 of the range between the source (transmitter) and destination (receiver) of the communication. Every time we reach the limit of the Shannon theorem,[40] we seem to find new ways to overcome it, whether using *ultra-wideband* (UWB) and MIMO (multiple input, multiple output) technologies, advanced coding, and other techniques.

Imaging technologies

Digital imaging has a significant potential impact on technology and market disruption. The main disruption caused thus far is the advent of the digital camera, disrupting the photography market, at all its segments, from the entry-level consumer to the high-end professional studio photographer. Military applications as well as industrial ones use digital cameras. Here, too, we observe several different performance parameter factors. There are several different types of digital cameras in the market at any point in time. There are high-end cameras as well as low-end cameras. There are cameras that use 1/2-inch elements and there are cameras that use 1/3-inch elements. There are CCD imaging elements, as well as the lower-cost CMOS elements. When I looked for a chart that would show the trends, I could not find one. Instead, I did find a lot of information pertaining to the market introduction of digital cameras from the different manufacturers.[41] I will therefore use one of the methods described in Chapter 5. I used the *camera resolution* as the performance parameter for digital image capture technology. I collected the following data about product releases:

1986—Cannon RC-701, 96 Kpixel
1986—Sony ProMavica MVC-2000, 380Kpixel
1987—Canon RC-760, 600Kpixel
1987—Konika KC-400, 300Kpixel
1987—Olympus V-100, 360Kpixel
1988—Canon RC-470, 360Kpixel
1988—Nikon QV-1000C, 380Kpixel
1989—Fuji DS-X, 400Kpixel

1989—Sony ProMavica MVC-5000, 720Kpixel
1990—Olympus V-102, 360Kpixel
1991—Konika KC-DX1, 400Kpixel
1992—Canon RC-570, 410Kpixel
1992—Kodak DCS2000, 1.54Mpixel
1994—Fuji DS-505, 1.3Mpixel
1995—Kodak DCS-3, 1.3Mpixel
1998—Fuji DX-10, 800Kpixel
1998—Canon PowerShot A5, 800Kpixel
1998—Canon PowerShot Pro70, 1.54Mpixel
1998—Kodak DC220, 1Mpixel
1998—Kodak DC260, 1.54Mpixel
2002—Canon EOS D60, 6.3Mpixel
2002—Canon PowerShot A40, 2Mpixel
2004—Canon PowerShot A75, 3.2Mpixel
2004—Canon EOS 20D, 8.2Mpixel
2006—Canon EOS 30D, 8.5Mpixel
2006—Canon PowerShot A630, 8Mpixel

The next step is to plot those product introductions on a chart, where the X-axis is the linear time, and the Y-axis is the logarithmic *performance parameter*, in this case the camera resolution.

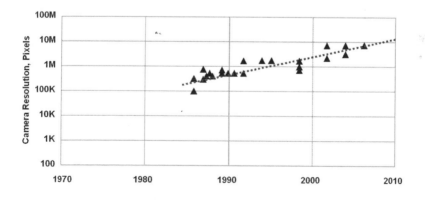

Figure 15—Digital camera resolution trends

You will notice there are several resolutions that existed at any given time. Those represent cameras for different market segments. In 2002, the consumer-grade camera had 2Mpixel, while the professional-grade camera had over 8Mpixel, at a completely different price point. You will also notice that the trend will change over time. If you take the average

1988 camera resolution of 380Kpixel as the basis, and 2006 cameras (with 6Mpixel) as the next reference point, it represents an annual growth rate of 17%. Take the 1998 average of 1Mpixel, and you will see an annual growth rate of 25%. The trend accelerated over time, but not dramatically. With a 25% annual growth rate, this *performance parameter* barely makes it to the list of trends we should observe.

In 1997, the "above average" laptop computer had a color LCD screen size of 12" (diagonal), with a 4:3 form factor, and a screen resolution of 800x600 pixel (SVGA). In 2007, ten years later, the "above average" laptop computer has a color LCD screen size of 12.1" (diagonal), with a 16:9 form factor, and a screen resolution of 1,366x768 pixels (WXGA). If you take the LCD *pixel density* as a performance parameter to project, it will represent growth from 6,960pixels/in^2 in 1997 to 16,920pixels/in^2 in 2007. While this seems like significant growth, it shows a trend line of only 9.3% growth annually.

Specific predictions—2014

For now, I will assume the time horizon for the predictions needs to be seven years, as this is when the technology we harness will disrupt a new market. I am writing this book in 2007, which means I need to be able to predict 2014. The following will show what the different *performance parameters* of the different technologies will be in 2014:

Technology	Performance parameter	Current value	In year	Annual growth	2010 value	2014 value
Digital Camera	Camera resolution at the high-end of cameras [Megapixel]	8.5MP	2006	+17%	15.9MP	29.8MP
Semiconductor	Process node	65nm	2007		45nm	32nm
Hard Disk Drive	Aerial density [Gigabits/in^2]	10Gb/in^2	2005	+40%	54Gb/in^2	207Gb/in^2
HDD	Price per Gigabyte (Desktop)	40¢	2006	-40%	5.2¢	0.7¢
HDD	Price per Gigabyte (micro drive)	$15	2006	-40%	$1.94	25¢
Flash memory	Price per Gigabyte	$50	2006	-40%	$6.5	84¢
HDD	Desktop HDD Top Capacity [Gigabytes]	750GB	2006	+40%	2,900GB	11,000GB
HDD	Micro-drive capacity [Gigabytes]	10GB	2006	+40%	38.5GB	148GB
Flash memory	Flash (SD) card capacity [Gigabytes]	4GB	2006	+40%	15.4GB	59GB
Processors	Desktop processing power, Personal Computer	10,000 MIPS	2003	+47%	148,000 MIPS	693,000 MIPS
DSP	Processing power, MMACs – cutting edge	10,000 MMACs	2006	+37%	35,000 MMACs	124,000 MMACs
DSP	Max frequency analyzed (@100 MACs/Hz)	50MHz	2006	+37%	176MHz	680MHz
DSP	Cost per MMACs	2¢	2002	-29%	0.9¢	0.1¢
DSP	Power consumption [mW/MMACs]	0.1mW (100µW)	2002	-32%	5µW	0.1µW
DSP	Cost of analyzing a High Definition Video signal	$80.8	2006	-29%	$20.5	$5.2
DSP	Cost of analyzing a 3GHz radio signal (SDR)	$4,847	2006	-29%	$1,232	$313
DSP	Power consumption of handling HD signal	673mW	2006	-32%	144mW	31mW
DSP	Power consumption of handling 3GHz signal	40.4W	2006	-32%	8.6W	1.8W

Figure 16—2014 technology predictions

You need to distinguish *main* trends from *derivative* ones. The *main* trends are the ones that the industry is "obsessed" with as the improvement target. The *derivative* trends are those that result from the improvements in the main trends. For example, in the hard disk drive industry, the main driving performance parameter is *aerial density*, the density of storage over a certain surface area. This is the *main* parameter that the hard disk drive industry is trying to improve and optimize. The *derivatives* of it are the overall capacity of hard disk drives with the same size, the size of HDD with the same capacity, the cost per a capacity unit (GB), the connectivity speeds, and others. The semiconductor industry focuses on the *process node* shrinkage. The derivative trends will be the memory capacity over the same size of, say, a flash SD card, the size of a memory card of a certain capacity, and the cost per capacity (GB) of any memory card. It will further be the size and cost of an integrated circuit capable of certain functionality, or the amount of functionality that can be included in an integrated circuit of a fixed size and cost.

What does the information provided in Figure 16 mean? I will take a few data points and give examples of what the possibilities will be:

- The micro hard disk drive capacity in 2010 can hold a full high-definition movie. A flash card (SD form factor) could probably hold this amount in 2011. A 2014 microdrive can hold six high-definition movies.

- A DSP in 2014 can manipulate a high-definition movie (with 100 MACs per sample) for the price of $5.20, consuming 31mW (which, on a standard 800mAh battery would most likely allow operation for thirty-one hours, not considering anything else).

- In 2014, the highest frequency analyzed by a DSP could be just shy of 700MHz. A software-defined radio (SDR) handling 3GHz radio frequency would not be available commercially.

Low-tech trends

From 1990 to 2005, the *aerial density* of hard disk drives grew at a rate of 100% every year. At the same time, the *gate count* (or transistor count, the density indicator in the semiconductor industry) grew at a rate of 100% every two years. In 1990, a 1600cc car engine produced close to 90BHP (breaking horsepower). If the automotive *engine power* parameter evolved as quickly as the semiconductor *gate count* evolved, by 2005 we would have seen the same 1600cc engine produce 23,000BHP. Furthermore, if it had evolved as quickly as the hard disk drive industry, it would have produced almost 3 million BHP. It is safe to say it did not. In fact, if in 2005 the average 1600cc car engine produced 120 BHP, the rate of change would have been slightly less than 2% a year.

The semiconductor and hard disk drive industries evolved at unusually fast rates. No other technology or industry evolved at this rate. What does it mean for this analysis? While it doesn't mean we should completely ignore those trends, it does mean that they will not be the technologies that will enable disruptions for several reasons, the main one being that they are highly predictable and easy to envision. This prevents *disruptive* competition. All competitors in a market are aware of the progress made, over a long period, which gives them plenty of time to prepare. Furthermore, since the performance requirements of consumers grow too (explained well by Clayton Christensen in his books), the "low-tech" technologies merely play "catch-up" with consumer requirements. Consumers do require more powerful car engines over time, for the same price and, therefore, the improvements over time satisfy a need that is already there, without enabling a new dimension of value.

You should focus on technologies that are *hard* to envision (note that I am *not* using the word *unpredictable*, as this book explicitly describes how and why even the fastest-moving technologies are, in fact, *predictable*). Focus on technologies that grow at a pace of at least 25% annually. A *performance parameter* that changes 25% annually will increase in value four times in seven years. Low-tech trends will most likely never make it to become trends we should observe. Or, will they?

Will the *performance parameter* be ready in time for the disruption to occur? The basic rule of thumb to use (in most cases) is that as long as the technology reaches the target required for a disruption within 50% (plus or minus), the disruption *can* occur. For example, if the hard disk drives had not reached 6GB at the introduction of iPod, and reached only 3GB, Apple would have still invented the iPod and would have disrupted the portable music player market. The evidence for that lies in the fact that we *do* use the iPod Nano today, with as little as 2GB.

However, there are situations in which meeting a certain, very specific bar will enable a disruption, and being only 5% below it will not. The evolution of jet engines and the market disruption in the form of the *very light jet* (VLJ) category is an example. The aviation market did not offer anything between regional travel (fifty-plus-seat jet or turboprop airplanes), connecting smaller airports, and private aviation, consisting of two very distinct types of airplanes: the private/business jets, costing $10 million and more to own, or the private piston-engine planes, costing from under $100,000 to over $1 million. The operational expenses associated with the private/business jets made them suitable mostly for a very high-end business and private market, while the short range and slow speed of the piston-engine airplanes made them suitable mostly for recreation, and very limited business markets.

Jet engines had to reach a certain size, power, and price to create another market. The Pratt & Whitney PW610F offered more than 900 pounds of thrust, weighing less than 100 pounds. It enabled the disruption of the aviation market by introducing the VLJ, a small jet carrying five to six passengers at altitudes, speeds, and ranges of commercial jets. The operational expenses are close to those of general aviation piston-engine aircraft. They allowed a completely different type of aviation: the *air taxi*, and the *personal jet*. It could not have happened if the engine power had been 50% less than what the PW910F delivers. The bar that needed to be crossed was much higher, and most likely within 10% or less from the value it has today, enabling the VLJ market.

A further refinement of the rule of thumb will therefore be discussed next:

- A disruption can happen even when the *performance parameter* is within 50% (plus or minus) of the value we believe it needs to have to cause that disruption.

- *Low-tech* trends do not have disruption capabilities, as their relatively slow pace will merely catch up with increasing consumer performance *expectations.*

- In rare occasions, low-tech trends *will* have disruption capabilities, only if there is a *certain value* their performance parameter needs to reach to enable disruption, and then the 50% rule above does not apply.

---

[36] Wi-Fi is a registered trademark of the Wi-Fi Alliance.

[37] Bluetooth is a trademark of the Bluetooth SIG, Inc.

[38] WiMAX is a trademark of the WiMAX Forum.

[39] Dr. Lawrence G. Roberts, "Internet Growth Trends," 2000.

[40] Also called the *channel capacity theory*: $C = BW * \log2 (1+P/N)$ [bps].

[41] Information sources: http://www.digicamhistory.com/, and the Canon Camera Museum at http://www.canon.com/camera-museum/.

Chapter 5
Predicting Future Technology Trends

The previous chapters provided some of the key, fast-moving technology trends. Those chapters not only described the rationale behind those trends, they also told you what to expect the *performance parameters* of those technologies to be in the next decade or so. However, in many cases, those trends will not be sufficient for you, and you will need to seek out relevant trends for the application or market you wish to disrupt. In some cases, you will need to address different *performance parameters* for those technologies, rather than the ones I described before. The process of collecting reliable technology trend data consists of several components:

- Identifying the technology and the performance parameters sought
- Finding credible data sources
- Collecting data
- Selecting the appropriate history time span
- Deducting a trend curve
- Identifying the target time horizon

Identify the technology and performance parameters

This is a case of "chicken or egg." On one hand, you need to know where specific technologies and performance parameters are going to be, while on the other hand you do not know which parameters to focus on if you do not know which market you intend to disrupt. Chapter 8 discusses how to identify market segments that are in need of disruption. The process is iterative.

One part of your work will be academic and empirical, when you search for "interesting" technology trends that carry the potential to disrupt the market. It is somewhat similar to the work of a meteorologist. She is looking for weather patterns (technologies) that carry the potential of disruption to communities (markets). She also identifies the direction and patterns (performance parameter trends) of that weather system, to be able to know how the weather will affect the different communities. What will be the magnitude of a storm forming in the Caribbean when it "lands" in Florida?

The other part of your work is similar to playing the role of the community "protector." You care only about the impact (disruption) of the weather system (technology) on *your* community (market). You want to see how the technological trend will affect a specific market, creating an opportunity for disruption.

Those two things happen in parallel. The process I would recommend pursuing is made of (1) identifying markets that are "vulnerable" to disruptions (see Chapter 8), and (2) looking at technologies that might disrupt them to achieve the breakthroughs in those areas of "vulnerability" to create new dimensions of value. As you identify the combination (market + technology), you will have to focus on the specific performance parameter that, once it reaches a certain value, will enable the disruption. *This* is the parameter you are looking for. There will be a lot of "dancing around" while you go from market analysis to technology analysis, until you lock down the specific technology, performance parameter, and target market. Where you start this research is not necessarily where you might end it.

Credible data sources

Once you select the *technology* and the *performance parameter* you are interested in investigating, you will need to identify *credible* data sources. Remember that your projections are as accurate as the data you choose. Trusting the wrong source of information can lead to making false assumptions on the future progression of the target technology and the performance parameter you are researching. Later in this chapter, I will show the potential impact of wrong assumptions. On the other hand, you will need to balance the accuracy of the information you need with the efforts (time and money) required to obtain it. Try to get confirmation of the information you find by getting it from more than one source (assuming independently developed items). You will be surprised at how much data you can find, and how accurate it will be, within one thorough Internet search session. You have to use all the right terms, and you have to verify the information you find, but you will find what you are looking for during a few hours of focused search. You can start with simple things such as entering "what are the hard disk drive capacity trends?" with www.ask.com, or "hard disk drive trends" with www.google.com. Later you should find the organizations, people, and companies involved. Find the market research firms that cover the field. A good rule of thumb is that if you run across some names (analysts, market research firms, manufacturers, organizations, individuals) significantly more than other names, and no obvious advertisement is involved in those occurrences, you got the right data sources. Before long, you will get the accurate data points you need. Some of the more credible data sources I know and use often are:

- *Market reports*—market research firms publish reports on different topics. You may have to combine reports to get the data you need, and you may have to call the analyst who wrote the report to get clarifications (their names usually appear on the front page of the report). Leading market research firms include Forward Concepts, iSupply, InStat, Strategy Analytics, Ovum, Frost & Sullivan, IC Insights, and others. Different firms specialize in different markets and different aspects of those markets. Some specialize in the semiconductor industry, while others focus on consumer behavior and end-product consumption. Make sure you choose a firm that specializes in the area you need.

- *Trade publications*—different industries have trade publications (magazines, online newsletters) that may contain the data you need. Again, you will need to identify the leading publications in the field to find data you can trust. The information you need might be "hiding" in a short article, but it may still be enough. You may want to contact the reporter to confirm the accuracy and sources (as much as they will reveal to you) of the information.

- *Leading manufacturers*—the leading manufacturers of a technology will typically have products tracking the technology progress very closely. Identifying those leading manufacturers is not hard. If it is, use market-share reports that will identify the leaders in their field. To get a roadmap of *data processing power*, you should search Intel's Web site. To get a roadmap of *digital signal processing (DSP)*, you should search Texas Instruments' site. Search for flash memory data at SanDisk, Toshiba, or Samsung. Semiconductor progress roadmap information can be found at Texas Instruments',

TSMC's, and UMC's Web sites. The information can be found through press releases (companies tend to announce the introduction and even pre-introduction of new products), archived presentations, and white papers.

- *Industry organizations*—different industries, especially those that involve standard-based technologies or those that involve pre-competitive inter-company cooperation create organizations, supported by the leading players in the industry. Part 3 of this book discusses those organizations in detail. Those organizations hold a lot of helpful industry-related information. The person to contact would most likely be the *executive director* of the organization, a person whose full time job is to promote this organization and the industry it represents. Information I found from ITRS, SIA, and FSA assisted my research into the semiconductor industry. My research into the hard disk drive industry used information I received from IDEMA and its executive director, Ed Grochowski. Other industry organizations include the Wi-Fi Alliance, IEEE, TIA, ITU, the Consumer Electronics Association (CEA), the USB Implementers Forum and its chairman, Jeff Ravencraft, and many others. For the most part, the information those organizations gathered originated at the companies involved. Make sure that the organization seems to be representing the major players in the industry. Sometimes a few companies—not representing the majority—create organizations. The sources of information are similar to those of the leading companies themselves: press releases, presentations, and white papers.

- *Trade conference proceedings*—the different industries typically hold conferences, at which ideas are exchanged, companies introduce their latest and greatest products, and the industry leaders, carefully selected by the conference organizers, present their ideas, products, and projections. If you cannot attend in person, those proceedings may be available through the conference Web sites.

- *Industry evangelists*—every industry has people who drive it. It is not just companies that do that, but also individuals in those companies. Texas Instruments' Gene Frantz is one such evangelist in the area of *Digital Signal Processing*. Ed Grochowski (formerly with IBM, and now the executive director of IDEMA) is yet another one. I did not know Ed until I researched the

Internet for "hard disk drive roadmap." After finding quite a few of his projections, history descriptions, and technology trend papers, and presentations, I realized that Ed was the person with whom I needed to speak. The next search of "Ed Grochowski" revealed his position as the executive director of IDEMA, which is where I eventually found him.

Collecting data

The easiest way to collect data would be if the data you are looking for is actually available from the sources you identified and in the format you need it. However, often you will not be so lucky, and you will have to combine multiple data sources and manipulate the data to extract the *performance parameter* you seek.

Keep in mind that while the *time* axis is *linear*, the *technology performance parameter* axis is *exponential*. All industries (I cannot think of one that does not follow this rule) improve their performance by a *multiplier* rather than an *adder*. The semiconductor industry finds ways to have the silicon process node shrink by 30% every two years, and not decrease by 10nm every two years. The hard disk drive industry seeks to increase the *aerial density* by 40% every year, not by $100Mb/in^2$ every year.

Theoretically, you only need two data points to draw a trend line. While the trend might not be a straight line, it is safe to assume that it is very close to it. Only over periods longer than ten years (typically) may technology trends become non-linear curves. Then the question is if we should care what happened more than ten years before. I will return to this question later.

Relying only on two data points can be dangerous though. Figure 17 below describes some of the possible errors that might result from using such a small number of data points. Assume *data points A* and *B* are both accurate. The *accurate* trend line will go through both points and allow us to predict the value of the technology parameter in the future. However, what if instead of *data Point B* we get erroneous data points *B1*, *B2*, or *B3*? Data points *B1* and *B2* represent errors in the value of the performance parameter. *B1* represents an *undershoot*—the assumption that the technology has progressed *less* than it did in reality. *B2* represents an *overshoot*—the assumption that the technology has progressed *more* than it did in reality. Either way, we will draw the wrong trend line, which might be overly *conservative* (if we rely on an *undershoot* data point), or too *aggressive* (if we rely on an *overshoot* data point).

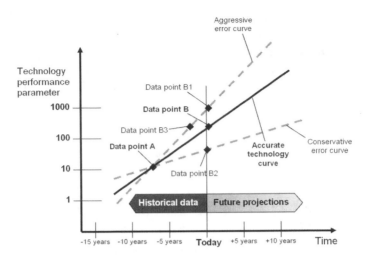

Figure 17—Data errors

The risk of using a *conservative* technology trend line is that we will miss the opportunity for disruption, simply because we do not believe the technology will move fast enough to enable the disruption in time. It will prevent us from disrupting, and open an opportunity to our competitors to move first. On the other hand, the risk of an *aggressive* technology trend might force us to disrupt when the technology is not mature enough, once again letting our competitors catch up with us in time for the technology performance parameter to reach the disrupting value. Unfortunately, I have firsthand experience with that. The InterHome Internet Telephony adapter my own company, Solram Electronics, developed in 1996, was ahead of its time. We developed it on the promise that the quality of service the Internet could offer over an international link would be reasonable (both in terms of overall end-to-end latency, as well as latency consistency). By 1998, the year Solram Electronics closed, the Internet had not yet delivered on that promise. Today, Skype™42 phones deliver on exactly the same promise, because the Internet quality of service improved and the use of broadband connections became pervasive. The InterHome came ten years ahead of its time due to an *overshoot* assumption.

Data Point B3 represents an accurate performance parameter *value*, but is assumed to have occurred at the wrong *time*. The impact is the same, causing us to project the wrong technology trend line, whether it is overly aggressive or overly conservative.

In general, recent data is more accurate. The data sources are still "live," and easy to retrieve. The older data, as important as the new data, is harder to obtain accurately. Ten-year-old press releases, articles, white papers, or presentations might be harder to retrieve, and mistakes are more likely. I recommend gathering as much old data as possible, and use the *average* of that data as a reference point.

The "sweet spot"

When collecting data points to draw a technology curve, you will find that multiple data points exist for almost every single technology parameter *at any given time*. There are several reasons for this phenomenon:

- Sometimes there are issues of *backward compatibility*. When Ethernet reached a speed of 100Mbps,[43] manufacturers could not build products that supported only 100Mbps and not the previous 10Mbps standard. If my computer supported 10Mbps and I bought an Ethernet router that supports only 100Mbps, they would not be compatible. Therefore, 100Mbps and 10Mbps products existed at the same time.

- There are different *applications* and different *form factors* of products for different purposes. A hard disk drive for different applications will exist in different capacities and sizes. For example, in 2004, the average desktop 2.5" hard disk drive capacity was 160GB, while the average 1.5" laptop hard disk drive was only around 60GB. Both disks existed at the same time for different applications.[44] A similar example is the amount of storage a single flash memory card can hold. A microSD™ card, the smallest size card in 2007, would go only as high as 2GB, while the larger compact flash holds 8GB.

- Sometimes, certain applications simply do not require better performance. If an application, for example, requires no more than 256MB of flash memory, there is no need to have a 4GB flash card. There will, therefore, be a need to maintain both products as offerings by a company that manufactures flash cards. When I discuss the "sweet spot" concept in the following text, you will note that while the cost per capacity parameter does have its "sweet spot," a point at which $/GB is optimized, the overall cost of flash cards with smaller memory is lower. If the application requires only 256MB of memory, a manufacturer would rather use a $25, 256MB card than a

$100, 2GB card, even though the first will have a *cost-effectiveness* factor of only $0.10/MB while the latter has a factor of $0.05/MB.

- In some industries, there are tradeoffs between technology parameters. For example, while smaller silicon process nodes offer better pricing (hence, the great progress along the technology curve of Moore's law), the larger silicon process nodes offer better power handling. While digital circuitry-intensive components will tend to move to the most advanced (and therefore smallest) process nodes, power components[45] will require "older" technologies. In 2006, while people used 65nm process nodes for highly complex digital integrated circuits, people typically used 250nm processes for power components.

- Given the advanced nature of the technology, the quality of products using the "cutting edge" might be marginal. Companies may sometimes disqualify a product as a "cutting-edge" product, while qualifying it as a lesser-performing product. For example, if an Intel 133MHz Pentium processor did not completely pass the quality tests for operation at 133MHz, operation at 120MHz was tested. Passing 120MHz quality tests allowed marketing it as a 120MHz processor. Not passing 120MHz tests but passing 100MHz tests allowed marketing it as a 100MHz processor.[46]

Drawing an accurate technology trend curve requires taking the same "position" in the range of products available at any given time. In Figure 18, you can see that for each point in time there are several products at different positions along the technology performance parameter. For simplicity, I show only three products at a time: the *cutting-edge* product, representing the *highest* possible performance product; the *sweet-spot* product, representing the *optimal* price-performance product; and the *low-end* product, representing the *lowest* performance product that is still economically viable. When drawing the technology trend curve, you must use the same product position for all points on the curve. Figure 18 shows three curves: the *cutting-edge* technology curve, the *sweet-spot* technology curve, and the *low-end* technology curve.

Something to keep in mind—the introduction of products actually takes place in *steps* and not along a *constant slope*. A product (or technology) might be available in the market with the same performance for a few years before there is a jump in performance.

For example, the silicon industry typically releases a new process node on a two-year cycle. This means that if the 90nm process appeared in 2004, and the 65nm process appeared in 2006—there was actually no 76nm process introduced in 2005. The *cutting-edge* process in 2005 was still 90nm. This would be a good reason to assure that when drawing a *cutting-edge* curve line, the points taken match the times at which new technologies appeared, rather than arbitrarily selected points in time. The same applies to the *low-end* curves. Low-end products become unavailable when manufacturers decide it is not cost effective anymore to keep those products in production. This trend line is harder to track, as manufacturers typically do not announce the discontinuation of product manufacturing to the public (although they do inform their customers, the OEMs, through "end of life" messages). Furthermore, sometimes there are oddly priced products available in stocks held by distributors, due to different economics of "stock dumping." As a rule of thumb, do not rely on *low-end* technology curves. Typically, those curves will not be a good source for innovative disruptions as those rely mostly on cutting-edge technologies or, at least, the *sweet-spot* technology curves for best economics.

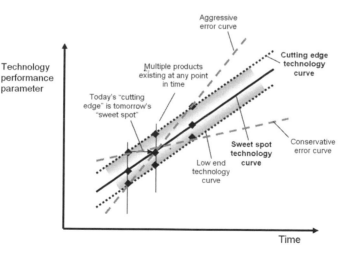

Figure 18—Technology parameter curve range

Figure 18 demonstrates that today's *cutting-edge* technology will become tomorrow's *sweet spot.* You can see that the three different trend curves are parallel. This will not always be the case, but it is generally a good rule of thumb.

The most important lesson from this chart is that relying on different positions along the technology performance parameter axis at different times will result in erroneous technology curves. Using a *cutting-edge* product at one point in time and a *low-end* (or even a *sweet-spot*) product at a later time will result in too *conservative* a trend line.[47] Using a *low-end* (or even a *sweet-spot*) product at one point in time and a *cutting-edge* product at a later time to project the technology curve will result in too aggressive a trend curve.[48]

To understand better the concept of *sweet spot,* I started researching hard drives. I went to the Flash Memory Store[49] to research external hard disk drives. There were many different types of hard disk drives available for purchase. Some were internal drives and some external. Of the external drives, there were drives with high-speed USB 2.0 interface, drives with high-performance FireWire interface, and other parameters. To ensure consistency and relevancy of the data points, I chose hard drives of the same form factor, the same interfaces, and from the same manufacturer, QMemory. I looked for the price points of the different disk drives and, with everything else being equal, I normalized them to their capacity. The prices I found were as follows:

Memory Capacity	Overall Price (MSRP)	Price ($) per GB
750GB	$525	0.70
500GB	$339	0.68
400GB	$259	0.65
250GB	$139	0.56
200GB	$135	0.68
160GB	$132	0.83
120GB	$123	1.03
80GB	$110	1.38

Figure 19—Hard disk drive price-per-capacity

The hard disk drive capacity parameter can help better explain the *sweet spot* concept. If you look only at the overall price of hard disk drives of similar form factor with the only varying parameter being the capacity of the drive, you see that those prices increase as the capacity increases (from $110 for a 80GB drive to $525 for a 750GB drive). However, when normalizing those prices to the capacity of the drives, you find an interesting phenomenon: moving from the smallest available disk drive to the largest one available, the price-per-GB initially decreases, and then starts increasing again. Eventually, this ratio reaches its optimized point, which I refer to as the *sweet spot.* In the research I did, I noticed that the "cost-effectiveness" of the HDD of the type researched started at $1.38/GB for the smallest available hard disk drive of this form factor (80GB), gradually declining to $0.56/GB for a 250GB drive, and then climbing back up to $0.70/GB for a 750GB hard drive. This makes the 750GB drive the *cutting-edge* drive, the 80GB drive the *low-end* drive, and the 250GB the *sweet-spot* drive.

There are several reasons for the existence of such an optimized point. As we move closer to the *cutting-edge* technology position, the cost of manufacturing increases, due to more expensive manufacturing facilities, and the yield decreases, due to lower quality of the cutting-edge process.[50] On the *low-end* side of the range, there are other, "fixed" costs that, when amortized over a smaller value of the technology parameter, will create an increased cost element in the cost-effectiveness factor. In a hard disk drive, the cost of the electric motor, the electronic circuitry, and the package, among other elements, remains the same.[51]

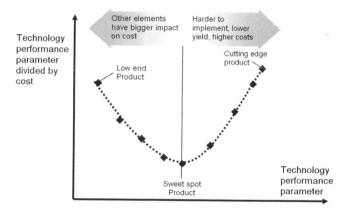

Figure 20—Technology sweet spot

Similar phenomena exist for silicon production. The yield of an advanced, *cutting-edge* process is typically lower than the yield of a more established process, free of its infancy problems. Furthermore, the cost of *photomasks* is higher for smaller geometry designs as the lithography technology is more complex. The cost of a more advanced production facility is much more expensive, requiring amortization over a smaller number of production units. On the other end, the testing costs, wire-bonding costs, and integrated circuit packaging costs (along with other such "fixed" costs) do not change with the process node, and, therefore, they become a bigger burden on the unit cost. A good rule of thumb is that the cost of a die of a new silicon process is 30% more than the same die of the previous process. With 100% more functionality, it should still be worth it.

Gordon Moore, in his article from 1965, observed, "Reduced cost is one of the big attractions of integrated electronics, and the cost advantage continues to increase as the technology evolved toward the production of larger and larger circuit functions on a single semiconductor substrate. For simple circuits, the cost per component is nearly inversely proportional to the number of components, the result of the equivalent piece of semiconductor in the equivalent package containing more components. But, as components are added, decreased yields more than compensate for the increased complexity, tending to raise the cost per components. Thus, there is a minimum cost at any given time in the evolution of the technology. At present [1965], it is reached when 50 components are used per circuit." Figure 21 is taken from Moore's article (courtesy of Intel) and shows the concept of "sweet spot" as observed by him.

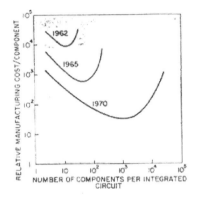

Figure 21—Moore's "sweet spot" diagram

After conducting the hard disk drive research, I went on to research the prices of flash cards for digital cameras, by looking up prices from the SanDisk catalog. Like HDD, there are multiple types of flash cards.[52] I chose the somewhat "standard" SD™ Card form factor. Still, there were multiple variants of the same form factor.[53] I chose the Standard SD™ memory card, and retrieved the following prices:

Memory Capacity	Overall Price (MSRP)	Price per GB
4GB	$199.99	$49.75
2GB	$99.99	$50.00
1GB	$59.99	$59.99
512MB	$39.99	$79.98
256MB	$24.99	$99.96
128MB	$17.99	$143.92

Figure 22—Flash memory price-per-capacity

There are two conclusions from the flash card example. The first is that for some technologies, the *sweet spot* actually exists with maximization of the technology performance parameter. How can that happen? Typically, when different instantiations use the same technology, the best economics of scale result with the maximum capacity (in this example) with amortization of the "fixed" costs (such as a package) over the highest value. The second conclusion is even more interesting. Not only is the total capacity of hard disk drives in a different order of magnitude than its solid-state competitor, the flash memory,[54] but the price/GB is close to a hundred times cheaper. On the one hand, as Chapter 7 will discuss, there is an overall trend from electromechanical (e.g., hard disk drives) to solid state (e.g., flash memory). There will be an interesting dichotomy in the use of storage in electronic products, where different applications use the two different storage methods.

The beginning of time?

To draw a technology trend line, you first need to take the most current technology performance parameter that you can find. You will use this as your anchor point. This is the most accurate data that represents, hopefully, the "state of the industry" today. To project a line with a certain angle into the future, you now need to find the angle. If you take only a data point that is a year old, you risk significant errors. The answer to "How far back do we need to look?" is not straightforward. You need to consider the rate of changes in the technology. If changes occur every ten years, then you should look more than ten years, or even twenty years back. If the rate of change in this industry is annual, then five to ten years will give you a good and reliable trend indication.

You should *not* go back to the "beginning of time." During the first years of a technology, the rate of change is very erratic. There is no history or pre-competitive cooperation, and companies will improve along any rate they can. Multiple instantiations of the technologies will occur, competing with each other, until the industry settles down on standards, and pre-competitive cooperation takes place. This is the point in time you are looking for. By then, the leaders (companies, industry organizations, but mostly people) have realized a rate of change they can live with, and started solving barriers that prevented them from staying along the prescribed technology trend. Another phenomenon to keep in mind is that the technology trends may change over time. Figure 23 demonstrates this point. Taking *all* data points into consideration (back to the "beginning of time") will cause you to observe *trend line 1* and project it into the future.

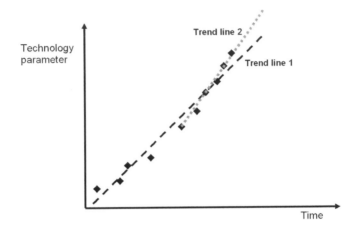

Figure 23—Technology trends changing slopes

However, observing data points over a shorter (yet reliable enough) timeframe, may actually reveal changes in the slope of the technology trend line. There are many reasons for this change of slope, but the main one is psychological; the leaders of the industry *decide* it is time to change the slope. They will increase the slope to increase competition, and they will decrease the slope when the technology commoditizes. While Moore's law originally indicated a 50% silicon area decrease every eighteen months, it was not long after that when the trend found itself "riding" a twenty-four-month cycle. ITRS indicates that starting in 2007, the cycle will become a thirty-six-month cycle. Similarly, while the hard disk drive industry maintained an *aerial density* growth rate of 25% annually from the mid 1960s to 1991, it changed its slope to 60% between 1991 and 1997, went as high as 100% annually from 1997 to 2001, and appears to have stabilized at a 40% growth rate from 2001 to 2006, and probably beyond. It represents a perfect example of why you should focus on a period of five to ten years.

Shoot in front of the duck

How far ahead should you aim? Problems of aiming too far out are (1) accuracy, (2) other "surprises," (3) competitors catching up. Releasing a new technology to market takes three to four years, at best. However, things will take longer in reality. Add two to three years for market development. The first period will be a trial, an early adoption period. Prices can be higher, capacity can be lower, battery life might be shortened, and size might be bigger. Two to three years later, real market adoption is where you should shoot (in front of the duck). One of the basic lessons when learning how to conduct air-to-air combat (dogfight) is to shoot in front of your opponent. If you aim exactly where your opponent is, by the time your bullets reach that location, your opponent is no longer there. This is why you need to shoot *in front* of your opponent. By the time your bullets reach that place in space, so will your opponent. Use this as guidance regarding where you aim with your disruption.

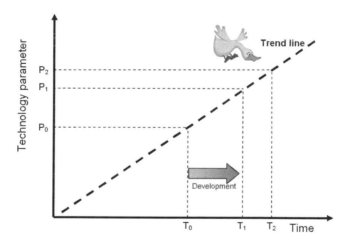

Figure 24—Shoot in front of the duck

In Figure 24, T0 represents today, the time in which the development of the new disruptive implementation needs to start. At this time, the current technology parameter value, represented by P0, is not yet viable for the new implementation. At first look it appears that, if it takes the time from T0 to T1 to develop the new implementation, you should consider the value of the available technology P1 for the new implementation. However, I would strongly recommend looking further out in time and, as a rule of thumb, look two to three years further. There are two reasons for this. The first is that markets always take longer to develop. When I first got involved in the ultra-wideband (UWB) ultra-high-speed wireless connectivity market in 2003, the expectation was that UWB-enabled products would be on retail shelves by the end of 2004. As of 2006, the market has not developed yet, not even to fulfill the needs of early adopters. I suspect, at this time, that this market will address early adopters in late 2007 to early 2008. You may start developing an implementation in 2006 to address a market in 2010, relying on a projection of the required technologies in 2010. However, the market will most likely develop only two to three years later. At that time, the technology would actually exceed the value required to address the implementation, and your competitors, relying on the technology in 2012 or 2013, will deliver products that outperform yours. The second reason to shoot further out in time is that, even if the market starts developing in 2010 as expected—only the early adopters buy the products. Surprisingly enough, at this point, a product that is a little too big, a little too expensive, and consumes a little too much power (since the required technology has not achieved the performance required for the new implementation) would still be acceptable. Early adopters are much less sensitive to the performance of the product. They are driven by the new possibilities it encapsulates assuming, and rightfully so, that the performance will only improve in time.[55] The first BlackBerry communicators did not have the capabilities they have today. The first cellular phones were bulky,[56] had very short battery life, and the infrastructure had less than adequate coverage. However, the markets developed assuming, rightly so, that the underlying technologies would improve and the products would be what they are today.

---

[42] Skype is a trademark of Skype Limited.

[43] Later it reached 1Gbps, and recently a standard known as 802.3an was released, increasing the Ethernet speed to 10Gbps.

[44] The data density of both drives was the same, at approximately 8.5GB/in^2.

[45] Such as USB line drivers, wireless power amplifiers, and more.

[46] Those in the silicon industry sometimes refer to this as "binning." Instead of only *passing* or *failing* a component during final quality tests, components go into bins after final tests. There will be the top performing components bin, as well as the less-than-top-performing component bin. This does not mean that the less-than-top-performing components have no value. Applications that require less than the top

performance use them, and their price is lower to reflect their lower performance. It still is more economical than to scratch this material. (Manufacturers can still generate revenue off less-than-perfect components as well as OEMs that use components that, while less than the maximum available performance in the market are sill satisfactory for the specific application for which they are used by this OEM. The price is less than if those were components performing at the best-in-class performance available in the market at the time.)

[47] For illustration, assume that in 2000, the cutting-edge hard disk drive (HDD) had 20GB, the sweet-spot HDD had 10GB, and the low-end HDD had 5GB. In 2004, assume that the cutting edge HDD had 100GB, the sweet spot had 50 GB, and the low end had 25GB. Projecting a technology curve based on the cutting-edge capacity in 2000 and the low end capacity in 2004 will lead you to believe that the four-year capacity growth factor is only 25 % (from 20GB to 25GB), and therefore to believe that in 2008 that capacity will be only 31GB. If the disruptive application requires that the capacity reach 200GB, you will find that point in the year 2044, almost 40 years from now! On the other hand, using the correct cutting-edge curve, you will find that the 4-year capacity curve growth factor is 900% (a number closer to reality), and that the 2008 capacity will be 1,000GB. Based on this curve, a 200GB capacity appears in 2005 or 2006, almost 40 years different than when using the erroneous conservative trend line. Furthermore, even relying on the correct *sweet-spot* trend line, it is possible to reach the 200GB mark in 2006 or 2007.

[48] Using the same example data as in the previous footnote – Projecting a technology trend line based on the low-end 2000 capacity and the cutting-edge 2004 capacity will result in believing that the four-year growth factor is 3900% and that in 2008 the HDD capacity will be 8,000GB. In reality, using the data above, the cutting-edge capacity four-year growth rate is only 900%, and in 2008 that capacity will only reach 2,000GB. If the product planning relies on HDD capacity to be 8,000GB (as if, for example, the product planning relies on the ability to store 320 full-length high-definition movies), you might be planning for this capacity to be reached in 2008, whereas in reality this capacity will be reached only in 2011 or 2012. Although the error is only three years – it can still make or break a business.

[49] www.flashmemorystore.com.

[50] If, for example, the yield (number of good, selling-quality units divided by total number of units manufactured including the failing ones) is only 80% and the cost of manufacturing a single untested unit is $10, we should consider this cost to be $12.50, accounting for failing units.

51 If, for example, the cost of those elements is a fixed $5, then burdening a 100GB hard disk drive with them will result in a $0.05/GB "tax," while burdening a 20GB drive with them will result in a $0.25/GB "tax." At some point in time, it is no longer economical to manufacture drives with such a small capacity in which this "tax" becomes prohibitive.

52 I found SD™ cards, Memory Stick PRO™ cards, CompactFlach®) cards, xD-Picture Card™, miniSD™ cards, microSD™/TransFlash™ cards, RS-MMC™ cards, MMCmobile™ cards and Ultra II™ Mobile cards. These are all different form factors for different applications and connections. Some are for pure digital cameras, some are for cellular phones, etc. They also carry different price points.

53 The different flavors were SanDisk Extreme II® SD™, SanDisk Ultra II® SD™, Ultra II® SD™ Plus, Standard SD™, Shoot & Store™ SD™, and Gaming SD™ cards. Even those all serve different purposes and have different parameters (such as access speed), other than the main parameter which, in this case, is the memory size.

54 HDD reach capacity of 750GB while flash cards reach capacity of 4GB. Keep in mind that the form factor or those HDD is significantly larger than that of the SD card.

55 For further discussion on the behavior of early adopters, see Geoffrey Moore, Crossing the Chasm.

56 Users typically referred to them as "brick phones" due to their shape, size, and weight.

Chapter 6
Understanding Non-technological Trends

There is no doubt that technology—and specifically high-technology—moves very fast. When you draw the technology trend lines into the future, consistent with their behavior in the past, you will have a hard time believing the numbers you see. Figure 16 is an example. Can you believe all the 2014 numbers there? Well, they represent straight trend lines. However, other driving forces do not move this fast. For example, it takes the Federal Communications Commission (FCC) some eighteen to thirty-six months to change its rules from an initial *notice of proposed rulemaking* (NPRM) until the new rules are in place and, even then, sometimes the overall impact on the industry might be marginal.

This chapter covers a few driving forces that, while moving much slower than high-tech, may have a significant impact on many industries. Those forces can make or break markets and business models. They can turn the future prospects of companies and technologies around. There is no way to say the following without causing you heartburn, so I'll just go ahead and say it: even major catastrophes create opportunities. To be clear, I am not trying to guide you to create a catastrophe, nor do I ever wish one would happen. However, when they do happen, there are opportunities that, while easing a terrible situation, will also create opportunities and new markets, as well as change the way markets behave. The events of September 11, 2001, are one example. Many people realized that we in the US lived under the naïve belief that we were safe. But 9/11 proved us wrong, creating a whole new market for defense equipment and security products for airports and aircraft. This market almost didn't exist before. Global warming, on the other hand, would take a long time to create an effect that would create new markets. Over time, the gradual temperature increases will increase the opportunities in the air-conditioning market, but will they do much more than that?

You need to evaluate four major factors when you consider those forces:

- *Gradient*—are those forces changing gradually, or do they have an "on/off" effect? Global warming, for example, has a *gradual* impact. Things will happen over a long period. Of course, there could be specific events resulting from global warming that will have a dramatic and sudden impact, but for most cases, the changes will be gradual. Gradual changes let you prepare. They are easier to predict. They typically change very slowly and, therefore, pose little opportunity for market disruptions.

- *Impact*—certain events might have devastating impact on the markets you are targeting. Others may have an enabling impact, or very little impact. The Telecommunication Act of 1996 had a dramatic impact on the telecommunication industry in the US. It enabled new players and changed significantly the competitive landscape and business models for existing, incumbent players.

- *Controllable*—do you have ways to affect those events, or are they completely out of your control? FCC (and other government agencies, US and otherwise) regulations can be influenced through lobbying, alliances, and other political activities. To influence regulations, you must first know there is an opportunity to affect them. I am a big believer in *controlling your own destiny*, and will always preach that even government actions can be initiated by industry. Global warming, on the other hand, is probably out of your control. No lobbying will stop it.

- *Permanency*—are those forces temporary or permanent? Temporary changes in regulations, nature, or society, will create temporary opportunities that might be short lived, not justifying the investment made in harvesting them. You should consider changes that last less than five years as temporary. If your planning time horizon is five years or more, you should not consider them at all.

The most important trends to observe are those that have a *significant impact*, are *permanent*, and *change quickly* rather than gradually. You need to consider the possibility to influence them in a favorable direction, if they are *controllable* too. Otherwise, you should simply prepare for them.

I arranged those non-technological driving forces into three categories, as discussed in the following paragraphs.

Government, global, political, and regulatory

These forces are "man-made." People in government or other institutions decide them, and then create laws, rules, and standards. I can argue whether they are *gradual* or not. On one hand, legislation can make an immediate impact and cause a step change in an industry. The Telecommunications Act of 1996 was such legislation. Other pieces of legislation can be gradual, and change the scenery over a long period, allowing the industry to adjust. For example, the FCC decided to convert all the UHF TV frequencies from analog to digital, and mandated the transition to digital TV. Congress passed the law in 2006, with the compliance deadline in February 2009. This gives enough time for industry to prepare, and for no single company to gain a significant disruptive, competitive advantage.

As stated before, the impact can be significant. You need to remember that the government creates rules to support its constituencies, and those include parties interested in change, as well as those who resist it. The government must be impartial to all legitimate interests, and, therefore, will typically not make dramatic moves.

Of the three forces discussed here, government, political, and regulatory, government is the most "controllable." After all, the purpose of government legislation, as stated above, is to create a better environment for the people. If the people manage to convince the government and other regulatory agencies of the importance of a certain legislative or regulatory act, the government will implement it. Such "controlling" is done through lobbying. Since the government wishes to comply with the needs of the widest base of the people, the probability of success of lobbying depends on the amount of external support you garner before approaching the government. Before starting to lobby, you should secure the support of other companies with similar interests, and demonstrate such support to the government. The government will immediately consider whom the legislation will hurt. You may have to secure the support (or at least "don't care") of those, too. Even then, the government will take time to create such legislation in a fair and effective manner, as equitably as possible, and as much as possible in a way that will guarantee reelection for another term.

Government actions are reversible—whether through later legislation that will reverse the effects of the previous one, or by supposedly unrelated legislation, that might nullify the effects of the previous one. Much like the original legislation, the government will typically not create reverse legislation unless there is significant support for it from outside the government, which goes back to the fact that government and regulatory actions are somewhat "controllable."

That said, governments worldwide confront "hot button" issues, which receive higher priority than others. Those are typically (not in any special order),

- Privacy
- Globalization
- Security
- Freedom of trade

I already gave an example (the Telecommunications Act of 1996) of how government and regulations can affect industry and markets. Another example is the never-ending regulatory debate over the frequencies and power outputs allowed for the ultra-wideband wireless technology. While the US FCC was very liberal in its ruling in 2002, it took the rest of the world more than five years to reach some clarity. While writing these lines in 2007, worldwide regulatory support for such products is not in harmony, a fact that delays the adoption of the UWB technology.

One morning early in 2006, a California senator learned that his Wi-Fi network allowed unlawful and malicious access into his computers connected to his network, which was unsecured. I should add that the Wi-Fi technology includes very robust security mechanisms but, at the same time, users typically do not activate them, leaving their networks vulnerable to such attacks. After a very quick legislative process, the California bill became law. While causing some industry (well, the Wi-Fi industry) concern, the impact was not as dramatic. Protecting the consumers' privacy, the California bill required securing Wi-Fi equipment "out of the box," or including very clear labeling instructing to consumers to protect their wireless networks. Criticized by the media ("Can we legislate away consumer idiocy?") the "Wi-Fi user protection bill" still allowed some eighteen months before manufacturers had to implement it.

Society

The term *society* is very wide and covers a lot. The aspects of society that are of interest to you in the context of this book focus on technology consumption habits. When you look at Christensen's charts of disruptive technologies, and Figure 1 in the introduction to this book, as well as many other charts throughout the book, you will notice that the *market* is described by a line indicating *demand* for certain performance. You will see that this line shows a gradual incline, which means that consumers demand *more* with time. However, you should also note that this incline is very gradual and mild. In fact, consumers *resist* change. Later in this book, you will find a discussion about this resistance, along with ways to overcome it. When I discussed the future of DSPs with Gene Frantz (in Chapter 3), he stated, "We can deliver a 600,000 MMACs DSP *today*, if we want to, but engineers will not know what to do with it." The gradual and slow change in consumer behavior and demand for performance is also the opportunity you have to disrupt, as covered in the introduction to the book. When BMW comes up with a new line of cars, it takes time to get used to the new look. They are an *acquired taste*. When we do get used to the new look, we don't want to go back, but it doesn't happen overnight.

The impact that society and consumption habits have on disruption is dramatic. After all, you build disruptive products for consumption. The consumption trends (as described in Chapter 7) will enable those innovative products. Those society trends likely have the most impact on the success of your products—more than any government action or natural event.

Are society and consumption habits *controllable*? To some extent they are. The media influence consumers. Multimillion-dollar commercials and advertisements can reach billions of consumers, but will affect society very slowly, while allowing competition to organize. Grassroots efforts reach a small number of consumers and adoption takes forever. Wi-Fi started as a grassroots effort. Consumers bought Wi-Fi gear in retail stores, and charged the expense to their expense reports. One day, enterprises found themselves with installed Wi-Fi networks and had to catch up.

How permanent are social changes and consumer habits? They are *not* permanent but, as stated above, change gradually. Unlike government legislation that can be reversed, society trends typically do not go back.

Nature

Natural events typically take place in a gradual manner. The effects of global warming will span across generations. Even the most rapid effects of global warming will take ten years or more, and there will be time to prepare. A fuel shortage does not happen overnight. No doubt that fuel shortages and environmental concerns, gave rise to the market for hybrid cars. However, this market is slow to develop. Government incentives for hybrid cars are not significant enough to influence the rate of adoption. Fuel prices increase very gradually. When I moved to California in 1998, the price of a regular unleaded gallon was $1.23 (and $0.99 in Texas). In 2007, I paid more than $2.10 per gallon, representing an annual increase of 8.7%. Even when the prices rose above $3.00 in 2006, they would still have represented an annual increase of less than 15%. It would not have changed the way consumers use products, dramatically and instantly breaking markets apart while creating new ones where none existed. People still buy SUVs for personal consumption. I did. At the same time, there can be natural events that cause immediate changes. The tsunami of 2004 had an immediate and devastating effect. I don't believe it created new markets or demand for new products that didn't exist before. Having said that, I believe a sudden natural event could be so fundamental and permanent that it would create new markets. A highly contagious flu epidemic would put a lot of pressure on the telecommuting infrastructure, video conferencing, and other relative components.

The impact of natural events is dramatic, and can be devastating. However, the world "goes back to normal" after these typically short-lived events. Hardly ever does a sudden natural event change the world significantly enough to create new markets.

Of the three driving forces (government, society, nature), this one is the least controllable. I wish we could do something to stop global warming, but I don't think there is anything we can do in the short term that will reverse it. One thing about society's ability and willingness to change things—the impact must be relatively immediate for us to pursue. One of the reasons that by February we drop our new year's resolution to lose weight this year is that we don't see an immediate impact on our hard work. Will we stop driving SUVs? Will we all take the train to work? I bet that if we could immediately observe our impact on global warming, we would. So it is not really that we *cannot* affect nature, it is that we are not *willing* to, given the long time from action to results.

The permanency of natural events is twofold. The fundamental changes (e.g., global warming), are permanent (unless six billion people commit to do something about it). Local changes (e.g., a hurricane, a tsunami, or a flu epidemic), on the other hand, will have a temporary effect, after which things will go back to normal.

Can we predict non-technological trends?

The answer will be different for the three different driving forces. We can predict (and even influence) some government and regulatory events. Those are, to some extent, open to the public. As an example, before the FCC changes its rules, it published a "Notice of Proposed Rulemaking" (NPRM). If you monitor FCC publications, you will know about it, most likely years ahead of any change. The industry had more than three years to prepare the digital television transition, and even more, as the legislation work started long before 2006, taking effect only in 2009.

Society is the easiest to predict. It doesn't change overnight. There are very specific trends in which society consumption habits change, and the next chapter describes those in a way that will allow you to predict them. Hardly ever in history has society changed dramatically, and somewhat unexpectedly, as during political and industrial revolutions, and even those took a relatively long time and, some will say, are somewhat predictable.

We have tools today to allow us to predict natural changes, specifically weather and climate changes. Predicting slow changes (such as global warming) is based on historical and empirical data, projecting those trends into the future, much like predicting technology trends, except at a much slower pace. Predicting faster changes (such as local weather) is improving, predicting weather a few days ahead. Those changes, though, are not so fundamental as to create market opportunities, so they will be outside the scope of our interests in this book.

Part 2
Inventing The Future

Chapter 7
Product And Market Evolution Trends

You will note than I am using the term *disruptive implementation* rather than the conventional *disruptive technology*. So what is the difference between a technology and an implementation? I consider *technology* as the enabling component of disruptive implementations. The semiconductor silicon process is an enabling technology for a *system on chip*, which is a complex integrated circuit that implements an application or a product (e.g., MP3 player). A *technology* and an *implementation* actually depend on the place the product has in the value chain. For example, for the personal computer industry, the *microprocessor, hard disk drive* and *memory* are the enabling technologies. A company in the business of building personal computers (Dell, Apple, Hewlett Packard) monitors the processing power of microprocessors as the underlying technology. The improvements in processing power is the *performance parameter trend* to watch for, as it may give rise to new types of personal computers. Such new types of computers would represent a *disruptive implementation*, as it will be a non-linear implementation of that enabling technological improvement. Companies in the business of building microprocessors, though, look at the silicon process as the enabling technology and the shrinkage of this process as the performance parameter trend to monitor. Those companies will create non-linear disruptive implementations based on the silicon process technology trends. The iPod was a disruptive implementation based on the hard disk drive capacity technology trend.

So how do you find opportunities for disruptive implementations? There are four components to your ability to create such disruptive implementations:

- Prediction of the enabling technology trends. While very steep in nature, as described before, those are highly predictable due to the psychological nature of those trends.

- Assumptions on the behavior of non-technological driving forces. Those can be unpredictable and uncontrollable, but may also vary gradually, and more likely will not have an impact on the future for four to eight years.

- Understanding of the general customer and consumer behavior trends. Those trends occur in every market. In order to identify the opportunity to disrupt, you need to identify those markets in which the natural trends have not yet occurred. This chapter will discuss those in detail.

- Finally, the ability to visualize the future for which you are planning. Collins and Porras, in their legendary book *Built to Last*,[57] wrote about *envisioned future*. To them, only the ability to create a vivid description of the future, to the point of almost "living it" is the key to achieving the "big hairy audacious goals" (BHAG). To me, only the ability to create a vivid image of the future, based on the technology trends, consumer behavior trends, and driving force trends, will help the innovator identify the opportunities for disruptive implementations. Envisioning your customers' behavior in the future will allow you to find what is missing—and that is what you want to innovate. Not believing in the envisioned future will prevent you from doing so.

So how does a technology disruption occur? The following diagram might help explain the dynamic. Simply put, a disruption occurs when a technology developed for a certain market exceeds the performance level required for that market and, with continuous investment, improves along its trend line to the point of disrupting another market, which is on a trajectory to improve performance along a different performance characteristic.

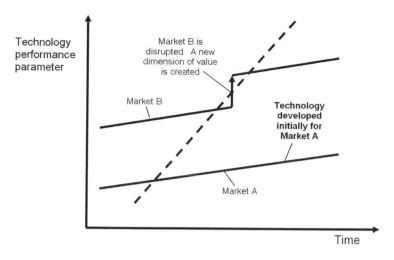

Figure 25—How disruptions occur

Keep in mind that, just as new technologies fuel the market for new products, demand for those products fuels the investment in those technologies, creating a down-the-value-chain demand for those technologies. If the market for electronic products was not as big as it was, there would not have been such a great demand for semiconductors, and the investment in developing the semiconductor technology would have been small to the point that semiconductor technology would not have been where it is today. The size of the electronics end-product market was close to $1.3 trillion in 2006, which fueled a $250 billion semiconductor market (which also means that the semiconductor content of electronic products is close to 20% of its overall retail price.[58] With the investment in research and development averaging 10%-15% of revenue for semiconductor companies, the industry-wide investment in semiconductor R&D was close to $25 to $38 billion in 2006. This investment allows the semiconductor process roadmap to continue to be as steep as it is and, in return, continuously disrupt market segments and enable all the new consumer electronics products you see at the Consumer Electronics Show in Las Vegas every year, coincidentally, on my birthday.

Clayton Christensen, in his books, *The Innovator's Dilemma* and *The Innovator's Solution*, describes the concept that a technology advances faster than the consumers in the market require. At a point, according to Christensen, the technology and product performance overshoot the needs of the consumers in that market, even at the high end. After serving *market A* to a point of overshooting its needs,[59] the technology, which exceeds the needs of *market A*, all of a sudden offers a new value to *market B*. Before this point in the development of Market B, the technology does not merit consideration, because it does not meet the absolute *minimum* requirements of products in *market B*. At that point, *market B* undergoes a disruption. A new dimension of value-enhanced products enters the market, and the rules of the game change. The technology will continue development to the point of disrupting another market, most likely. A few examples are in order.

Take the hard disk drive (HDD) technology. The investment in the HDD market would not have been made if it weren't for the mainframe computer market. It was obvious that those computers required memory that was much more than could be stored in solid-state random access memory (RAM), and needed to be accessed much faster than a magnetic tape drive could have offered, and needed to be non-volatile. However, the HDD industry became an almost independent industry, continuing to evolve beyond the needs of the mainframe computer market. It was quite apparent that the performance dimensions for the HDD technology would be mainly (but not solely) the data density and the cost of capacity, measured in \$/MB. The HDD technology evolved beyond the need of the mainframe computers, and beyond those of the minicomputers. After all, what value would the mainframe computer or minicomputer market have to disks with a diameter of 5¼"? 3½"? Less than 1"? One might claim that it was the HDD industry, developed for the mainframe computer market, which disrupted it. The 5¼" disk drives enabled the introduction of the microcomputer (personal computer) market, which disrupted the mainframe computer markets, and even its successor, the minicomputer market. One might also claim that is was the introduction of 2½" disk drives that gave birth to the portable laptop PC that disrupted the desktop PC market. After all, most PC users use only one computer, either a desktop or a laptop, and most of them are moving away from desktop computers to laptop computers. In fact, while desktop PC sales grew 7% from 2002 to 2006, laptop PC sales grew 19% for the same period.

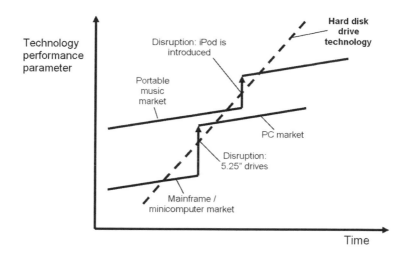

Figure 26—HDD technology, from mainframe computers to iPod

The HDD technology did not stop there. Fueled by revenue from the PC market, the technology continued to produce smaller disk drives with higher density. The PC industry had no need for a disk smaller than 1½", and definitely not one smaller than 1". However, it was a 6GB, 1½" HDD that disrupted the portable music market, and allowed Apple to introduce the iPod, adding new dimension of value to that market, and creating a $6 billion a year opportunity for Apple. Will the HDD technology evolution stop there? I don't think so. With HDD smaller than 1", I expect them to enter digital cameras and cellular phones, adding enormous amounts of content capacity, and introducing new applications, some of which will most likely be disruptive. In 2005, JVC was the first to introduce the "Everio G" camcorder series, the first digital camcorder that uses a hard disk drive instead of a tape or a DVD writer.

One of my favorite market disruptions is the cellular phone. Wireless technology evolved for markets other than the telephony market. Military communications, and later civilian communications, benefited from wireless technology advances. The first radio communication devices relied on vacuum tubes. They were bulky, heavy, pricy, and consumed a lot of power. In its initial form, the wireless technology could not have disrupted any other market. A military tactical radio weighed over 100lb, had a price tag of tens and hundreds of thousands of dollars, and consumed thousands of watts just to reach a target a few dozen miles away. Military equipment is very expensive. But there was no doubt, the radios did their job. The military vehicles could carry those radios, and had enough "juice" in their electrical systems to power those radios.

The radio technology continued to evolve, though. The invention of the solid-state transistor dramatically reduced the size, power consumption, and cost. All of a sudden, a radio carried by a soldier on foot became a reality. After that, radios revolutionized automobile fleets, allowing taxi drivers to receive assignments while on the road, tracking truck drivers, and alerting security vehicle drivers. Powered by an auto battery, the radios were too heavy to carry manually. Then, with the invention of the integrated circuits, the radios got even smaller, and the hand-held "walkie-talkie" radios were introduced. In fact, military communications provided the source of almost every new wireless technology, starting with *narrow-band* radio communications, and continuing with *spread spectrum* communications that allow multiple radios to share the same radio frequencies. The latter was adopted for wireless networking (Wi-Fi) and wireless headset (Bluetooth) markets, just to name two.

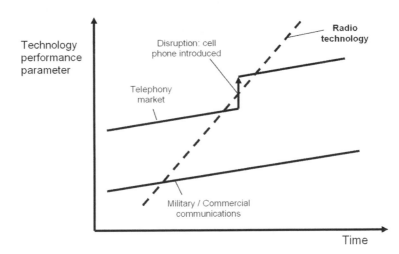

Figure 27—Radio technology, from military communications to cell phones

The continuous evolution of the radio technology disrupted the telephony market the most. The telephony market was in a mature state. New telephones offered continuous (non-disruptive) improvements. Some of those improvements were small and some were large, but they were all continuous. The tone dialing, answering machine, caller ID, and the cordless[60] telephone had the biggest impact on that market. Those innovations paled in comparison with the cellular phone disruption. When the radio technology reached a point where it was small enough, cheap enough, low-power enough, and high-quality enough (although the first cellular phones had a price tag of over \$3,000 with a service cost over \$1/minute, and with batteries that lasted less than one hour of "talk time"), it disrupted the telephony market dramatically. In 2006, more than one billion cellular phones went to almost three billion subscribers, half the world population.

The opportunity here is that the technologies that will disrupt markets are *already in existence,* serving other markets. Our task is to identify those technologies and see how they can disrupt other markets than those they are currently serving. I would even be so blunt as to state that the HDD, semiconductor, memory, and DSP technologies will cause most consumer electronic disruptions. The first part of this book was a guide to understanding the technology trends, and estimating their future performance. Now the question is where are the opportunities for disruptions that those technologies present when taken out of the markets that fueled their fast evolution?

In the last few decades, there have been parallel disruptive implementations that repeated themselves over many different markets. Those disruptions conditioned the consumers to expect them in more and more markets. This chapter will address the key disruptive implementations that took place with examples for each. In order to find opportunities for disruptive implementations, we must look at different products and markets, and position them along a vector of improvements that happened in other markets. The closer the product (or market) is to the left side (*"from"*), the more likely it is to find an opportunity to innovate and disrupt the market. However, the closer a product (or market) is to the right (*"to"*) direction, the less likely it is to find an opportunity for disruption.

In the next paragraphs I will provide the *from-to* vectors for the trends I will describe. I went beyond what is available today, to what I think the future can offer if technologies can provide support. However, I have to admit, my imagination is limited too. Do not consider my *"to"* as the end of the road for those trends. Think about what may come after that.

Flexibility: From analog to digital to software

Many electronic products moved from implementing *analog* electronics to *digital* electronics. The technological improvements that supported this trend included the invention of the integrated circuit, higher-scale integration, and faster signal processing. Hand-held radios used to have several crystals for the different radio channels, which made them bulky, expensive, and limited to a small number of channels. Newer radios include digital circuitry called *frequency synthesizer,* allowing selection of multiple frequencies (channels) with a single crystal and digital circuitry. The new value created was lower cost, higher flexibility (from ten channels to a thousand channels), and smaller size. Digital camcorders used to record in an analog way. Newer digital camcorders are recording digitally.[61] The value added is higher video quality, ability to edit the movie, and longer retention of the quality over time, especially with magnetic tape cassettes. Music used to be played with vinyl records (analog), then with magnetic tape (still analog), and then moved to compact disk (CD—digital) and solid-state MP3 players. The value came in the form of dramatically improving sound quality, longer retention time (cassettes tend to lose the sound quality over time), easier handling, and lower cost, as well as new ways to obtain content. For video recording and playback, analog videocassette recorders (VCR) worked, advancing then to digital DVD players and recorders (digital). The new value created was higher quality, longer life span, lower cost, and easier handling. The smaller size and easier handling made the mailing of DVD movies cheap enough to allow the emergence of companies like Netflix® and the online unit of Blockbuster®, which would probably not have emerged if movies were still stored on VHS cassettes.

The invention of the microprocessor and the digital signal processor (DSP) introduced another level of flexibility. While the traditional digital integrated circuits were good for only one purpose and not modifiable, today microprocessors and DSPs reach processing speeds that allow them to perform quick tasks previously done with dedicated logic. This level of flexibility reduces end product cost, as general purpose processors allow for economies of scale cost reduction in their production. It further allows more complex features, and field upgradeability and programmability.

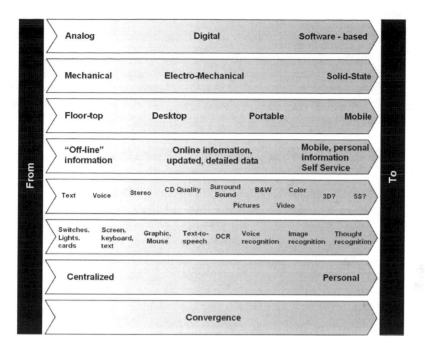

Figure 28—Evolution trends

Another example of the trend to software-based applications is the migration of more applications from dedicated products (such as calculators) to PC-based programs. I don't remember when I last used a calculator as a stand-alone device. Every time I needed one recently I used the one available as part of Windows, or the one available in my cell phone.

Mechanics: Mechanical to electromechanical to solid-state

Many products that started life as mechanical products transitioned into electronics ones. The digital camera is one of the most obvious examples. It completely changed the photography landscape and profession. From cellulose film to memory storage, the new value offered had many dimensions. First, it allows taking pictures and viewing them immediately after shooting them. How frustrating it was to shoot a picture to find only after it was developed and printed that it was far from perfect. Digital photography turned the process of developing and printing pictures (the "dark room") into a low-cost and simple printing process using a small, affordable, portable desktop printer. Storing the pictures is simple. Now you can print an unlimited number of copies without worrying about carefully storing the original negative. The ability to manipulate the picture with a personal computer is within everyone's reach. No doubt this transition from mechanical to electronic added significant value. In fact, I cannot recall the last time I saw someone using a film camera.

The term *electromechanical* refers to a system (or subsystem) made of both mechanical and electronic components, combined. A CD or DVD player is one example where there are mechanical parts, including the CD/DVD loader and optical head, and the electronic part of translating the information read into video signals. Solid-state electronics refer to electronic systems (or subsystems) with no moving parts. Examples of transitions from electromechanical products to solid-state products include the transition from CD music players to MP3 players. This transition started with the implementation of a music-compression algorithm called MP3. This algorithm allowed reducing the size of a typical CD-quality, four-minute song from approximately 40MB to 4MB, a ratio of 10:1. Using flash memory (solid-state, silicon-based) allows storing multiple songs in memory rather than on a CD (or even a hard disk drive). Apple Computers noticed this trend, and although their highly disruptive iPod (capitalizing on a trend from analog to digital and higher capacity of hard disk drives) was less than four years old, they introduced the iPod Nano, using 2, 4, or 8 GB flash memory, introducing a much smaller device, still capable of storing thousands of songs. The main value delivered with the transition from electromechanical to solid-state is smaller size and less susceptibility to mechanical "trauma." Dropping a CD or HDD-based music player will most likely hurt it to a point of irreparable malfunction. It will not affect a solid-state product that way where a precise, delicate mechanical system does not exist.

In 1989, I had an idea. To help my memory and help me plan my day as I drove to work, I used a microcassette-based voice recorder. It was relatively bulky, but it was the best anyone could hope for at that time. That same year, Intel announced the first flash memory component, a 1 megabit component in a single package. That component cost $45, whereas the entire voice recorder I bought had cost me about $50. Calculating the amount of time that can be recorded over 1Mb of storage using a 4Kbps voice compression algorithm showed that I could store 250 seconds, or 4 minutes. That was enough for the task. The new value dimensions that this technology would offer were numerous: it would be smaller, would not have the electromechanical mechanism associated with the cassette tape and, more than anything, would provide direct access to any message, allowing the deletion of a specific message without deleting the entire tape. My wife named the proposed product *memcorder*, as it was a combination of a solid-state *memory* and a voice *recorder*. I even built a prototype, using an answering machine voice compression integrated circuit and the Intel flash component. It worked! Unfortunately, I did not have the courage required in 1989 to start my own company. Today, many of those recorders are available from Sony, Panasonic, Olympus, and others, capable of recording hours of messages, and at retail prices of less than $50. In fact, the flash-based MP3 player market was an extension of that product.

Mobility: From floor-top to desktop to portable and mobile

Many products and markets started their lives standing on the floor. Mainframe computers occupied halls, and minicomputers occupied rooms. Music players came in special cabinets (from long-play vinyl records to magnetic-tape cassette players). The next step of evolution was turning them into desktop products. The computer became a desktop computer. The music cabinet became a desktop cassette tape recorder. The telephone started as a public telephone booth, and became a desktop product.

In many cases, there is still a significant market for those desktop products. However, as we become mobile, we need those products to move with us. Possibly one of the biggest opportunities for disruptive innovation is in turning desktop and stationary products into portable or mobile ones.

You probably noticed that I use both terms, *portable* and *mobile*. It's not a mistake. They are different. *Portable* is something you can carry or move easily, but not necessarily while operating. *Mobile* is something you can carry or move easily, *while operating*. A laptop computer is *portable*, while a cellular phone is *mobile*. One of the trends observed today is the adoption of the Windows mobile operating system and applications suite on cellular phones. Having the ability to manipulate Office® documents on a cellular handset will offer the ultimate *mobility* of the personal computer. BlackBerry is an example of taking a desktop application (e-mail) and turning it completely mobile. There is no doubt that the laptop computer offers tremendous value over the desktop computer. It can be turned on anywhere (well, anywhere comfortable) to process documents. With the wide availability of Wi-Fi "hot spots"[62], you can even access the Internet and electronic mail. However, the time it takes the laptop computer to start, and the inconvenience of its size (compared to a cellular phone or a BlackBerry), left it in the *portable* zone rather than moving it all the way to the *mobile* zone, where the cellular phones and BlackBerry communicators are today.

Keep in mind that not everything needs to be portable or mobile. You need to consider carefully the value of turning a product mobile. I am sure that at some point we will see portable printers. In fact, you can find a few in the market, but those offer poor quality compared to the desktop printers, and are not especially portable. As I write these lines, I am involved in the global launch of a new technology to broadcast live TV to mobile phones. Will this transition from living room TV to mobile TV work? Will it provide value? Time will tell, but I will describe what makes me think it will. Clayton Christensen described the success of the BlackBerry as the ability for "killing time productively."[63] The ability to watch TV on your cell phone will offer a relatively similar value. It will offer ability to "kill time enjoyably." Both devices (and applications) offer this ability. One distinction is that the BlackBerry allows you to *communicate* to kill time, while the mobile TV allows you to receive information or *entertainment* to kill time. Mobile TV is not a new thing. The Sony "Watchman," introduced in the 1980s, did not turn out to be a great success. Why will it be a success now? The answer lies in the definition of "killing time." How does one "kill time?" In today's busy schedule, the time to kill is on the order of minutes. I don't believe anyone will watch one-hour episodes of NBC's "Law and Order" just to kill time—definitely not on a screen as small as the cellular phone's. However, CNBC, CNN, ESPN, and similar "live" content sources is viewable two minutes at a time. Furthermore, having "headline" channels that keep offering headlines whenever people watch will be key to that ability. This content simply did not exist before. The content that the Watchman could receive was the free, over-the-air programming, filled with one-hour programs. It also required extending the antenna in an uncomfortable manner, and offered very poor reception quality.

Connectivity: More communication links, immediacy, and richness

In 1998, America Online (AOL) bought a small Israeli company by the name of Mirabilis for $407 million. In 1998, a sale like this should not have been a surprise, as we were still two years *before* the "dot-com" bubble burst. It was interesting to know that Mirabilis did not have any revenue. All they had was a small communication program called ICQ (pronounced "I seek you"). That program offered something not offered by any communication device (or software) available at the time. It offered the ability to know if your counterpart to the conversation, anywhere in the world, was online right then, and allowed you to send a message that would pop up on his or her screen immediately. The immediacy of this program earned the category the name *Instant Messaging* (IM). Just before acquisition by AOL, ICQ had a subscriber base of over 12 million users. I was one of them. Initially, I was skeptical about the need for this program but, once I had it, and once people I knew had it, I saw the value. Today, people worldwide use IM. AOL called ICQ by the new name: AIM (AOL Instant Messenger). Yahoo! has the Yahoo! Messenger, Microsoft Network (MSN) has the MSN Messenger, and then there is Skype, and beyond. Until that point, there was no ability to send a message immediately. The only way to communicate immediately was via phone. That could have been much more expensive (especially when international calling is involved), and it lacked the ability to discretely send a message. The problem with an IM program is that computers do not have fixed Internet addresses (or "telephone numbers"). The service provider dynamically assigns an IP address.[64] It is equivalent to having a different telephone number all the time. How can anyone call you if your telephone number keeps changing? ICQ introduced the concept of a server with which every computer, once connected to the Internet, registers with a known (fixed) user name, and lists the current IP address assigned to it. Every other user wishing to communicate with this user, knowing the fixed user name, will automatically find the IP address through this registration server. Is it a disruptive technology? Not really. It is a disruptive implementation of an existing concept. It did not require any cutting-edge research. All it required was an understanding that people desired a new way of communication that improved on other available means. It offered people with computers, connected to the Internet, the ability to seek each other out and send instant messages to each other while doing other things. It became a great success. The cellular phone market followed suit, and introduced the SMS.[65] SMS offers the ability to send a short text message to another cellular subscriber, without the need to have the phone ring and place a long conversation. MMS,[66] on the other hand, capable of delivering richer content than the simple SMS text messages thus far has not turned into a great success. Text, apparently, was enough.

People like to communicate. New techniques and network topologies were invented to offer the ability to innovate ways of communicating. Some of them offer more value to the users, and some less. One opportunity to innovate is to find new ways to communicate, in a way that offers value.

During my childhood in the late 1960s, we relied on mail as the way to communicate. The turnaround time for a letter (sending a letter and receiving a reply) was two to four weeks. Later, in the early 1970s, we could rely on the phone booth down the road. That is, of course, assuming that the person whom we were calling had a phone. We waited about five years to get our first telephone. In the 1990s, we transitioned to cellular, personal phones. Today, Sprint Nextel is offering *"push to talk*" functionality, allowing you to connect to another person without even dialing. One of the biggest disruptions the Internet created was the electronic mail (e-mail). The *transaction cost* was down to almost zero. The turnaround time was down to minutes. Instant Messaging and SMS are immediate.

Another aspect of communication is the *richness* of delivery. From letters to voice, and then to video. At some point, I expect more senses to be involved (touch, smell). Talking with a Texas Instruments' IT manager one day, I asked why we don't use video conferencing. The answer was that the IT department was afraid of the system overload associated with the bandwidth required for video conferencing[67] if the company's 35,000 employees used it. Here is a good disruption target, I thought.

The communications market trends, therefore, involve improvement along three lines, each creating disruption opportunities:

- More *coverage*—offering more links to more people, wherever they are;
- *Immediacy*—quicker turnaround of interactive communication;
- *Richness*—involving more senses (from text to voice, to video, to—?).

An interesting side effect of increased communications is less face-to-face time. I should warn you, though, that until *rich-conferencing* allows me to observe the body language of the person I am communicating with, I will personally not replace face-to-face meetings with video conferencing for delicate and sensitive interactions.

Immediacy: Availability of live content and information and self-service

I flew internationally out of Israel for the first time in 1989, when I was twenty-four years old. Flying internationally was a big deal. It was also a long process. I had to call a travel agent. I didn't have any information to allow me to compare airline prices or select the right schedule or route. I was completely at the mercy of the travel agent who booked my flight. I had to trust her to get me the best price and schedule. I arrived at the airport early enough to get a good seat on the plane.

Last week my wife and two daughters flew to Israel for our annual summer family visit. I booked their tickets online. I got a list of all the possible routes going to Israel with the different airlines, at the different times, with their prices. I chose the best route for them, with reasonable prices. While still making the reservation I was able to choose seats for them. As it was an international flight with two different airlines, it had to be a paper ticket. Otherwise, like all my domestic flights, single-airline international flights these days, an electronic ticket would have been enough, which means that I would have printed my tickets with my desktop printer right after completing the reservation process. I could even print my boarding pass twelve hours before my flight, and avoid the check-in hassle. Then I took my family to the airport and headed back home. When home, I monitored www.flightview.com. There I was able to know when the plane took off, and could track it all the way through to JFK. When the plane was about ten minutes away from touching down at JFK, I turned to www.liveatclnet and found a live feed of the JFK tower frequency.[68] A few minutes later, I heard, "JFK Tower, American heavy 462 is with you for runway three-one right." Then I heard, "American heavy 462, clear to land runway three-one right." When I heard the tower handing the flight over to the ground control frequency, I knew the plane was on the ground. As I expected, within two minutes, my wife called me to let me know they had landed safely at JFK. I already knew that. I probably knew more about her flight than she did.

One of the most powerful consumer trends is the need for available information, detailed information, and immediate information. How do we buy books? We go to www.amazon.com. We have all the information we need about the books. We can see comparable books. We can see other books from the same author. We read recommendations from readers who read this book. We can see how high this book is on the bestseller list. Best of all, we can virtually open the book and look inside to see the cover, read about the author, see the table of contents, the index, and even read an excerpt from this book. We have all this information to help us make a smart decision, and it's available immediately at the tip of our fingers.

Where can you find a piano store in Dallas? The easiest (and probably only) way twenty years ago was to open the *Yellow Pages* and look for it. Today, an easier alternative would be to look up "Piano Stores" in Yahoo! maps. That option was not available to me on the weekend, while driving with my seven-year-old daughter who decided she wanted to start learning how to play the piano. I had to find a piano store, preferably without driving home to do some research. No problem. My car is equipped with a GPS navigation system. I hit the "NAV" button, and then a menu popped up on the screen. I chose "Point of Interest" then "Type," "Shopping," and "Musical Instruments," Then it asked me if I wanted to sort the results by name or by distance from where I was. Not planning to make a long trip, I chose "by distance." Three names within fifteen miles showed up. I chose one. The store's telephone number was there, and I chose to call them. The navigation system, connected wirelessly via Bluetooth® link to my cellular phone on my belt, dialed the number. I asked for the working hours of that store, and found the store was open late enough for me to pay it a visit. I then directed the navigation system to guide me, turn-by-turn, to that store. Twenty minutes later, my daughter and I were checking out pianos. Once again, the information was available at the tip of my fingers, this time in my car. The immediacy, availability, and comprehensiveness of the information added a lot of value, for which I was willing to pay when I bought this car. Navigation systems are installed in many cars today and are not considered a luxury item as they used to be ten years ago.

So what can you add next to capitalize on this consumer/innovation trend? For one, the weather can be available on the navigation system's screen. Moreover, you can add traffic conditions. Both types of information are available today over local radio stations. The ability to move this content into the navigation system's screen in a visual manner combined with making recommendations of the best possible routes to avoid traffic jams and maybe even bad weather will add value and move along this trend line.

We are becoming junkies for immediate information. We can get our children's school grades over the Internet. We can see what our neighbor's house is worth with the county tax appraiser's office. Some schools offer live video camera feed of the kids at school, although there are potential privacy issues with that. Finally, we can buy almost everything online, whether from an established retailer (Amazon.com), or from the world's largest flea market—eBay.com. Our need for immediate information went to the extreme when JetBlue differentiated itself by offering live TV to its passengers. This never got much media coverage until September 2005 when JetBlue flight 292 descended with its landing gear facing sideways, with 140 of its passengers watching their own plane landing in Los Angeles live on TV in front of their seats.

We see more and more personal content available online. The production costs are minimal. From photo sharing (ofoto.com) to video sharing (YouTube.com), more content that is personal appears online for billions of Internet users. With cellular camera phones and videophones, the day is not far off when live content will air from handheld devices to billions of users.

Rich content

In October 2005, not long after releasing the iPod, initially used only for high-quality music, Apple announced the Video iPod. With an upgrade to iTunes®[69] to allow the download of video content for the high-quality video display, the content stored and viewed on the iPod became richer.

The information we consume will move along a path of content *richness* improvement, much like the interpersonal communications described above. The early days of Internet information were text based. Most of the information we consumed was through newspapers and books, filled with text. At some point, we started consuming information and content through voice. Then came stereo. I remember my excitement listening to my first stereo system, being able to sense that the lead guitar was on my left, the base was on my right, and the drums in the back. You could still hear the "hiss" associated with vinyl records or cassette tapes. That hiss disappeared with the invention of the compact disk and digital recording. Surround sound followed, which located the sources of sound along three dimensions. Images moved from still pictures to video clips, and from black and white to full and rich color. Even the depth of color pictures improved over time. While the first color screen PCs had 256 colors,[70] they have millions of colors today. I owned the first Microsoft flight simulator. It was a black and white version, with relatively low resolution, but it provided a primitive virtual sense of what flying is. Today, with Microsoft's Flight Simulator X, with the processing power, memory, and disk storage capacity available in PCs today, and with the screen resolution and quality, you can see virtual elephants walking underneath your low-flying virtual plane. I remember playing very basic video games using an Atari device, and when I look at the picture resolution, detail, lighting, and motion of today's Sony PlayStation 3 or Microsoft's Xbox 360, I can't help but wonder how far we are from not being able to tell whether the movie we see is real or a high-quality animation.

What's next? Obviously, three-dimensional visual representation. Remember how R2-D2 projected Princess Leia's 3-D image to deliver a message to Obi-Wan Kenobi? I believe there is still more to come even beyond 3-D visualization (not that we reached 3-D visualization yet). The next step should be to involve all our five senses in experiencing information. The question is how detailed does it need to be to fool our senses into thinking we are experiencing "the real thing"? While real-life motion is smooth and continuous, video is transmitted one frame at a time. When a video has more than eighteen frames per second, it feels like real motion too.

While CD quality is notably better than cassette tape quality (and our ear *can* tell the difference), we cannot tell the difference between CD quality and MP3 quality, compressed by a ratio close to 10:1. That compression, while saving significant memory and disk space, does it in a way that our ear cannot tell the difference, even though parts of the original sound are lost.

Natural man-machine interaction

There is an interaction between machines and the people who operate them. I use the term *machines* loosely here. It represents any products, mostly electronic, that require some kind of interaction with its human *operator.* I cannot think of a single machine that operates without any human interaction of one type or another. That interaction is called *human interface* (HI) or *man-machine interface* (MMI).

The first machines had very simple interfaces. The interface was in the form of lights, switches, and even a punched card. In 1977, when I was studying computer sciences, I had to punch my FORTRAN programs on punched cards, carry them to a punch-card reader, feed them to the huge NCR computer, and then wait for my program to run and for a printout of the results, which went to the output bin (which was, literally, a bin).

As technology progressed, those computers were equipped with terminals. Those terminals had no processing power themselves, and included black and white (well, black and green mostly) CRT displays, command-line interactions,[71] and a keyboard. The interaction required text only, and no graphics were involved. Invented by Xerox, first adopted by Apple, and later by Microsoft in its launch of Windows 3.0 operating system in 1990, the graphical user interface and *human interface devices* (HID) replaced the command-line, text-based interface. The first HID was the mouse that we still use today. Over the years, other *pointing devices* emerged, but probably the only other pointing device that became as pervasive was the laptop touch-pad. The light pen (used to point at the screen), trackball, and other HID never became as pervasive as the mouse and the touch pad. The HID and graphical user interface created a much more natural interface between the user and the device. The user would point at the object of interest on the screen, "click" on it and, in return, the computer performed the desired action, somewhat intuitive when you see the graphical *icon* of that object on the screen. We are all too familiar with the *recycle bin* on our Windows display. Its function is so obvious when you look at it. It looks like a trash can, and it has the universal *recycle* logo on it. Is it not clear that this is where the deleted objects or files go?

Computers are not the only machines that we, as users, interact with. Today, car navigation systems use voice prompts to guide the driver to the desired direction. Driving the car while hearing "in one mile, turn left into highway seventy-five" is not as unusual today as it might have been twenty years ago. At this point, I will separate the MMI into *machine-to-human* and *human-to-machine*. The *machine-to-human* interface, while I hope I do not do it injustice by trivializing it, is much simpler. The "thoughts" of the machine are very clear (to the machine, at least). They are digital and stored for easy retrieval to communicate them. The way to communicate (mostly through voice prompt) relies on pre-storing an audible vocabulary in the storage of the machine. When the machine needs[72] to communicate a message to the user, it will retrieve the stored voice representation of that message and play it to the user. Initially, such interfaces had a somewhat unnatural voice to them. The words, even though combined into sentences still sounded like individual words. The user could not hear the natural diction of a human. It was all too easy to recognize that this was a machine rather than a human. Text-to-speech systems have improved significantly, and today it is getting harder and harder to recognize when a machine, and not a real live person, is speaking to you. Given the "clear and known" state of the machine "thoughts," the *machine-to-human* interface requires a much smaller processing power than the other direction (*human to machine*).

A *Human-to-machine* interface is very hard to implement. There are theoretically four ways I can think of that allow (and will allow) us to communicate (with machines, or with other humans). First is the written word. I am not considering typing on a keyboard or pointing with a mouse "written word." I consider writing with a pen "written word." The Palm Pilot was one of the first products that allowed "writing" (although, not in a natural way but rather in a way called "Graffiti" by Palm) on its screen while understanding the written text. Tablet PCs use the entire touch-sensitive screen as an input device, allowing the user to write freely with a stylus while the computer understands that input. Understanding what another computer is "writing" is easy using OCR (optical character recognition), as computers "write" in a very clear and consistent manner, using fonts that were programmed into them by, well, users. Reading human handwriting is much more difficult. In fact, sometimes it is hard for humans to read what other humans write. In our favor is the fact that we can sometimes understand the written word out of the overall context of the sentence. Our handwriting is not consistent. It varies from person to person. It does not use standard fonts. We find it hard to write at the same size and on a straight line all the time. One user's handwriting can be dramatically different from another's. Simply scanning a handwritten page facilitates handwriting recognition. Given the diversity, vagueness, and less-than-clear nature of our handwriting, converting handwriting into machine "standard" text takes significant processing power. To date, the machines' ability to read our handwriting cannot emulate our own ability to understand our own (or someone else's) handwriting. It could be that the algorithms (developed by humans) to read and understand handwriting are not comprehensive enough. We find it relatively easy to *read* handwriting, but hard to explain how we do that and to "train" a machine to emulate it. It could also be that the processing power and storage required to completely emulate our ability to read handwriting is not available.[73] In my opinion, it is the combination of the two, imperfect algorithms and processing-power/memory shortage, that prevents a good emulation of our own ability to read handwriting by machines. Unfortunately, even reading other machines' "handwriting" is not a job done perfectly by a machine. Using the most advanced business card readers does not always produce the desired outcome, and we have to proof the conversion manually. Our own reading skill exceeds the machine's skill, even when it comes to reading the standard, machine-generated text.

The next level of *human-to-machine* interaction is using voice. In one of my MBA classes, I had to summarize complete textbooks. One day, I decided to buy a software tool that was capable (or, at least, this is what the software vendor claimed) of converting spoken voice into text. This would have helped, as I could say my thoughts and my PC would automatically turn them into a document. However, even the leading software vendor claimed the software was only 95% accurate (which was the highest of the available software tools), which meant that one in twenty words would not be interpreted correctly. In reality, it was even lower than that and, believe me, I am a very clear speaker. It was simply impractical to review the entire text to fix one word in ten.

To improve driving safety, some cars are equipped with hands-free telephone kits, allowing the driver to speak and guide the phones to dial. My car is equipped with such a system, built in originally,[74] but even there you cannot rely on the system's accuracy. It tends to misinterpret my commands. Often it confuses "call" with "cancel," for example. You have to be very clear when speaking to it. The same applies to *interactive voice response* (IVR) systems, often used as automatic user interface systems over the phone for different service providers. Call American Airlines to get details on a scheduled flight. Call your bank to get your account balance. Call your pharmacy to refill a prescription. In all those cases, you will not be talking with a human. You will speak with a computer, equipped with an IVR system. While recognizing your touch-tone keys is much simpler (as those are, like the machine-printed word, standard and limited in variety), recognizing your verbal input is not. Once again, the software programs we use cannot completely emulate the way we analyze voices we hear. Again, it is due to the same combination of factors: our inability to describe (and therefore guide a machine how to emulate) the way we understand spoken words, and the availability of cost-effective processing power and memory to perform the function.

Perhaps one of the most sophisticated types of *human-to-machine* interface is the visual one. We understand body language. We can tell if a person is happy or mad. We can tell if a person is uncomfortable, and sometimes even if he or she is lying. We cannot even begin to start instructing a machine how to do that, and for the same two reasons. There are some very basic, very dedicated *visual pattern recognition* systems used to perform very specific functions. The most pervasive one is the bar-code reader that can optically read a bar code. The automotive manufacturing process also uses visual pattern recognition. Those systems are highly specialized.

The bottom line is that we did not get to the point where our communications with electronic products is as simple as our communications with one another. Pressing a button is not natural. We can understand each other's handwriting (well, most of the time). Machines are not even close to understanding our handwriting. We can understand what others are telling us. Machines are struggling with that. We can interpret visual cues we are getting from others. Machines don't know where to begin yet.

One day, maybe there will even be a way to read minds. Currently, we do not know how to read each other's mind. However, with an ability to tap into the brain and an ability to convert our thoughts into machine-readable language, we will be able to guide machines with our thoughts. The key missing link right now is that ability to tap into our brains.

In summary, our ability to communicate effectively and accurately with machines is limited. While the machine can communicate *to* us relatively easily through graphical interface and even voice prompts, its ability to understand our cues (through written words, spoken words, and visual gestures) is severely primitive. This is mainly because of: (1) our inability to translate accurately the way we perform those functions into computer algorithms, and (2) the shortage of processing power and memory resources to perform those functions effectively. While being researched significantly, this is still one of the key areas where technology trends (mainly cheap processing power and storage) offer innovation opportunities. For now, instead of teaching machines how to understand us when we communicate in the most natural way, we taught ourselves how to communicate to a machine in a way it knows.

From centralized to personal

Popular Mechanics magazine predicted in 1949, "Computers in the future may weigh no more than 1.5 tons." IBM's chairman, Thomas Watson, predicted in 1943, "There is a world market for maybe five computers." Ken Olson, the president, founder, and chairman of DEC, said, "There is no reason anyone would want a computer in their home." Well, they were all wrong, weren't they? Granted, it was hard to predict the evolution of the semiconductor industry in the 1940s, especially since the integrated circuit did not appear until 1960. However, why do people see the need to own a computer at home? It is due to a trend of personalizing everything we own. It has nothing to do with mobility and small size. It is about ownership, personalization, and constant availability. A mainframe computer, and even a minicomputer, is "community property." You do not have access to it whenever you need. The personal computer is available to you all the time. In the 1980s, I used IBM's huge laser printers (the 3800 series). While still faster than any printer I know today, I always preferred to use a small (and slow) desktop printer. The quality was much poorer;[75] it suffered from many mechanical problems, but it was mine. I did not have to go anywhere to print. It printed on my desk, and it was readily available. Today, the quality of desktop printing is as good as centralized printing or publishing.

There is a general trend of moving from centralized ("community") products and services to personal, desktop or portable products. This trend followed computers from mainframe to desktop to laptop, telephones from public telephone booths to personal phones to cellular phones, and movies from public cinemas to family TV to personal, mobile TV. There are several reasons for this trend:

- There is an abundance of content. Only with personal devices will you be able to consume your own content.

- You can customize your experience. You like things in a certain way, and other people like things in different ways. We customize our "favorite" lists of Internet sites. We customize our cellular phone ring tones.

- We want things done exactly when we want them—not when everybody else is ready.

- We want things to come to us. We don't want to go to them.

Another trend we should note here is the trend from centralized content to peer-to-peer content. I am not referring to the network or communication topology, which might remain centralized, but rather to where the content really is. Some peer-to-peer services do not require a central "master" or "hub" to operate. eBay, for example, is a centralized service, but the content is distributed among all eBay members. The ability to access other people's content and assets (in a positive way, of course, and not in a way that violates privacy and property rights) is a trend we will continue to see. Skype, AIM, and Yahoo! Messenger are other examples of a service that, while centralized in topology (they will not work without the directory servers), connects individuals.

Convergence

One of the more controversial trends is that of convergence. You will find people arguing fiercely about whether convergence will take place or not. You will always find those who believe that convergence is inevitable. I will start with defining convergence. Convergence is the combination of multiple functions, otherwise served by different, independent devices, into one device—the *converged* device. There are converged devices in our lives right now. A digital camera is capable of capturing MPEG4 videos. A digital camcorder is capable of capturing still pictures on a flash card installed in it. Camera phones are becoming a hit, integrating a digital camera into a cellular phone. Motorola, in cooperation with Apple, introduced their ROKR phone in 2006, integrating an iPod into a slim phone. I was amazed when I got my Nokia N73 phone, integrating two digital cameras, a camcorder, an MP3 music player as well as a video player, an FM radio receiver and, of course, a telephone.

No doubt, converged devices exist. The advantage of convergence is obvious: it lets us carry a smaller number of devices, while maintaining the functionality of many more. However, how well do they perform all the individual functions, compared with the stand-alone, dedicated devices?

With 256KB flash, Motorola's ROKR is very limited in its capacity for music compared to the 2GB, 4GB, or 8GB iPod nano, not to mention the 40GB HDD-based iPod. The digital camera function of a digital video camcorder typically lacks the optical zoom capability of a *dedicated* digital camera, it lacks the powerful flash illuminator, and its resolution is significantly lower than that of a regular digital camera, typically by a factor of 5 to 10. The same is true for a camera phone. The camera typically lacks flash illumination, and the resolution and picture quality are too low to serve as a replacement for a 5 megapixel *stand-alone* digital camera. On the other hand, the high compression rate of the video capture feature of a digital camera adversely affects the video quality, and it lacks functions such as stability control that dedicated digital camcorders have.

Dedicated devices need to have specific attributes that will make them better in their "specialty." Converged devices must exercise tradeoffs to accommodate all the devices. Sometimes, those tradeoffs are not acceptable for competitive purposes, and we are forced to carry the converged devices as well as a few other dedicated devices.

Will there be a bright future for converged devices? Yes, but only as long as the performance level of each of the functions meets the *minimum acceptable level* of each one of the functions as a stand-alone device. If those tradeoffs are cutting too deeply, and cause the performance of each individual function to be significantly lower than the *minimum acceptable level* of the individual devices—they will fail.

Consumers would most likely love to carry one device capable of multiple functions, but only if those conditions are met with an overall compelling product.

---

[57] Jim Collins, Jerry Porras, "Built to Last: Successful Habits of Visionary Companies," HarperBusiness, 1994.

[58] And most likely closer to 40% of the overall cost of building the product, assuming the product is sold with a 50% gross profit margin.

[59] In fact, the technology does not need to exceed the higher end of expectations to disrupt another market. It can disrupt the other market while still underserving the original market for which it was developed.

[60] To be distinguished from cellular phone. Cordless telephone is the technology where the handset can be carried through the premises to a certain range from the base unit. This range is measured in hundreds of feet, at best.

[61] There are several digital methods employed by digital camcorders. The most familiar one uses magnetic tapes, while recording the video digitally, called MiniDV®. Other digital techniques include the use of DVD recorders in camcorders as well as hard disk drive camcorders, and even flash memory (completely solid-state) storage.

[62] A Wi-Fi hot spot is a place where Wi-Fi access is available. The Starbucks® chain was one of the first to offer Wi-Fi service. In fact, if you open your Wi-Fi enabled laptop (today, even a $499 laptop is Wi-Fi enabled) in a Starbucks store, you will be able to connect to the

Internet, for a price. Even the fact that there is a price to pay makes this function a lot more portable than before. T-Mobile was the first cellular operator in the US to offer those "hot spot" Wi-Fi services nationwide to its subscribers.

[63] Clayton Christensen, Michael Raynor, "The Innovator's Solution," Harvard Business School Press, 2003.

[64] Internet Protocol address. It is made of 4 bytes, and therefore can support theoretically 4.3 billion different combinations. While this number could serve a significant part of the world population, the way those numbers are assigned to users is determined by service provider, geographical region, and, in fact, cannot be allocated to users on a permanent basis. In December 1998, the Internet Engineering Task Force (IETF) created a standard number RFC2460, called "Internet Protocol version 6", also known as IPv6. The big difference between IPv6 and the current IP address scheme (also known as IPv4, as defined in RFC791) is that it supports 16 bytes of IP address, thus allowing each computer (and any other device connected to the Internet) to have its own, fixed IP address, just like a telephone number. IPv6 is in a very long adoption process.

[65] Short message service.

[66] Multi-media messaging service.

[67] While voice encoding requires between 4 and 12Kbps, video encoding requires some 384Kbps for a reasonable, small-screen (less than a PC screen) video-clip. It has almost 100 times more bandwidth!

[68] An Internet user most likely provides the live feed with an air frequency radio scanner tuned to the appropriate frequency, connected to a personal computer and streaming the soundtrack constantly. The ability to deliver this live feed requires only relatively cheap equipment.

[69] iTunes is a registered trademark of Apple Inc.

[70] As much as could be represented by one byte of memory per pixel

[71] The user responds to prompts to enter commands. Once entered – the computer performs an action and displays the results on the next line (or lines). Then it prompts the user for another command. Those commands are scrolled down the screen one after the other, and there is nothing done in parallel. The last operating system to use such command-line interaction was DOS.

[72] The machine really does not have "needs." The program running at the machine guides it to prompt the user with the appropriate message at the appropriate time.

[73] Or, at least, not available in a cost-effective manner. After all, using a super-computer, while possibly providing the required processing power, is not "affordable" or "cost-effective" regardless of criteria

applied. This needs to be a function that can be performed by devices costing less than $100.

[74] Therefore should be optimized to the car as much as possible as opposed to after-market kits that might not be optimized to any specific car.

[75] Compared with today's desktop laser printers that can be purchased for under $100.

Chapter 8
Finding The Disruption Opportunities

It is time to start identifying market disruption opportunities. By now, you have identified the direction of fast-moving technologies and identified consumption trends. Now it is time to find where they intersect and create the disruption opportunities. Remember, this is only the beginning. Once you identify the opportunity, you still need to define the right product, the *whole* product, and create a value chain and ecosystem that will support it. The following chapters will cover that. For now, focus on finding the opportunities.

The disruptive innovation process

The process will include the following steps:

- Identify a market segment by the *job* it is performing.
- Rank products in that market by how evolved they are.
- Identify the expected performance of the key driving technology trends and ways in which those technology trends can move the products along the evolution path in the market segments.

The opportunities may improve along one evolution trend, or along several. The more evolution trends you will disrupt, the bigger the market will be. However, even disrupting a single evolution trend is enough. After all, the cellular phone disruption happened along one line only—mobility. And it moved only from *desktop* to *mobile* (although it skipped *portable*).

Identifying a market segment

Here, you will have to generalize the *job* that the market you are interested in is performing. The more granular your identified market (or *job*), the harder it will be for you to identify lagging consumption and market evolution trends, as specific segments have already evolved to a certain degree along those trends. For example, you can generalize the iPod as a "mobile music player," as a "mobile media player," or as a "media player." The first will represent an advancement along the *mobility* dimension (see Figure 28), representing no opportunity for value enhancement there. Categorizing the iPod as a "music player" will falsely indicate a possibility for enhancement along the *rich content* dimension, which, of course, the iPod has already migrated into. Categorizing it as a "media consumption" device will probably open us up to as many opportunities as possible, as demonstrated in the next paragraph. The *job* that the iPod does is to allow us to consume media.

Ranking the evolution of the products

Once you categorized the market, you should take all eight evolution trends described in Figure 28 and rank how well this *job* performed in this market, by how close it is to the right side (the "evolved" side). Wherever the product/market is closer to the left, there is an opportunity to move it to the right, along the natural market and consumer evolution trends:

- Is the iPod *software based*? Yes. Based on a processor, software updates are available from iTunes.

- Is it *solid-state* based? It depends. The iPod nano is *solid-state* based, using flash storage and no moving parts. The video iPod, on the other hand, still uses an HDD and, therefore, is *electromechanical* in that is has moving parts in it. Opportunity to innovate? A flash-based *video* iPod?

- Is it mobile? Yes. It doesn't get much more mobile than the iPod nano.

- How *immediate* is the content availability? I believe there is a lot that can be innovated there. Along this dimension, the iPod (and all other music and video players) ranks poorly. The content is available only *offline*. How can we get any content we wish, immediately? Will the convergence with the mobile phone help? Will the business model ($0.99 per downloaded song and $1.99 per downloaded video) receive support?

- How rich is the media? I believe the iPod reached *CD quality* and *color video* quality. Opportunities to innovate might be in adding surround sound and possibly 3-dimentional video.

- How advanced is the user interface? Unfortunately, it is not very advanced. I would at best put it in the same category with the graphic user interface that a Windows-based PC has with a mouse. Plenty of opportunities to innovate here: support voice recognition, and maybe even tune recognition, and beyond. The way to discover the innovation opportunities is to think of what would be a natural way to communicate with the device, that cannot be conceived of today.

- Is it *personal*? You bet!

- Is it *converged*? We see an interesting trend of converging the music (and video) *job* with other *jobs*. Motorola was the first to launch a cellular phone (ROKR®) that included an iPod. Nokia released its N73 phone with music and video playback capabilities, and Apple released the Apple iPhone earlier this year, 2007. Are there any other devices that make sense to converge *media playback* into?

Finding intersections with future technology performance

Once you identify where a product/market can use some "evolution," review the technology trends that can allow such evolution, and identify the required value they need to reach. Then find the time in which they will reach the required value. I will use the iPod example, in which moving the *video* content to *solid state* will be the dimension we seek to improve. The enabling technology is the flash memory. Assume that the progress you think is required is to hold twenty-four hours of video content at 768Kbps (a good quality video for a small iPod screen, and roughly the quality provided by iTunes' video clips). The memory capacity you will need is 8.3GB. 8GB flash cards are available even in 2007, but at a very steep price of more than $350. Now assume that you think the market will emerge only when the price of that storage would be no more than $20 (or $2.50/GB). With a flash memory price of $50/GB in 2006, and with a trend of -40%/year (see Figure 16), it will reach that price point in 2011 to 2012.

The next example will discuss *software-defined radios* (SDR). This term (mostly theoretical today) describes the ability to implement a complete radio using *digital signal processors* with the radio frequency directly converted into digital samples. The advantages of such a radio are enormous. Today, radios are limited to specific frequencies by the limited capabilities of the analog components. The radio spectrum is becoming crowded and so *smart* radios, capable of finding unoccupied frequencies and using them, can come in handy. In fact, for quite a few years, the FCC has been investigating (in conjunction with industry and academia) the concept of such "cognitive radios." The majority of radio communications today (2007) and in the near future are taking place under 3GHz.[76] When will a DSP be capable of handling such a frequency?[77] When its performance is 600,000 MMACs. With DSP capabilities of 10,000 MMACs in 2006 and growth rate of 37%/year, this will happen in 2019. If we limit the DSP price from exceeding $10, this would not happen before 2016. In fact, as you can see, the DSP processing power will be the limiting factor, not the price.

Opportunities

Writing this section was probably the most rewarding part of the book, as it allowed me to let my imagination run wild. Some of the ideas will sound wild and unimaginative. If this is the case, just wait a few years. Some of them will light the much-sought-after "light bulb." Some of them will probably sound trivial. They were worth writing about anyway.

Identify songs by a few notes

When I am looking for a song to download from iTunes, I do it by the name of the song, the name of the band, or the album title. The first time I downloaded a song, I didn't know if I was downloading the right song. For 99 cents, I took a bet. As it turned out, I downloaded the wrong song. Later, I learned that I can actually preview any song for 30 seconds free of charge. This certainly helped. However, how many times have you tried to download a song without remembering the title, the artist, or the album? Probably quite a few times. I know it's happened to me. Wouldn't it be nice if the user interface to iTunes would include the ability to say a few words from the song, or sing a few notes, and have iTunes be able to map that against the database to help us find the right song? Would it add great value? Probably not, as we do find most of the songs we like by the name of the song, artist, or album. However, it will move the music player market along the *man-machine interface* evolution path from keyboard, display, and audio playback to speech (and music) recognition.

Innovation Profile:
Market: music players
Evolution improvement: MMI *(from keyboard, display, and audio playback to speech recognition)*
Technology gaps: faster processing, increased storage capacity

Video conferencing

The concept of video conferencing is not new. So why did it never make it to the mainstream market? Perhaps my *InterHome* experience will help explain. Internet telephony in 1996 had very poor quality. It was choppy, the latency was too long, and dropped calls were the norm. Today, eleven years later, Internet telephony has quality equivalent to, and even better than regular voice telephony. What changed? The Internet capacity reached a point in the late 1990s where it was quadrupling every year. The ability of the Internet to support more traffic, faster, with lower latency grew. Bottlenecks disappeared, from the home Internet access (from dial-up to high-speed broadband) to the Internet backbone—the ability of the *public* Internet to support voice applications improved. When you use Skype or Cisco®[78] IP Communicator® today, the quality is very high. But when you add to it video conferencing, the picture is choppy, and the voice quality drops with it. Video communications, even at relatively low quality, requires bandwidth that is fifty to one hundred times more than that required by simple voice communication.[79] The Internet capacity and traffic capability has to catch up with that demand. I believe it will. Take 2004 as the year in which the Internet traffic capacity was enough to support good-quality voice communications, and assume that the capacity growth continues to double every six months. If the quality needs to be between fifty and one hundred times that of voice in order to support video conferencing, then by 2008 the capacity will be enough to support video (small screen) over the Internet with the same quality in which voice was delivered in 2004.

Innovation Profile:
Market: Interpersonal remote communication
Evolution improvement: Richer content—from voice to video
Technology gaps: Internet traffic capacity

Maskless lithography

In Chapter 1 of this book, I briefly described the semiconductor lithography process. It includes the ability to project an image on the silicon wafer. It uses glass masks for the process. With smaller geometries, those masks become very expensive to manufacture. While the cost of a single wafer comes to a few thousand dollars, an advanced-process mask set can cost a few million dollars, and take a few weeks to produce. With the exception of the design team labor cost (and sometimes even without making this exception), the mask costs are the single most expensive cost element in the design of an integrated circuit. During the development process of a new component, there might be several mask sets involved for the different versions of the product until it reaches production readiness. Given this prohibitively high cost, semiconductor designers work extra hard to assure they do not need multiple iterations of the product until it reaches such production maturity. The ability to make "simple tweaks" to the product even once in production is very expensive.

Maskless lithography is a very new area of research. Instead of projecting light through the expensive glass masks, it generates the image electronically, through scanning or any other method of dynamically deflecting light or other radiation to which the photoresist material will be sensitive. Maskless lithography will eliminate the need for the expensive masks, replace them with a zero direct-cost alternative, and reduce the cost of a "test chip" from a few million dollars (over 95% of which will be the mask costs) to a few tens of thousands of dollars. It will allow small start-up companies to quickly prototype, and even productize new and innovative components. The *fabless* business model allowed semiconductor companies to go into production without billion-dollar investments in fabrication facilities, relying on the pure-play foundries to allocate their capacity to them. *Maskless lithography* will allow companies to go into production as cheaply as if they were pure software companies. The level of innovation, creativity, and competition in the semiconductor market will grow.

Innovation Profile:
Market: Semiconductor manufacturing
Evolution improvement: From mechanical (optical) to solid state
Technology gaps: Optical abilities

Wireless video projection

Video content is becoming mobile. Whether mobile TV or portable media players, small devices are carrying video content. In most cases, this content is for personal consumption, but in many cases, we want to share it. Laptop computers carry video content, as well as pictures and presentations and other visual content, often being shared using a projector. The ability to connect wirelessly a video content source to a TV or projector has value—the value of true mobility. Today, wires enable transfer of video content. Be it FireWire, USB, DVI, HDMI, Ethernet, or even the old analog RCA or composite video—they are all wired. The USB connection has already made it to the wireless domain with Wireless USB. The main problem with video content is that it typically is not transferred compressed, and uncompressed, high-definition content, requires data rates above 1 Gbps. At the 2007 Consumer Electronics Show (CES) in Las Vegas, a few technology vendors demonstrated rudimentary uncompressed, above 1 Gbps wireless video transfer. The range is short, and the wireless medium is susceptible to interference and spectrum sharing. A group of consumer electronics manufacturers, including LG, Sony, Samsung, Toshiba, NEC, and Panasonic, are promoting Wireless HD™, a new wireless standard. Operating above a frequency of 60GHz, this standard, while allowing uncompressed high-definition wireless communications, is less than efficient, highly directional, and costly. The problem with compressed communications is that you need to compress the content on one side, and uncompress it on the other, requiring processing power.

Will the quality of compressed video content be significantly lower than uncompressed content? The easiest answer to that is that DVDs contain MPEG2 compressed content. Cable and satellite TV, as well as IPTV, all carry compressed content, and even the two new and competing high-capacity DVD standards, Blu-ray and HD-DVD, carry compressed, high-definition content. You never see low quality there.

I think it is safe to assume that wireless video communications, with "living room" or "conference room" range of up to 30 feet, will enhance the value of mobility. The question is, will it be compressed or uncompressed, raw video? If I had to bet (well, more like predict the future), I would say compressed. It is a more efficient use of spectrum. We moved to compressed content in many aspects of our lives, including voice communications,[80] high-quality music (MP3), high-quality still pictures (JPEG), and high-quality video (MPEG2 and MPEG4). I have never seen media that moved from being compressed to being uncompressed. Using that as a reference, I would have to conclude that we will see compressed wireless video communications.

What are the challenges? The wireless technologies required to deliver compressed video exist today. There is a high likelihood that the source device will already hold the content in a compressed form (whether on a DVD, a hard disk drive, a flash card, or any other form). The destination device does not necessarily have an *uncompressing* mechanism. With digital signal processors (DSP) prices dropping, adding the uncompressing mechanism should be straightforward. Another issue to address would be the suitability of the MPEG2 (or MPEG4) compression standards for slide shows, requiring higher resolution and better color separation than a motion picture.

Innovation Profile:
Market: mobile video players
Evolution improvement: Mobility
Technology gaps: processing power, silicon cost, and video compression algorithms

Movie downloads

Video-on-demand has been available for some time, but had a few disadvantages compared to DVD. It could not be viewed over and over again, stopped, restarted, or entered at any desired scene. Downloading the whole movie will have the same effect as owning a DVD; much like music download is succeeding CD sales. Movie downloads are available now, but mostly illegally. Just like the initially-pirated Napster gave way to iTunes, the same would happen with movie downloads. Movie and Video consumption started in movie theatres, where one had to go to the centralized theatre to watch the movie. It then transitioned to video rental facilities such as Blockbuster stores that allowed consumers to view movies at the convenience of their own home, albeit after going to a public store to rent the movie. A further improvement was the mail-in movie rental, started with Netflix, and soon followed by Blockbuster's "Total Access". The industry had made significant progress from *centralized* to *personal*. The next step would be to download movies over the Internet, advancing the industry along the *immediacy* dimension. With a standard-definition movie size of some 5GB, and using a relatively high-end broadband Internet link of 5Mbps—it would take over 11 hours (theoretically) to download a movie this way at that quality. Movie downloads are already available with shorter download time, but at lower quality than standard definition movies. Movie download will become pervasive when Internet links will allow such download to occur within 1 minute or so, which requires a data rate of 670Mbps. Does 670Mbps sound impossible? So did 5Mbps, less than 10 years ago. While impossible today, it would certainly be possible in the future, most likely with fiber-optic infrastructure. The question is only when.

Innovation Profile:
Market: video/movie consumption
Evolution improvement: From centralized to personal, and immediacy
Technology gaps: Broadband Internet speed

---

[76] Cellular phones operate at 800-900MHz, 1.8-1.9GHz, and 2.1GHz.

Wi-Fi and Bluetooth operate at 2.4GHz, WiMAX operates at 2.5GHz. Digital TV operates at 700MHz, and GPS operates at 1.5GHz.

[77] With the definition of "handling" meaning performing at least 100 MACs per sample, with the sampling rate twice the highest frequency.

[78] Cisco is a registered trademark of Cisco Systems, Inc.

[79] Cellular phone voice throughput is 12.2Kbps. Reasonable quality mobile video requires some 384Kbps. Video iPod uses some 600-700Kbps. All use a very small resolution screen or 320 x 240 pixels (QVGA) or less.

[80] Voice communications carried over the cellular network, as well as over the Internet, is compressed.

Chapter 9
Creating Disruptions Or Riding Them?

There are many opportunities for disruption in the annual $1.3 trillion electronic product market. In fact, every small change to the market presents a huge opportunity. The iPod represents close to $7 billion in annual revenue for Apple. While it represents a major consumer electronics market disruption, it accounts for only half a percent of the overall electronic product market. The cell phone market disruption created a market that represented over $100 billion in 2006 in annual revenue from phone sales, of which the semiconductor content represented over 30%, or over $30 billion. The annual revenue from cell phone services is most likely close to $1.7 trillion. With over a billion cell phones sold annually, it is clear that adding a single dollar of value (or content) to it will represent $1 billion in market disruption. With almost three billion cell phone subscribers worldwide, every one incremental dollar of monthly service value chargeable to a subscriber (thus increasing the monthly service value by only 2%) represents $36 billion. The personal computer market, although smaller, at close to 200 million devices sold in a year, but at higher prices (averaging over $600), represents a $120 billion market, of which the semiconductor content is over $50 billion.

You can categorize disruption into three types: major disruptions, minor disruptions, and derivative disruptions.

Major and minor disruptions

Both *major* and *minor* disruptions are described here as the *main* disruption, to differentiate it from the *derivative* disruption. While the distinction between the *main* disruption and the *derivative* disruption is easy to describe, the difference between the *major* and *minor* disruptions is a hard one, as well as a subjective one. What are the criteria to set the two apart?

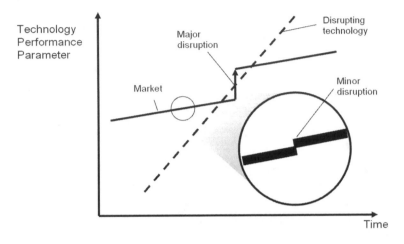

Figure 29—Major and minor disruptions

One criterion is the size of the market created by the disruption. The market size can be incremental to the market size for products that filled the same job. However, sometimes it is not very clear. The new, disrupting products may only *replace* the current products in the market, not increasing the overall revenue created by products serving this market. Should you consider that disruption? You should, but as a zero-sum game. In this case, the disruption *cannibalized* an existing market. The previous products simply ceased to exist while new products replaced them for the same functionality, only better, faster, cleaner, cheaper or safer (or any other dimension of value added). The manufacturer of the previous product loses, while the manufacturer of the new one wins. In most cases, though, the previous product survives to some degree. It finds a niche, as small as it might be, and continues to exist in that niche. However, when over 90% of market "disappears" for a product, then, for all intents and purposes, you can say that the product was *replaced.*

Another criterion defining a *major* disruption versus a *minor* one is the percentage of the original product that remains in the new product that replaces it. Take hybrid cars, for example. They add several dimensions of value to disrupt the automobile industries, such as fuel efficiency (especially in a world where oil prices are going up and oil supply is diminishing) and environmental friendliness (less emissions that might contribute to global warming). However, the majority of the original vehicle remains intact. The vehicle still needs a steering wheel, airbags, antilock breaking system (ABS), doors, seats, and the rest of the vehicle. Only the engine changes, and even there—a significant part of it is still the same. If you look at the iPod—it changed the mobile music player market more significantly, but still it had a lot of resemblance to the Walkman®[81] and mobile CD player. It still has the headset, audio amplifier, and user interface. Only the media changed. The transition from horses and carts to automobiles was a much larger disruption, as only a few components and features of the horse and cart remained in the automobile[82] market.

A third criterion identifying a major disruption is the *usage* of the new product. How different is the usage of the new, disruptive product from the old, incumbent one? The transition from phone booths to desktop phones was significant. Although still used to make calls, the availability to consumers increased dramatically. The next migration to cellular phones, increasing the availability of making calls beyond homes and offices, added significant value to the same functionality. The usage (of the same functionality) became very different from before, indicating a *major* disruption.

A fourth criterion is the magnitude of *incremental performance*, and the value of the *added dimensions of functionality* that the new product introduces. Increasing speed for a networking application by 20% might not warrant any premium. Even multiplying the Ethernet speed by a factor of 10 (from 10Mbps to 100Mbps) did *not* warrant a price premium of more than 10%. In fact, due to backward compatibility, consumers were willing to pay the 10% premium only for products that supported *both* the 10Mbps and 100Mbps functionality, automatically. The migration from USB 1 ("full speed") to USB 2 ("high speed"), although it offered a performance improvement by a factor of 40, did not attract much higher premiums. You should challenge what the *real* impact would be on the consumer experience when using the product. If, for example, the performance improvement allows new functionality that was unavailable before the added performance, it would warrant a more significant premium than if the performance improvement enhanced experience linearly.

The fifth criterion is the ability of the new disruption to enable new business models, and change the *distribution of profits* in the value chain. A hypothetical example: imagine there was an *all-in-one* printer that could print and bind a complete book at the quality level of a regular printed book, and it could do that for the same cost as printing one copy of a million-book print run. Imagine further that the printer could have printed different books, one at a time, one after the other. This would eliminate the need for publishers. Amazon.com could have a printer like this installed in every distribution center, and print books completely on demand, collecting the profits that would have otherwise been collected by the publisher and the printer. Furthermore, it would eliminate the cost of maintaining an inventory, and shipping books from different publishers to Amazon's distribution centers.

Why do we care about classifying the disruptions into *major* and *minor* ones? The answer is that while *major* disruptions may create dramatically more wealth than *minor* ones, they face much more resistance all around, and are much harder to realize. I will list a few of the resistance sources to *major* disruptions.

Consumer resistance

First, the more different the usage of the new technology or product is, the more *consumer education* there will need to be. Educating consumers is not a preferred route. Consumers do not like learning new ways of using products. Only a small number of consumers (the ones Geoffrey Moore[83] calls *early adopters* or *innovators*) are willing to learn new things. According to Moore, the *innovators* will learn new things simply because they are new, while the *early adopters* will learn new things when they believe they can realize added value. Either way, the majority of consumers will resist learning new "tricks." The more different the use of the new product is from the incumbent one, the slower the adoption will be, and the slower it will move from the hands of the few *early adopters* and *innovators* into the hands of the *mass consumer market*. Consumers also fear that the data they might have stored in "the old way" will no longer be reliably stored. With all the attempts to reduce paperwork, people prefer hard copy for some records because they do not trust the electronic media to retain the important and sensitive data as reliably. Computers and hard disk drives have been known to crash or be hacked into (although paper copies have been known to burn, fade, get wet, get misplaced, or otherwise be destroyed).

So how do you avoid educating consumers and delaying the adoption of the new technology? There are several ways. One is to retain all the existing features and use cases of the old, incumbent product. Try to make the user interface as similar as possible to that of the existing product. If you want to deliver the TV experience into a new form factor product (such as a cellular phone), you must maintain as much consistency as possible with the existing service (the regular, living room TV). You must keep the same operating buttons (TV on/off, channel up/down, volume up/down). It took time for cellular phone consumers to realize that with a cellular phone you do not wait for a dial tone before you start dialing, but rather dial the number first and then wait for the ring tone. Sure, you can change the way you use television on your cell phone, but consumers will not adopt it quickly. You can add features that will be available only in the new product, but not in a threatening way. Let the consumers start to consume the *regular* features they are used to, and gradually transition into the *new* features, offered only by the disruptive product. The ability to "rip" music CDs through iTunes and listen to them on iPod was, in my opinion, an ingenious way to let consumers transition into the "real" advantage of the iPod—the ability to download (and pay for) new music they do not own. Initially, consumers were able to upload the CDs they currently owned into the iPod. Gradually, the consumers explored the iTunes store, and started downloading music, a much bigger source of revenue than iPod product sales. The consumers had to first adopt the iPod, before they started using the new features.

We must consider that some disruptions occur with *non-consumers* (a Clayton Christensen term). The new product or service might be like nothing you ever used before. When a new technology disruption puts products with certain functionality into the hands of consumers who never used anything like it before, the above is not applicable. Maintaining the same way of operation is meaningless because there was no way of operating a similar product before. Take the personal computer, for example. Sure, some of the users of the personal computer (probably the early ones) used mini-computers or even mainframe computers at work or college, and the transition to personal computers was somewhat smoother. For most, though, the use of computers, personal or otherwise, was completely new. There was no *previous* way of doing things, so anything was possible. Companies were competing on "creating legacy," or inventing ways that consumers will do things. DOS established itself, later replaced by Windows. IBM created a competing way of operating the computer, and so did Apple. As it turned out, Microsoft's way won. When considering disrupting into a *non-consumer* market, we must assume it will still take time for consumers to adopt it. Not because it works *differently* from products they are currently using, but because it works *nothing* like anything they used before. Either way (new ways of doing similar things or disrupting a *non-consumer* market), consumers will resist the new product.

Ecosystem resistance

When the disruptive technology or product is significantly different from existing products, most likely, someone will need to create a new ecosystem, a value chain, or infrastructure. Motorola in the US or Ericsson in Europe could not have introduced the cellular phone only (which initially was called a *car-phone* and not many believed it could become truly handheld). They had to build an infrastructure with coverage good enough to encourage consumers to use it. Although requiring major efforts in electronic miniaturization and product design, the hardest part was building the infrastructure. Building it in a single city would not have been enough as consumers travel, and the value of the cellular phone arises typically during that travel. With modern transportation, travel takes us beyond a single city, so the value of the cellular phone would have materialized only when the deployment was on a national basis. With the cellular phone infrastructure optimized for voice, the delivery of data (e-mail and Internet) and television into cellular phones might require separate infrastructure. The deployment of such infrastructure could be as painful (if not more) as the deployment of the initial cellular phone infrastructure. Metricom's Ricochet service is an example of an excellent product idea that crashed due to insufficient infrastructure deployment.

How can we avoid the extensive, long, and capital-intensive infrastructure deployment of such a service? The best way is to leverage an existing infrastructure. While the initial cellular infrastructure was analog, the *second generation* (GSM, CDMA) was digital. Voice was converted to digital signals. The network was more suitable for data transmission too. RIM's success with the BlackBerry exactly where Ricochet failed was due to leveraging an existing infrastructure, namely the digital cellular phone infrastructure. Will mobile TV be able to benefit from leveraging the *third-generation* cellular phone infrastructure? The 3G network has a lot higher capacity than the second-generation one. However, the number of subscribers is growing, and with cellular service pricing declining, and more data usage of the network, this capacity might not be enough to support the extremely capacity-intensive television services. Voice services require a low-rate (although low-latency) capacity, between 4Kbps and 12Kbps. The cellular networks operate optimally to allocate those small capacity "chunks" while assuring low-latency. Data services (such as Internet, e-mail, and instant messaging) are asynchronous, and can live with longer latency, allowing the network to allocate capacity to them on a *best effort* basis. Television broadcasting, on the other hand, requires high capacity, high *quality-of-service* operation. The bandwidth of a reasonable video stream is 384Kbps, or between thirty and one hundred times the bandwidth of a voice call. This can severely cripple the capacity of the existing network, if used to carry TV broadcasting. New infrastructure might be required.

When considering leveraging an existing infrastructure for new products, technologies, and services, you must consider:

- Can the existing infrastructure support the essential features of the new product, technology, or service?

- Will the new product, technology, or service allow the existing infrastructure to continue and support its originally intended use?

- Will the new products or services displace the existing ones using the same infrastructure?

The latter factor nullifies the second one. If the new product or service displaces the existing one and uses the same infrastructure, we should not be concerned with the ability of the existing infrastructure in serving the "old" products or services, as those will disappear.

Unlike leveraging an existing *infrastructure* is the leveraging of an existing *installed base* of products or services. Let me define *installed base* first. Product manufacturers focus on the *annual shipment* of those products rather than on how many of those products are in use by consumers at any time. There are several phases in the life cycle of a PC. First, it is new and completely active, and being used as the *main* computer (for home or office, for work, study, or play). This phase will typically last up to three years. In the second phase, the PC is still operational, but not updated with the latest hardware and software. At this point, most consumers will opt not to go through the trouble of upgrading some of the PC components, and would rather buy a new one. The "old" PC is still operational, for some secondary purposes. This phase ends when the PC does not work anymore. If the first phase lasts three years on average, there is an installed base of all the PCs shipped in the last three years, close to 500 million computers. For cell phones, it is easier to know the magnitude of the installed base, as a subscription is required, and we know there are close to 3 billion subscribers worldwide, which means the installed base is 3 billion phones.

Why are those numbers important? As stated before, product manufacturers will care only about the number of new products that will ship in a year, as this is their total available market. After-market accessory manufacturers[84] care about the installed base for *main* products that those accessories can complement *once the main product is already in the hands of the consumers*. An example is the market for external backup hard disk drives. Less concerned with the number of new PCs shipped in a year, the manufacturers of those external drives focus on the number of PCs already deployed. With its huge *installed base* size, the cell phone market should have represented a much larger *after-market* opportunity. However, since cell phones in general do not have many after-market accessories, there is less additional hardware. Headsets (wired and wireless), batteries, memory cards (for smart phones) and downloadable applications (the leading one being *ring tones*) target this installed base of cell phones.

To maximize an *installed base*, consider as a target market the features that the largest part of the installed base of products have, which might be features of products manufactured twenty-four months ago (in the case of cellular phones), three to six years ago (in the case of PCs), or even ten years ago (for cars). If you target only features that were included in products less than one year ago, you may exclude parts of the installed base, limiting the total available market for your disruptive market or product. When Solram Electronics built the InterHome product, it had to connect to a PC. The year was 1996, and the newly released USB standard was not included in the entire installed base. When considering the interfaces available in PCs over the last three years (1993 to 1996), only three interfaces made sense: the parallel printer port, the serial COM port, and the gaming/MIDI port. Because most used the parallel printer port, and the mouse or other device used the COM port, Solram chose the MIDI port to communicate with the device.

There are other aspects of the need to create a new ecosystem to enable the market for the new product, technology, or service. You may need to create new distribution channels. There are many different types of distribution channels available today for different products, so there is a high probability of using an existing distribution channel for your new products or services, requiring only minimal adjustments to support the new products. Retail channels today are set up to sell everything, including cell phone service contracts. eCommerce channels are available for sales of almost everything. When you think of distribution, think in both directions of the value chain. Not only distribution of *your* product or service, but also distribution of components required for those products or services. You must ensure that there are more suppliers than there will be vendors of the new product to assure the bulk or bargaining power will be with your company and your competitors.

Incumbent product resistance

Highly disruptive products are different from any other product they replace. IF the product is less disruptive, there is a higher probability that the "older" product can still compensate for the difference. The existing (or *incumbent*) products, currently performing the same job, will always "resist" the introduction of the new product. *Major* disruptions will introduce strong incremental value and typically new *dimensions* of value.

When wireless LAN (IEEE 802.11b standard-based, later called Wi-Fi) surfaced, it was competing with the established *wired* Ethernet. It was a major disruption, as it added a significant dimension of value—mobility—and the ability to connect as many computers as desired to a single access point, without the need to be near an Ethernet jack. It was definitely a significant new dimension, and the value it brought to consumers made it such a *major* disruption that the existing Ethernet could not cope with it. Ethernet is still widely used, but mostly as a *backhaul* technology, one that connects broadband connections to Wi-Fi access points. The Ethernet technology could do nothing to nullify the new value that Wi-Fi brought. It found its niche and stayed there. This niche will continue to be viable and healthy until, perhaps, the pervasive introduction of mesh networking.[85] On the other hand, the introduction of the next generation Wi-Fi, based on the IEEE 802.11g standard, was a *minor* disruption. While increasing the performance five-fold, it did not add another dimension of value. But 802.11b products resisted the change. Lowering prices of 802.11b gear kept the more expensive 802.11g products out of the market. With new players (Broadcom, Intel, and Atheros) using the new technology as an entry point to the Wi-Fi market, they quickly got sucked into a price war, reducing the prices of 802.11g products to the point of replacing the 802.11b products. Although they should have delayed the adoption of such a *minor* disruption, new market entrants used it to penetrate the market and changed the landscape, against common wisdom.

Company internal resistance

The creation of disruptions is difficult and laborious and also high risk. Established companies resist them, with stronger resistance to *major* disruptions than to *minor* ones. Start-up companies and their investors embrace disruptions, *major* more than *minor*. Start-up companies can succeed only when the rules of the game change, and that happens only with *major* disruptions. They can strive only if they outmaneuver the slow, large companies. For start-up companies, "bet the farm" is the only way. Large established companies are risk averse. They have shareholders to answer to. The employees focus on seniority. They (the companies and the employees) have a lot to lose, whereas start-up companies have nothing to lose.

Main and derivative disruptions

The second distinction is between *main* and *derivative* disruptions. The *main* disruption is the classical definition of the term *disruption*. It is the iPod, the cell phone, the PC, and beyond. The *derivative* disruption is something that results from the occurrence of the *main* disruption. It is a component that did not exist before the creation of the main disruption, but is essential to its existence. Often overlooked, those *derivative* disruptions may take on a life of their own and go on to disrupt other markets, as you saw in this book. The hard disk drive was not a *main* disruption. Mainframe computers needed mass non-volatile storage, which prompted creation of the hard disk drive. It took on a life of its own and helped disrupt its creator, the mainframe market, by enabling the mini-computer market. It continued to evolve to disrupt the mini-computer market and enable the creation of the personal computer market. It then continued to disrupt the portable music player market, by enabling the creation of the iPod.

Which comes first, the *main* disruption or the *derivative* one? The answer is both. Most likely, there is a technology trend that will disrupt the *main* market, and serve as a *derivative* for this market, while there will be a whole slew of new derivative components that are disrupted as a result of the creation of the *main* disruption. Another possibility is for a *main* disruption not to *create* a derivative disruption, but rather to change the economies and market size of an existing derivative component or service. Take Amazon.com and eBay, for example. They created *main* disruptions in the way business is done, and their impact on courier services such as UPS and FedEx was enormous. Amazon.com generates revenue of $9.7 billion annually (2006), and eBay generates $5.6 billion (2006), representing tens of billions of dollars in products shipped. Instead of direct buying by visiting a store, consumers receive products by using UPS, FedEx, and others. While in business before the eCommerce *disruption*, that disruption significantly (and very positively) affected their *derivative* service.

Will a *minor* disruption create *derivative* disruptions? It might, but since it is a smaller disruption, its creators will most likely try to leverage as many existing derivative components as possible and will not mandate derivative disruptions. The market size will typically not justify the creation of a new derivative product.

As seen before, a *derivative* disruption of a *major* disruption may end up continuing to disrupt other markets. While still maintaining the status of a *derivative* component, it may enable a new market, and contribute to the disruption of a market based on its capabilities. The best examples of such *derivative* products that enabled so many other disruptions while maintaining the *derivative* product status are the hard disk drive technology, the semiconductor technology (with the subsidiary processor and memory technologies), and the radio technology. Other *derivative* technologies that can help, although typically do not initiate *main* disruptions, are display technologies (LCD, DLP, digital ink, and more), and image capture technologies.

How do the factors described for the *major* and *minor* disruptions affect *derivative* disruptions? *Derivative* disruptions do not typically face *consumer resistance* since they are, by nature, not made for *consumers*. Engineers in the companies creating the *main* disruptions are the target customers for the *derivative* disruptions, rather than the consumers. Hypothetically, assume that there is a significant disruption in the memory technology, and a completely new technology allows increasing the memory capacity of the same size SD card by a factor of ten. As long as this is still a memory card, would the consumers care? Would they even know? The engineers who will use this *derivative* technology disruption for their *main* disruptive product would care and might actually be the ones who initiated and requested the *derivative* disruption, or they are merely "riding" the *derivative* disruption to create their *main* disruption product. Either way, the customers (not the consumers) will *embrace* the derivative disruption where consumers typically *reject* the main disruption, as described above.

Will a *derivative* disruption trigger the creation of a new ecosystem? If this derivative technology *enabled* the main disruption, it most likely already has an existing ecosystem and value chain, created when this derivative disruption first took place. If this derivative disruption is a *result* of the main disruption, an ecosystem and value chain that supports the production of such a derivative component might be required, but it will most likely be limited in scope, especially since only a part of the whole, *main* product would need the value chain. The value chain of a hard disk drive (not the ones distributed in retail directly to consumers) is relatively simple. The value chain for Texas Instruments' components, although constituting the most critical part of the cell phone, is much simpler than the value chain and ecosystem of the cell phone itself. There are no services required, and the distribution is very simple, only to the cell phone manufacturers.

Is there resistance from *incumbent* substitute products to the new *derivative* disruptions? The derivative disruption is, as the name suggests, a derivative of the main product. As described above for the *main* disruptions, the developers of such disruptions are trying to maximize the utilization of existing components and address an existing installed base. This warrants the usage of *incumbent* components and technologies as much as possible, avoiding new components. The new components create a burden of qualifying them for the new products. They also eliminate the possibility of addressing an installed base, as they do not exist in the installed base. The decision to create (or request) a *derivative* disruption is therefore made only if there is no incumbent technology or component that can deliver the value needed for the *main* disruption. Once such a decision happens, there is probably no alternative to the *derivative disruption* and, therefore, it will not receive any resistance from such.

What about company internal resistance? Well, if the *derivative* technology existed *before* the creation of the *main* disruption, then it is not really a disruption for the company creating it. It is simply a new market for the same product. Not many companies will resist finding new markets for their existing products. In fact, they will embrace it. If, on the other hand, the derivative disruption is new, then it will be disruptive to the company's line of business. However, since the company itself requested the derivative disruption, in this case for the creation of a new *main* market, then there is an inherent demand for this new component by the creators of the main disruption, and the risk is, therefore, lower. The risk is not zero, though. Remember that the fate of the *main* disruption is still unclear. It might have all the right elements and symptoms of a successful *major* disruption, but at the time the request for the development of the *derivative* disruption occurs, it is still a very early phase of adoption. In fact, the demand occurs before the adoption ever starts, and without the *derivative* component the *main* product will never see the market. While company resistance to *derivative* disruptions is typically lower than resistance to the *main* disruption (after all, companies that believe "the customer is always right" will build the derivative technologies for the customer who asked for it), you do have the responsibility to validate and quantify the risks associated with the *main* disruption. If the market for the *main* disruption will not materialize, neither will the market for the *derivative* product. The internal DSL experience in PCTEL is more proof for this assertion. The customer is not always right. Compaq and Dell's request for internal DSL modems (even though it was only a *minor* disruption) caused quite a few companies (PCTEL and Texas Instruments included) to invest tens of millions of dollars in the development of *derivative* components. But the market never materialized, and the DSL (as well as other broadband) modem market remained an external one and never became integrated into PCs. Another thing to consider in the context of the *demand* for the new derivative technology is that if you waited until your customer, the *main* disruptor, asked you for a derivative and disruptive product, it might be too late to be competitive. You are probably not the only company solicited for that derivative product. When Intel decided there was a need for USB *high-speed* (2.0), it invited several companies to join the USB promoters group. None of those companies was first. When I proposed a *derivative disruption* for TI's connectivity group, one of my peers asked me if there was demand for such a product by any of our "usual" customers. My answer was that if demand existed, it would have already been too late to take a leading competitive position in this market. It is *before* there is demand, that companies can establish leading competitive positions, even with a *derivative* disruption.

Can you project and plan a *derivative* disruption (small or large) ahead of the *main* disruption and *before* your customer asks? I will assert that you can. There are two ways to project such disruptions: to project future *main* disruptions, or to follow another *derivative* technology that already exists, so that there is interdependency between them. The first case is harder to predict, and if you *could* predict it, you would probably be better off creating the *main* disruption yourself, rather than creating a *derivative* component to that main disruption. If the company you work for is too conservative to create the *main* market disruption, you may want to consider creating a start-up company to create that disruption. The second option, though, is an easier possibility. You need to identify a major driving *derivative* force, such as the hard disk drive, the flash memory, or processing power. Then you need to ask how those *derivative* technologies will affect other markets, and what other technologies, possibly less *driving* in nature, will be affected. The best example that comes to mind is connectivity. With higher processing power, a processor will need to move more data. Data busses will have to be faster. Silicon Valley-based Rambus,[86] for example, noticing the trend toward faster processing, faster memories, and faster graphical applications, saw the need for faster memory interfaces and created a very successful and profitable company on that premise. In the very tough IP market, it managed to create a *derivative* disruption, based on its ability to project technology trends and understand where other *driving derivative* disruptions will occur, and developed *dependent derivative* disruptions of its own.

Major, minor, or derivative disruption?

After the discussion of the different types of disruptions, you still wonder—which disruption is better? For an existing company, whether a 75-year-old public company with 35,000 employees or a three-year-old start-up, the decision between a *main* and a *derivative* disruption is moot. Your company is already in a specific line of business, and has the competencies and infrastructure to support one of the two types.

Texas Instruments, with the exception of the Educational Technology and Calculators business unit, is a company that sells in a business-to-business (b2b) model. It is a company that sells components (always *derivative* components) to engineers in companies that build products. TI's main customers are the electronic product manufacturers, such as Nokia, Motorola, Sony, Samsung, and others. TI is well entrenched in the *derivative* component world. TI used to be very diversified, with businesses such as sensors and controls (a business that was spun off in 2005 to become *Sansata Technologies*), defense components, and even laptop computers. However, TI secured a leadership position because of its focus on the semiconductor market, especially in the market for digital signal processors.

Say a TI employee meets with Rich Templeton (TI's CEO) and suggests that TI start a new and disruptive mobile phone business—not a business that builds mobile phone components, but rather a business that builds the phones themselves. What would Mr. Templeton say? I believe he would ask that employee to try creating a partnership with a cellular phone OEM that would build this *main disruption* phone, while TI created a critical mass of intellectual property assuring a competitive position for TI as a *derivative* component manufacturer, because that is what TI does best. TI does not have the skills or the experience to build phones. Nokia, Motorola, Samsung, and others do. TI may benefit from them building the phone and might have to encourage them to build the phone, but they should not build the phone itself.

In summary, your company already positions you as a *main* or *derivative* disruption creator. However, whether you are a *main* disruption creator or a *derivative* disruption creator, you can look for *major* disruptions as well as *minor* ones. Figure 30 shows you the characteristics, impact, advantages, and disadvantages of each disruption type.

	Main disruption		Derivative disruption	
	Major disruption	Minor disruption	To a major disruption	To a minor disruption
Features	Adds dimensions of value, or a significant performance increase, replaces majority of products in the market, replacing large percentage of the previous product	Incremental in nature. Not a "major step for mankind"	Can be a major disruption by itself. Has the potential to continue and drive disruptions in other markets.	
Target market	Consumers, end customers, and non-consumers	Consumers, end customers. Hardly ever non-consumers	The developers of main disruptions. Engineers, most likely asking for the disruption	
Customer resistance	High – need education	Low – it is a "better mouse trap"	Low – the customers are the ones requesting the derivative disruption	
Market resistance	Medium – no substitute products can meet new dimension of value, but overall facing resistance to change	High – substitute products can potentially meet the performance increase	Low – since the initial bias is *not* to demand derivative disruption, and one is demanded only due to no alternative	A minor main disruption may not warrant the creation of a derivative disruption
Company Resistance	High – due to risk and visionary nature	Low – perceived as a natural extension to existing products	Low – since the disruption is made "on customer demand" and is therefore perceived as low risk	
Ecosystem creation	Will most likely be required	Little, if any, is required, as it is using the same ecosystem as prior products	A new ecosystem might be required, but it is limited in scope as this is a business-to-business model	
Revenue potential	The highest – it changes complete markets and replaces existing products with completely different ones.	Moderate to low, depending on the overall market size. Most likely suitable for new entrants to enter an existing markets	Moderate to low, depending on the market size for the main major disruption, and the role that the derivative disruption plays in the success of the main disruption	
Probability of success	Lowest. Too many unknowns. Too much resistance initially	Moderate – might not overcome hurdles of existing products improving in other ways	Low – depending on the success of the main disruption. *An often overlooked aspect!*	
Examples	iPod, Cell phone, personal computer	802.11g, 1Gb Ethernet	Hard disk drive, Flash memory, USB 2	

Figure 30—Major, minor, and derivative disruptions

The highest revenue potential, as well as the highest risk and highest resistance, comes from the *major main* disruption. The product (or service) delivered to the consumer attracts a higher value than the sum of all its parts (the *derivative* components). A *minor* disruption generates a smaller revenue potential, as it addresses a smaller part of the market (a *segment* of the market) or it offers only an incremental value to existing products rather than a new dimension of value. The *derivative* disruption components will always attract less revenue than the complete product, but their importance to the existence and performance of the whole product may warrant a significant percentage of the whole product price. The semiconductor value of a flash-based MP3 player may be as high as

50% of the selling price and the Intel processor may represent 20% to 30% of the overall PC price, for example. Even a *derivative* disruption may generate significant revenue. After all, *derivative* components account for Intel's position as the number one semiconductor company in the world.

Estimating price and revenue potential of a disruption

The following is by no means a scientific method for estimating the revenue potential from a disruption. However, I wanted to bring up some of the main factors that will help you in determining the potential revenue. Some of them are obvious, but some might not be.

- *Value*, not *cost*, drives price. This is true whether it is the price of the whole product, or the price differential for the incremental performance or new dimension of value. Often companies make the mistake of taking the cost, adding the desired profit margin, and calculating the price based on those. This could be a mistake in two directions: on one hand, you might be pricing the product or service too *low* since the costs are low. There is nothing wrong with higher profit margins if the value justifies it. On the other hand, you might be pricing the product or service too *high* due to its costs, exceeding the value potential that customers or consumers attribute to them. This is a tricky one; if the cost of offering the product or service does not allow you to offer them in a value-based price while maintaining healthy profit margins, you have a problem. A few examples: when the Wi-Fi technology moved from the 802.11b standard (at data rates of 11 Mbps) to the 802.11g standard (at 54 Mbps), there was incremental value, but most likely at 10%-15% beyond that of 802.11b. The main value proposition of Wi-Fi was with its *mobility*, and that did not change with the faster products. Even though the *cost* of an 802.11g product was more than 15% higher than that of an 802.11b product, the premium could not have been passed to consumers. When you wonder how much consumers will be willing to pay for mobile TV in their cell phones, remember that on average they are paying $50/month for their main service—voice. The incremental value of mobile TV could possibly be 30%, or an additional $15, allowing a non-stop TV experience. The cost structure of non-stop TV over the cellular network would be prohibitive.

- Will the new disruptive products completely replace the existing ones? You will need to estimate whether the product offers increased performance, functionality, or a value-added dimension to the point it will completely replace the existing product, or if it will replace only some. You need to segment carefully the market based on the added performance or functionality to quantify that. The added functionality might be appealing only to a market segment with specific characteristics. You should factor this in to quantify the total available market in size, as well as to determine pricing. When a new product addresses the *high end* of the market, it can typically attract better price premiums, although the volume is typically lower.

- Are you cannibalizing your own product in the market? If you do have significant presence in the market with the existing product, and the new product will potentially replace all of them, you may want to consider a price *premium* for the product. If you are holding a small share in the market, or you are a new entrant to the market, then offering the new, disruptive product for the same price as the existing product might be a successful market penetration strategy. This was the strategy that Broadcom used when entering the Wi-Fi market. Broadcom, without any significant market share with 802.11b products, offered the 802.11g products for the same price. They did not cannibalize any of their existing products, but gained a leading market share in this market as a result.

- Pricing a *derivative* component should follow the same guidelines. Although it does not offer direct value to the consumer, it does offer value to your immediate customer in the value chain. The pricing should reflect the importance (and incremental value) of the product to the existence and performance of the final product. In some cases, the value of the *derivative* component is visible to the final consumer, even though you do not sell directly to the consumer. When buying PCs, for example, consumers are aware of the value of the processor inside. They are aware of the brand (Intel or AMD) and some other key characteristics (processor speed, memory size, memory speed, and so on). A consumer campaign such as Intel's "Intel inside" and "Centrino®[87]" campaigns, and Texas Instruments' DLP campaign can increase consumer awareness. Causing consumers to prefer products with specific *derivative* components in them increases the value of those components to the immediate customers, the product manufacturers and improves the profitability of those components.

---

[81] Walkman is a registered trademark of Sony.

[82] A fact that will explain why the first automobiles looked very much like carriages without horses.

[83] "Crossing the Chasm."

[84] The term *after-market* refers to accessories that can be added to the main product after it was sold, and in the hands of the consumers. Do not confuse this with *secondary market*, which is the market for used products, where the consumer who bought the product in the first place is now selling it to a second consumer. While the latter is very active for vehicles and real estate, it is not very common for consumer electronics products.

[85] Mesh networking is an ability that wireless *nodes* have that allows them to route messages wirelessly to the right device, even though it is out of range for one access point.

[86] Rambus was incorporated in 1990. They specialize in the development of high-speed connectivity and memory interface intellectual property (IP). Licensing and royalties alone account for 83% of their 2005 net revenue of $157 million.

[87] Centrino is a trademark of Intel Corporation.

Chapter 10
The Time Horizon

The first step in searching for the disruptive implementation opportunities is defining the time horizon. Almost regardless of the nature of the disruption sought, different time horizons will warrant completely different strategies. Even if you plan a disruption only two years in advance, would it amount to a disruption that would change the rules of the game in a market? It would most likely be a *minor* disruption rather than a *major* one. You should consider several factors when deciding on the time horizon:

- Nature of the development considered. In today's high-tech world, unless the product is completely software-based, the development of an integrated circuit will be involved, as well as the development of an end product based on that integrated circuit. Most likely, some programming will be involved to release the final product. The time scale for such development will be four years, as a rule of thumb (see Figure 32). If a shorter timeframe is sought, the flexibility is significantly lower if using new technologies that are significantly different than existing products.

- If multiple companies in an industry or organization need to develop industry standards as a cooperative effort, this process will add significant time. Chapter 14 will review the concept of *standard-based products* and the process of creating industry standards, as well as ways to influence this process effectively and favorably. You will be surprised with how dependent are most products on standards.

- The certainty of the future envisioned decreases the length of the time horizon. The future trend predictions offer a wide range of possibilities. Although trend lines tend to remain constant, they are more susceptible to deviation from the historical trend line the further in time we project them. The non-technological driving forces, even though much slower than the technological ones, may have a profound impact. As an example, the September 11, 2001, events had a dramatic impact on many industries. While it hurt some industries almost beyond repair (aviation), it created new opportunities in others (security). The probability of competitors making unexpected moves is higher if we give them a long enough opportunity. Competitors, in this context, include *companies* and substitute *products.*

High-tech consumer products typically have similar components, as shown in Figure 31. They typically include an *application-specific integrated circuit* (ASIC). As the semiconductor process got smaller, that single component, also called *system-on-chip* (SoC), could take on more functionality.

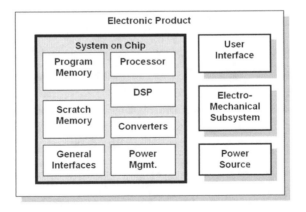

Figure 31—Electronic product and system on chip

The SoC typically includes an integrated general-purpose processor, capable of running the application to support the functionality of the end product, a digital signal processor (DSP) to process analog signals and turn them into data (and vice versa). It also typically includes some signal converters (converting analog signals to digital ones or vice versa), some "glue logic,"[88] power management circuitry, program memory, data memory, and interfaces.

Figure 32 describes the design cycle for such a product, from concept to product introduction. Different products may have different design cycles, but my experience shows that they are surprisingly similar.

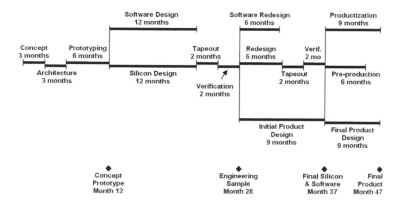

Figure 32—A typical product design cycle

The first development phase is the concept phase. When the concept evolves for the whole product, the requirements are defined, and initial specifications written. In the following three months, the design team will develop the architecture of the product. The architecture will include the different components of the SoC, the software structure. It will also calculate and identify the performance requirements and make technology choices. The next phase is an exciting one—the prototype phase. Now the design team, using off-the-shelf components and subsystems will build a concept prototype. The prototype is typically crude looking. It is too big, consumes too much power, does not perform exactly the way the production product is expected to perform, but it delivers the most important value: it allows the prospective customers to envision what it will do, as they would not be able to otherwise. Instead of the SoC, typically a FPGA[89] is used. When Qualcomm wanted to demonstrate the future performance of its CDMA telephones, its people built a prototype phone that had to be stored in a van and carried around town to demonstrate to the prospective customers (in this case the cellular phone operators) how it would work.[90] The prototype also has value in that it helps finalize the architecture of the finished product. The prototype will typically be operational within twelve months from the moment the team had the innovative idea and kicked off a committed development. At this point, development of both the SoC and the software is progressing. I saw development time of this phase vary mostly between nine and fifteen months, but it can also reach two years, or take only six months. On average, I used twelve months for this phase. At this point, the SoC will enter a phase called *tapeout*. The source of the name is the historic act of delivering a magnetic tape containing a file describing the physical layout of the integrated circuit[91] to the factory that creates the lithography photomasks used to fabricate the integrated circuit. The photomasks go to the fab, which in turn, creates the integrated circuits, which then will have to be tested and packaged. This process takes between two and three months, depending on the complexity of the silicon process. The *tapeout* moment is a very exciting one. It represents the transition from design to a physical integrated circuit. The days before the tapeout typically represent the highest amount of work, and you see engineers working around the clock to be ready for the tapeout on time. The moment when the first silicon arrives back from the fab is also an exciting one, as the engineers are anxious to see if the first samples work. There are times when the first samples return and do not work at all,[92] but in most cases most of the functionality is achieved. It typically takes up to two months to test all the functions of the SoC in the *verification* phase. A printed circuit board is built as a real-size prototype of the end product to accommodate the real SoC. In parallel with the silicon design process, and up to the moment of verification, software (or *firmware*[93]) is developed.

After the verification phase is complete, the engineering sample, at about two and a half years after the development started, goes to the customer (the OEM, Sony, Dell, Apple, Nokia, and others) who will now start designing the final product. Typically, the customers engage at an earlier phase than that, but when a disruptive innovation is concerned, they tend to wait until the engineering sample is ready. It takes them approximately nine months to build a form-factor[94] prototype of the end product. In parallel, the semiconductor company will modify the SoC design to eliminate any errors, modify features, eliminate "bugs," tapeout again, and verify the product again. Just over three years from the beginning of the development, the semiconductor company delivers the SoC as it will be in mass production. In the same time, the software will be mature enough to support preproduction. At this point, the OEM will enter the final product design phase, preparing the product for manufacture. It takes four years from day one until the *whole* product hits the shelves. I saw products that took less, but those were incremental improvements over existing products, rather than the disruptive implementations that this book addresses. Those products hardly ever take less than four years of development. Why assume four years? First, because that's the reality. Second, because the innovation is more disruptive when it addresses the technologies available four years away rather than less. Otherwise, it might be too obvious.

There are cases in which the innovative company is the sole believer in the disruption this product will create. A semiconductor company faced with this challenge might have to meet it by building the end product itself, and sometimes even offer associated service. While not within the core competencies of the company, and not supported by its business model, it might be necessary. In time, once there is a market for the product (and associated services, where applicable), the appropriate companies and service providers will step into the market and assume their roles. At that time, the innovative company may divest the unrelated businesses, sell them, or even simply shut them down once they have filled their role. Sometimes it's the product company that wishes to enter a market with an innovative product, being forced to design the SoC itself, or outsource its development.

---

[88] Generic logical blocks that perform relatively simple and non-flexible functions that the processor will not be performing.

[89] Field Programmable Gate Array. A component that has the highest level of programmability and can be programmed to emulate almost any possible function. It might not be able to run at the same speed as the final SoC, but it will be able to demonstrate the functionality. Those components can cost several thousand dollars and serve only as prototypes and development.

[90] Dave Mock, "The Qualcomm Equation: How a Fledgling Telecom Company Forged a New Path to Big Profits and Market," AMACOM/ American Management Association, 2005.

[91] In a format called GDS-II.

[92] The probability of that is dramatically reduced due to the semiconductor design tools, the simulation tools, and design rule check tools used prior to silicon fabrication.

[93] *Hardware* helps identify what cannot change (the SoC, for example). *Software* defines programs that are highly flexible and can change. The term *firmware* refers to software that runs on embedded processors and SoC, and as such is not as flexible as software that runs on personal computers and can be updated and changed at will. Between *hard* and *soft*, the term used was *firm* for *firmware*.

[94] A form-factor prototype is a prototype that will have the size and the look of the final product. While it can still change until it takes its final shape – it will look very similar to the final product. Prospective customers and consumers will provide feedback on this prototype.

Chapter 11
How People Use Products

The next two chapters will discuss the product and the value it should bring to make it successful, through three phases:

- Understanding the way consumers use products. If you develop products that are not easy to use, and do not add value as perceived by consumers, they will not create disruption. In fact, you will not sell anything beyond the initial hype.

- Defining the *whole* product. Most likely, the product you have in mind, which fits your capabilities, is not enough to satisfy the need that you are trying to create along the value chain. You need to understand the auxiliary components of the product that make it *whole.*

- Investigating the entire ecosystem. Products do not exist in a vacuum. There is a delivery mechanism (called the "value chain") made by multiple players that adds value to the product all the way until consumed by consumers. There are also companies and entities *outside* the value chain that impact the consumption of the product. Failing to assure there is an ecosystem in support of the delivery of the product assures no market for the product will develop.

The following examples in this chapter will make a case for the importance of understanding how consumers use products (and understand how they *don't* use products).

Internet telephony

In 1995, an Israeli start-up company called VocalTec went through a very successful IPO at NASDAQ. This planted success ideas in many high-tech entrepreneurs in Israel. I was no different. With the support of my wife, I decided to start a company called Solram Electronics. In 1995, the cost of an international call was over $1.50 per minute, and international calls were, therefore, rare, business related or personal. VocalTec pioneered the concept of *Internet telephony*. With a software application called *IPhone* (yes, neither Apple nor Cisco used this term first) running on a PC, they allowed two computers connected to the Internet to have voice communication between them. Of course, you had to know the IP address of the computer on the other side and both computers had to have people connect them at the same time, something that was much less than obvious since they used dial-up modems, sharing the telephone line with regular phones. VocalTec pioneered a concept known today as VoIP (Voice over IP). In principle, the idea is that a microphone picks up the voice, which undergoes digitization, compression,[95] and then transmission as payload over the Internet protocol (IP) link between the computers. At the receiving computer on the other side, the payload ships from the packets and is decompressed. Then the digital signal becomes an audible one, played by the speakers. The transmitted signal was broken into *packets*, rather than sent as a continuous stream, as the Internet protocol is packet-based rather than switch-based.[96]

Problems plagued the early days of Internet telephony. Somehow, you had to connect both computers to the Internet at the same time, you had to know the IP address of the other computer to be able to establish the initial connection, and then there were breakups, unintelligible voice problems, and dropped calls (pretty much every call was a dropped call due to Internet congestion at some point). People still used it. Why? Because international calls were very expensive. People used Internet telephony in places where an international call cost over $1 per minute, sometimes even $4 per minute. Internet telephony, as unreliable as it was, with the cost of a local call to your Internet service provider (ISP), was a darn cheaper alternative.

One night in 1995, I had an idea. I realized that people were willing to suffer through the poor quality of Internet telephony, but didn't use it for several reasons. First, using a PC to make calls was less intuitive than using the telephone. Second, the other person had to be online to accept the call. Third, it was not easy to find each other's IP address to establish the link. Overnight, I designed the architecture of a device that connected regular telephones to PCs, allowing the entire communication to happen using a regular phone, regular dialing, and automatically connecting the computers to the Internet for the call.[97] The device was a small box that connected the phone, the PC, and the telephone line. You could pick up the phone and dial the international telephone number for your destination. The box, later named "InterHome" by my wife, communicated with a similar box on the other side, alerting both computers to connect to the Internet. They registered their IP addresses with a server we had, established the link between them, and then allowed the users on both sides to hold the conversation. This was brilliant! (or, at least, that's what I thought). This would let people, familiar with using a telephone, to hold international calls using the most intuitive telephone, but at the low Internet prices.

It took three more years to build the products and start selling them. Solram Electronics built some 1,000 units before I shut the company down. It failed. The main reason was that I did not really understand the way people use the telephone and their expectations, which were unmet with the InterHome. While the main premise of the InterHome was to simplify the process of placing international phone calls over the public Internet, the installation and setup of the product was far from simple. At the time, the dial-up-based Internet connectivity was far from being stable, and you couldn't hold a long conversation without the link being dropped. Not only that, setting the product up required technical skills, but also sometimes placing the call itself required those skills just to understand what was going on and why a call was not complete. Combined with the quality of Internet telephony in 1998, suffering from long delays, choppy conversation and dropped links, the product ended up being a failure. When I use Internet telephony today (Vonage, Skype), the quality is superb and the user interface is simple; I have to wonder if the InterHome was not simply ahead of its time. Nevertheless, the important lesson is that the product did not address the way the target consumers would have expected to use it, and the quality was not what they expected to feel, compared with the alternative. There is no doubt, though, that Internet telephony applied significant pressure on the traditional telcos to reduce their prices.

Turning projectors off

One of the best (or worst) examples for not understanding user experience is the shut down process of an electronic projector. Electronic projectors take an input from a PC, a TV tuner, or any other video source (DVD player or VCR) and project it over a wall-mounted screen. Businesses use those projectors for slide presentations and at home they provide a replacement for a regular TV, projecting a larger image. Frequently shutting down the projector shortens the lamp's life and, therefore, the projector manufacturers added a step to the shut down process that requires user intervention in order to avoid inadvertent shutdowns. When you press the "off" button (either on the projector or on the projector's remote control), the projector will ask you to confirm shutting down by pressing the "off" button again. However, this message is displayed on the screen, while the user is facing the projector (either by pointing the remote control at the projector, or manually pushing the "off" button on the projector itself) and most likely not looking at the screen, where the confirmation request message appears. Often I watch users become frustrated, trying to understand why the projector did not shut down, even though the power off button was pressed. Although this example is not an example of why a product succeeds or fails, it is a perfect example of how manufacturers do not necessarily understand the way users use products.

Use cases and usage scenarios

A key element to the adoption of new technologies is understanding the scenarios in which users will use products, and how will they use them in those scenarios. RIM's BlackBerry is an excellent example. RIM understood that the consumer did not wish to have a separate e-mail account for mobile messages and manage two separate mailboxes. The BlackBerry shares the *same* e-mail account as the main computer and uses only one mailbox. RIM created the "BlackBerry Enterprise Server" software, an application that resides within the enterprise e-mail server and assures consistency between the two mailboxes. When a user deletes a message from the main computer inbox, it also disappears from the handheld device's inbox. When the user marks a message as *viewed*, the main computer inbox also shows it as *viewed*. This functionality evolved through a thorough understanding of the usage scenarios that contributed to the BlackBerry's success.

You understand the usage scenarios by putting the "average" consumer (a fictional entity that does not really exist, yet represents the typical behavior of the majority of consumers) in a reasonable scenario, and deducting from it the behavior, performance, and specifications of the product.

For example, assume you are developing a new connectivity technology that will connect a digital camera to a PC. You need to decide what the data rate should be. You should use the following process. First, figure out the memory capacity expected when the consumer wishes to upload the pictures from the camera to the PC. If you plan for a 2008 product, assume that the average SD flash card will have a capacity of 4 GB.[98] Further assuming that the average digital camera resolution in 2008 will be 8 megapixels, you will conclude that the average picture size will be close to 2MB. That means that the memory card can hold up to 2,000 pictures before it is full. On average, a consumer probably takes 40 pictures in a week, which means she will take a year to fill the memory card. However, it is still safe to assume that the average consumer will upload the pictures to the PC only when the memory card is full. Every now and then, and especially when users want to print pictures or create a slide show, they will upload them earlier, but our technology needs to be able to upload the full memory card. The next step is to determine a reasonable upload time. Is it thirty seconds? Two minutes? An hour? Given that the consumer may upload only once a year, you can be a little more forgiving. Still, you need to assume that it cannot be very long. An assumption of five to ten minutes is reasonable. Further assuming a protocol overhead[99] of 25%, the throughput required is 142 Mbps. USB 2.0 can perfectly handle this throughput.

An interesting phenomenon is that consumers sometimes use products and see value in a different way than you may envision. One example is the Microsoft fingerprint reader—a small device, capable of reading fingerprints, originally designed to add security to your PC by requiring fingerprint authentication before allowing the user to perform certain functions. However, PC users are not typically concerned about the security of their home computer, and IT managers are concerned with the less-than-perfect security that this fingerprint reader offers. It was another feature that made the product appealing. Today, we conduct a significant amount of our account management (bank, credit card, utilities, bill pay, and other) online. For added security, you have to go through a login page, requiring a username and password for authentication. Microsoft's fingerprint reader allows you to use your fingerprint to enter automatically the username and password instead of typing it. Using different usernames and passwords for different login pages creates a significant burden in terms of remembering all of them. Using the fingerprint reader, which stores securely all those usernames and passwords, and invokes them to get access to your different online accounts simply by pressing its surface with your finger, simplifies the process. Microsoft's fingerprint reader does not offer enhanced security, it offers simplification of your online account access, and it does a great job at it! This is only one example where a user-perceived value (simplified access) supplanted the manufacturer's original value (added security).

Educating consumers

As the creators of disruptive innovations, you are interested in rapid market adoption, before your competitors (the "fast followers") manage to catch up. The higher the adoption rate of a new technology is, the more entrenched the early mover is, and the harder (and more expensive) it is for the competitors to gain any share. On the other hand, it is in the interest of the fast followers that the technology adoption rate is slower, as it gives them an opportunity to gain market share with the non-users and pose a real threat to the first mover.

One of the biggest hurdles in adopting new technologies is educating the consumers how to use those technologies to their benefit. We tend to adopt new technologies faster if their operation is intuitive for us. An example I often use in lectures is asking people in the audience how to program a certain radio station on channel two of the car they just rented at the airport. Almost everyone answers immediately: "It's simple, just push in button number two for a few seconds and you're done!" They don't know the make of the car or the brand of the radio. It is the ubiquity of this function, across all (well, almost all) car models and radios, that makes this function easy to use. Otherwise, consumers would most likely not use it.

When the ultra-wideband (UWB) wireless technology was invented, it was clear that the function it would provide was that of high-speed, short-range connectivity. It was not clear, though, how it would be used. It was not until the USB special interest group (the same group that delivered the ubiquitous USB *wired* standard) launched a new specification called *wireless USB*, which behaves like USB, that the UWB technology was finally understood. People understand USB. It took time for people to adopt USB 1.0, as consumers had to be *educated* on how to use it. It was relatively simple when USB 2.0 appeared. Users understood that USB 2.0 was the same as USB 1.0, except that it was faster. It performed exactly the same functions as USB 1, and it had exactly the same user interface as USB 1. It even used the same cable and connectors as USB 1. It just worked faster. The adoption of USB 2.0 was, therefore, much faster, and the adoption of wireless USB follows suit.

The conclusion from these examples is that if you want a technology adopted quickly, you should avoid educating the consumers about this technology. It should operate like something they already know. Consumers will create the link in their minds between this technology and something they use often, and adoption will be quick.

While driving in a rental car in northern Italy in the summer of 2006, another thing hit me—you cannot assume that the consumers of a technology are all engineers. They are not like you. I was driving an Opel Vectra station wagon and noticed that the RPM gauge was showing the RPM number as 10, 20, 30, and beyond. Furthermore, it had "x100 min^{-1}" clearly printed on the dashboard. Was it clear? An engineer would immediately understand that the "x100 min^{-1}" means that the numbers (10, 20, 30...) needed to be multiplied by 100 and are given "per minute" (hence the min^{-1}, which indicates that the "min" is the *denominator*). Was the average driver supposed to decrypt this equation? Is the Opel Vectra fit only for engineers?

Always keep in mind—you are *not* the average consumer. You need to think about the *average* consumers and target your products and technology to make sense to them. I should have learned that *before* I developed the InterHome.

Signing up for service

The more disruptive a new product or service is, the harder it is to get consumers to buy it, use it, or sign up for it. When we formed the Mobile DTV Alliance, we were offering the vision of being able to watch high-quality TV on a cellular phone. The consumer response was, to say the least, interesting. When we took an average group of potential consumers and asked them if they were willing to sign up for service for a monthly fee of $19.95, the acceptance rate was close to 10%. This number significantly went up when we actually handed the target audience real phones with real service and live content. The probability of people who actually saw what the service looked like was significantly higher than 10%. This number was even higher after commercial trials. We gave people phones in a city that has service coverage and let them use the phones and experience the service for a month. After that month passed, we asked them if they were willing to pay $19.95 per month for the service.[100] The acceptance rate from these trials was at times above 60%.

Initially, those results were surprising. After all, our description of what the service would include, what channels would be available, and what the cost would be was very accurate. Why then did the numbers change? Before I answer this, I will give you an even more personal example.

Satellite radios had existed for quite a few years when I was about to buy a car in late 2004. I knew what satellite radio was, and I was aware of the offerings from Sirius and XM. I even considered buying a radio for $100, but always stopped when I thought of the $13 a month service fee. I was not ready to pay $13 a month just to listen to radio in my car. After all, isn't FM radio and a 6-CD changer enough for my thirty-minute commute to the office? Even when, in 2002-2003 I was driving to work for two hours each way, I was not ready to pay $13 a month to make that drive more interesting and enjoyable.

However, that car I bought in 2004 was already equipped with a satellite radio, which came with free service for a year. I am sure that the price of the radio and year of service were well hidden in the car's invoice price, but they were inseparable and I did not have a choice of lowering the car price to take out the radio and "free" one-year service. So I started using the radio. I found myself listening to CNBC on my way to work, getting a head start on the financial and stock markets, and listening to music from the '70s and the '80s on my way back home, totally unwound by the time I got home. After twelve months, I got a letter from the satellite radio service provider, who cordially asked me to renew the service agreement, but this time it was not free. I had to pay $13 a month. I did not even have to think twice—I immediately renewed the contract.

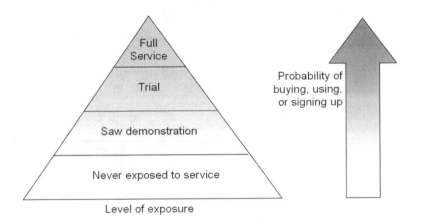

Figure 33—The link between exposure and probability of signup

What happened there? The answer goes back to that same problem we suffer from: limited imagination. Just as we cannot imagine what technology will look like only four years from today, we have trouble imagining an experience (a product or a service) to which we were never exposed, even if we have a detailed description.

It is not very complicated, actually. Initially, when we are *told* about new products or services, or when we *read* about them, we still don't really *get* them. We fail to imagine the *experience* we will have when using them. The second level of understanding occurs when we see a demonstration of what they feel like, or look like, and we get a better sense (although typically just a glimpse) of what the products or services will feel like. However, even then we don't really *get* them. We are still experiencing them differently from the way we will use them. Typically, during a demonstration we experience the products or services in a controlled environment, far from that in which we will use them in real life.[101]

The biggest incline in our understanding of the real experience comes with actually using them during the trial period in the real context of our lives. The fourth and last level of understanding comes with the use of the product or service for a long enough period of time (say a year), after which the initial usage habits give way to the long-lasting usage habits. At times, you may see a decline in the probability of usage during that last transition. The trial period is a time of excitement and experimentation, with users accepting some of the imperfections of the product or service. The probability of buying or signing up for service is the highest after the trial period. However, after the consumer has used the product or service for a longer period, some of those imperfections become annoying and the true value of the product is revealed. The most accurate "forecast" of acceptance rate comes only after a long usage period. Of course, it is no longer a forecast.

What can you learn from this? The more disruptive and unimaginable a product or service is, the harder it is to get an accurate early indication of the potential acceptance level. You can also learn that in order to get such a technology into the hands of mass consumers you sometimes must give it at no charge. At least until consumers understand the value of it and learn how to use it.

---

[95] A simple digitized (also called "Pulse Coded Modulation" or PCM) voice signal needs to be sampled 8,000 times a second with 8-bit resolution, totaling 64Kbps. With the top speed of dial-up modems being 56Kbps, transmitting PCM was not feasible. Therefore, voice compression techniques and standards were developed. Typically, the higher the compression ratio was, the lower the voice quality became. However, two compression techniques became pervasive for Internet telephony – G.723 (with a compression ratio of 10:1 resulting in a data rate of 6.4Kbps) and G.723.1 (a similar concept but with a compression ratio of 11:1, resulting in a data rate of 5.3Kbps), both capable of using standard dial-up modems without significant penalty to voice quality.

[96] "Classic" telephone is switch based. A series of "switches" (in the early days, those were really switches, manually operated by an operator) was required to create a link between the two phones communicating. This link existed as long as the conversation was ongoing. Today's telephony is transitioning into *packet-based*, which means digitizing the voice and breaking it into packets of data, transmitted from source to destination individually.

[97] Protected under US patent number 5,974,043.

[98] See chapters 1 through 5, which describe how to predict technology trends.

[99] Protocol overhead is the percentage of throughput lost due to protocol, handshaking, security and everything else that consumes throughput but doesn't qualify as "payload" – the data to be transferred.

[100] Some of the trials took place in Europe, where the monthly service fee proposed was twelve to fifteen Euros.

[101] In his book *Blink*, Malcolm Gladwell describes the New Coca-Cola taste focus groups. While the initial taste tests showed significant consumer acceptance, the product failed miserably and forced Coca-Cola to bring back "classic" Coke. Experiencing the product in the regular environment resulted in different perceptions than experiencing it in a demonstration environment.

Chapter 12
The Whole Product

Without iTunes, iPod would simply be a fancy, overpriced, cool-looking *external hard disk drive with a stereo headset*. But it's not. The iPod is, by far, the most successful portable music player on the market. Twice threatened by Microsoft,[102] iPod is still a mobile music player leader. We'll see if the Video iPod will be as successful with video content; there is no doubt about its success as a music player. To date, Apple has sold over 68 million iPods, generating about $14 billion in sales, representing nearly 40% of Apple's $19.3 billion in revenue in 2006.[103] That is success by any measure. Once you have used iPod with iTunes, you understand the importance of having both. iTunes allows you to download your favorite music using a comfortable and intuitive user interface, one that can be hosted only on a personal computer (PC or iMac®[104]). Connect the iPod to the computer with the cable provided, and the iPod will automatically synchronize with the computer. Not only will it get the new downloaded songs, you can also update it with your favorite playlists, and even your listening habits. This user interface and synchronization are simple to use, and target a very wide customer base. Apple guaranteed success by making it so easy to get music into the iPod. The relationship between the iPod and iTunes is similar to that between Tom Cruise and Renee Zellweger in *Jerry Maguire* when he told her, "You complete me."

The term *whole product* is more familiar to consumer product companies than it is to semiconductor companies. Semiconductor companies tend to focus on delivering integrated circuits. While considered the "brains" (and possibly the "heart") of electronic products, they are far from being the *whole* product. The whole product includes many elements we should not overlook. Those elements may include:

- Industrial design
- Software
- Infrastructure and back-end services
- Associated services
- User interface
- Media
- Distribution

Industrial Design

The industrial design of a product can add value in two dimensions: *aesthetics* and *functionality*. Apple Computers long ago earned a reputation for unique, aesthetic product design. Apple makes significant investments in industrial design that is appealing to consumers. The aesthetic design of laptop computers is critical to Apple's success, and so is the design of the cellular phone. Motorola's RAZR did not offer special functionality. It offered unique design. Launched in November of 2004 for a price of $800 ($500 with a service plan), by July 2006, less than two years later, Motorola had shipped fifty million RAZR phones. The phone's "must have" fashionable design accounted for the major success of this phone, which contributed significantly to Motorola's major "comeback" into the cell phone market.[105] Likewise, the iPod's sleek, plain industrial design strongly appealed to buyers. However, the iPod's industrial design also supported *functionality*. The special *scroll wheel* made the product easy to use, and added further to its sleek and fashionable appearance. Industrial design can add to the functionality of the product to the point that the product has less value with inappropriate industrial design. DLP® televisions must have special optical design associated with them to create a high-quality viewing experience. Cellular phones must have special audio design associated with them to allow high voice quality. Panasonic's Toughbook™, a rugged laptop computer, must have the right industrial design to protect it against drops and other accidents and help it live up to the differentiation offered through this feature.

Software

In today's electronic product market, almost every product has one or more *processors* embedded in them. Including a processor instead of fixed logic components allows for increased functionality, field programmability, and future revision updates. An average car has dozens (if not hundreds) of processors embedded in it. With a low-end microcontroller, capable of relatively simple functionality, for less than 50¢, they are a better alternative to the older hard-wired logic modules. However, this also means that a product manufacturer cannot sell a hardware product without software support. iPod will not have value without iTunes, running on a PC or iMac. We have established that. But the iPod also has an *internal* processor, responsible for the basic functionality of the product itself, regardless of the PC. If Apple had not developed the firmware, the iPod would not have been operational at all. When a company develops hardware that attaches to a PC, the company must also develop software drivers that will become part of Windows and allow applications to get access to that product.

Infrastructure and back-end services

Not all products require infrastructure. We can separate products by two types: those that require infrastructure, and those that do not. Most of the products that do *not* require infrastructure are those used for personal and local consumption and experience (media players, shavers, hair dryers, and on and on). Most of the products that require infrastructure are communication devices and real-time media devices (phones, radios, GPS receivers, and others). When the main functionality of a product depends on the existence of an infrastructure, there can be no significant market before that infrastructure is in place. Often it is not enough to have a *partial* or *local* deployment of the infrastructure. A full-scale, *national* or *global*, deployment is required to realize the potential value of the product. The telephone would not have realized its potential value without the telephone companies (telcos) building the telephone network. In the same way, cellular phones would not have realized their value without a cellular network deployed. RIM's BlackBerry would not have realized its value without the existence of the cellular network, and GPS receivers would not have even begun to realize any value whatsoever without at least twenty-four satellites in orbit. Some of those infrastructure deployments require investments of billions of dollars and are definitely beyond the capabilities of a single company, be it a Silicon Valley start-up, or a Fortune 100 company.

The best way to address the existence of an infrastructure is to use an existing one, even if built for another purpose, as long as it will still be suitable for the new use case. This was exactly the difference between the Ricochet failure and the BlackBerry success. While the Ricochet service required the deployment of a new infrastructure, one that was beyond the financial capabilities of Metricom, RIM utilized the existing cellular infrastructure for its highly successful BlackBerry service, although both products offered the same functionality.

In the early days of the Wi-Fi technology, a few companies wanted to offer Wi-Fi services in public locations, called "hot-spots." The first company, MobileStar, appeared to be very promising. Its planners realized that one of the best places to offer those services is in coffee shops, and started "wiring" the entire Starbucks chain. However, given the enormous investment required in the infrastructure, the company went bankrupt before finishing the deployment, and T-Mobile eventually bought the entire infrastructure.

When considering the use of existing infrastructure to offer new services, (1) the existing infrastructure should economically support the new service, and (2) the new service should not create an adverse impact on the current applications using this infrastructure (unless the new service is aimed at replacing the existing service using the same infrastructure). Several cellular phone operators decided to offer mobile TV using the cellular infrastructure. While intuitively this sounds like a good incremental use for an existing infrastructure, allowing the operators to generate more revenue from a new service without a significant incremental infrastructure investment, the current cellular infrastructure does *not* meet those two requirements. First, the economics of the cellular network will not support the broadcasting of high-quality, full-length TV shows. The cellular network *technically* can support it, but at a prohibitive cost to the operators or consumers, a cost that makes those services impractical. Second, since the network capacity required for a single TV stream to a single cellular phone is thirty to fifty times more than the capacity for a single phone call, it is clear that when mobile TV services become pervasive, it will adversely affect the voice services of a cellular network.

Sometimes the value of a product requires the availability of back-end services, rather than a full-scale infrastructure. Those are typically hardware and software components that reside somewhere while connected to the main communications network. A few examples are the BlackBerry server software, installed at the enterprise server to allow the synchronization of the BlackBerry and PC-based Outlook®; and directory services, connected to the Internet, allowing two users of Voice over IP (VoIP) to find each other over the network. Typically, the availability of such back-end services and components requires a significantly lower investment than the investment required for building infrastructure. Note that one advantage of back-end services is that they offer a continuous connection with all subscribers. This allows for advertisements, surveys, software upgrades, and other incremental revenue opportunities for the service provider.

Associated services

As you will notice throughout the discussion of *media, distribution,* and *infrastructure,* those components typically intertwine. In fact, it is hard to draw a line that will tell when *infrastructure* becomes *services,* or when *media* becomes *distribution.* However, it is not important. The important part is that you determine what constitutes the *whole* product. We can refer to the delivery mechanism of iTunes as *infrastructure* (or *back-end services* as described above), as it requires a server loaded with the content, and it requires all the right communication tools to allow an iPod to download the music. We can call it *media,* as the songs and videos stored at the iTunes server are the content for which the iPod exists. We can call it *distribution,* as it represents a path from the content owners to the final consumers, who create value. Finally, we can call it *service,* or *value-add service.* With iPod nano holding 8GB of storage (equivalent to 2,000 songs), costing $250, it is clear that the value created by downloading songs for $0.99 (almost $2,000 to fill an iPod nano 8GB with songs) is greater than the value created by selling the iPod itself.

It is important to identify where the infrastructure, distribution, or back-end services are an *enabler* of the product, and when the product is actually the enabler of the services. In fact, oddly enough, the *product* often enables the service rather than the other way around. This fact allows cellular phone manufacturers to give free phones: (taking the $100 phone cost "hit" for a two-year service contract valued at $1,200[106]), satellite radio providers such as XM and Sirius to offer free radios ($100 radio for a two-year, $300 contract), and satellite and cable television operators to offer set top boxes for free ($100 value, for a $720 contract).

User interface

You must pay special attention to having the right user interface. Too often technology companies rely on educating the consumers about using new products. The user interface tends to be highly technical and, while suitable for the engineers designing it, it will not be suitable for the consumers using it. Some companies differentiate their products or services through a unique user interface. None of those assures quick adoption of a new product, technology, or service. Whenever talking about the importance of user interface and the avoidance of educating the consumers, I use the same example of programming a station in a rental car radio. Consumers know how to use this ubiquitous user interface.

I used MP3 players for some time from many different manufacturers. They had different user interfaces, and it took me time to get used to each one. Finally, I caved in and bought my first iPod. I was surprised to see no user manual. How did Apple expect me to know how to use this device? The answer was—they just knew. It was amazing to discover how intuitive using iPod was. It is as if they knew exactly how I *expected* to use the device. I have to admit, this was the best user interface for a mobile device I had ever experienced—hands down!

Media

Products that store and play content require some kind of media. The tape recorder, camcorder, digital camera, DVD player, and many other products require magnetic cassette tapes, optical media (CD/DVD), hard disk drives, or flash-based media (SD Cards and others). Building the product itself is not enough, if consumers will not have access to the media required for its operation (with the exception of the HDD, which is an integral part of the product). There are two types of media—blank media, which the consumers will use to record and play their own content, and prerecorded media, that has content prepared for viewing or listening. There would not have been a successful DVD player market if there were no content available to view, including an entire distribution channel such as Blockbuster® or Netflix®. There would not have been a successful VHS VCR and tape-based camcorder market if blank cassettes were not available at retail stores.

Distribution

Whether it is the product itself, the media that the product needs, the content that the product needs, or the services associated with the product—there has to be a mechanism in place to get those into the hands of the consumers in as *friction-free* a manner as possible, and where they would naturally expect to find them. If the users are unaware of the existence of the products, services, media, or content, or if they find them hard to obtain, they will not use them. Advertisement is not enough to promote adoption. Creating easy access is. A company must create the appropriate distribution channels when developing a new product, technology, or service.

Make vs. buy and strategic partnerships

The most important lesson from this chapter is that in order for a product to become successful, you have to assure the product is *whole*. Forget something, and the product will not be a hit. Once understanding that, a company realizes two things. The first is that the scope of creating a *whole product*, along with all the different accessories, derivatives, options, and support, is a huge task that requires substantial investment, much higher than initially perceived. The second is that the company does not have the capabilities, skill set, or resources to perform some of the tasks required. Intel could not have caused the PC market to materialize by itself. It needed Microsoft, among other players, to complement its microprocessor offering with a compelling operating system. Apple is somewhat an unusual player, with multidisciplinary capabilities, ranging from product to software, but without semiconductor development capabilities, for example.

The decision to develop the *whole product* is not optional. If you do not develop the whole product, consumers will not buy it. However, the decision whether to design, develop, and build components of that whole product *internally* or use other companies to do it is one of choice. There are several factors affecting that decision, and several action paths a company can take to execute it. The factors affecting the decision of how to develop a component of the whole product are:

- *Central to the existence of the whole product.* Is the component in question critical to the main value the whole product adds? For example, how critical is iTunes to iPod? The answer is, if you didn't guess it already—very important. As I stated before, without iTunes, iPod would not have much value. It is the ability to get access to songs you do not own and download them to the device that makes the iPod stand out from previous mobile music players such as the Walkman. It is also worth noting that the more central a component is to the existence of the whole product, the higher part of the overall profitability of the whole product (or the value chain) it will attract. I will take the iPod example again. The iPod nano, with a capacity of 8GB, generates revenue of about $250. At the same time, with a capacity of 2,000 songs at a value of $0.99 each, iTunes will generate close to $2,000 from the same iPod.

- *Criticality to product performance.* In 2000, Texas Instruments acquired a company called Alantro. Later it became TI's wireless LAN business unit. However, Alantro brought only the digital components of the complete wireless LAN solution, and not the radio front end. There is little value in the digital components without the radio, as the radio will significantly affect the overall performance of the WLAN system. As this impact grows, the customers get more involved with the selection of this component of the overall solution, and a tighter relationship between the offerings of the two components is required. For TI, this initially led to a relationship with companies such as RF Micro Devices and Maxim, and then to a tighter partnership with the Silicon Valley-based Radio Communications, that eventually led to the acquisition of Radia.

- *Competency and bargaining power of a third party.* The existence of a third party competent enough to develop the required component is an important factor in determining the development alternative. If no company has ever developed the component, and no company has the required competency to develop it, there is no point in considering any of the third-party development paths, and the only two viable paths still left are to develop internally or outsource it to a company that has the right skill set for hire. Along with competency, the bargaining power of the third party has a similar impact on choosing development alternatives. Michael Porter thoroughly describes bargaining power.[107] Some of the sources of this power come from the existence of a single company with this product, or patents that the company might have on the specific technology. The more bargaining power a company has, the more reliance develops on that company.

- *Ability for independent development.* This is the dependency of the development of the two components evaluated. The clearer the boundaries between the different components, the easier it is to separate development teams and have the two components developed by different teams, or even different companies. Defining hardware interfaces, software interfaces (also called API[108]), and clear specifications will reduce the interdependency and allow true separation of the work.

- *Alignment with core competencies.* While the complementary component might not be one that is developed exactly in its desired form internally by the company, it might be somewhat similar to other components currently in development by the company. This similarity affects the ability of the company to transition existing resources to develop the new components, as skill set, processes, equipment, and other resources are already in existence and ready for transition. The transition from the development of FireWire components to the development of USB components was relatively easy for TI, and, therefore, the company could have developed USB components internally.

- *Confidentiality of the project.* Some projects are more confidential than others. The more disruptive the product is, the more secretive the company tends to be around its development. Having part of the whole product developed by an external entity can potentially leak some critical information to the world. Carefully partitioning the external work to maintain confidentiality around the nature of the whole product is critical to have any part of the product developed externally. Sometimes an acquisition can hint at a new direction the company is pursuing.

- *High number and diversity of complementors.* You need to consider the number and diversity of the components you need to complement your *core* component to create a *whole* product out of it. There might be a large number of complementors, and they might be highly diversified (i.e., fulfilling different tasks of the whole product). For example, if your disruption focuses on a new type of processor or DSP, you will need a wide variety of software applications to support it and make it compelling to customers. There will need to be many different types of software applications, most likely created by a wide variety of suppliers, each focusing on a specific area.

- *Customer interface and "ownership."* A part of the *whole product* will eventually be interfacing with the customer. That interface might take different forms. It varies from the user interface that software offers on a display, to the retailer who sells the product to the consumer, and the service provider who offers service associated with the product. If the product is sold from business to business (integrated circuits, for example, are sold to engineers in the product company rather than to consumers), the customer interface might be in the form of the offering of a reference design, an evaluation, and development board including the sold component, allowing the engineers at the product company to develop their product. Customer interface can be very important to a vendor, as it may offer a link to the customer and opportunities for future sales to the same customer, which is much cheaper that acquiring a new customer. Yahoo!, Google, and others create toolbars and other means of "customer ownership" to be able to directly approach consumers later.

- *Price sensitivity of overall solution.* Some of the development alternatives have an adverse impact on the price structure of the overall solution. IP licensing that has royalties associated with it is one example. Partnership and third-party referencing cause a potentially impossible three-way price negotiation, that benefits the buyer, but hurts the two suppliers, both forced to make price concessions.

There are several alternatives for developing, manufacturing, and selling the complementary parts to the main component of the *whole product.* Companies typically oversimplify those alternatives into the well-known term "make versus buy," as if there are only two such alternatives when, in reality, there are many more alternatives, as will be described here. While the terms *develop internally* (*"make"*) and *acquire* are interpreted quite consistently by all, the terms *partner, outsource,* and *contract* are interpreted differently by different people. Many times, when having a discussion involving one or more of those terms, I found myself having to "go back to basics" and agree on the definitions of those terms just so that the rest of the discussion would make sense to all participants. Even the word *partner* sometimes lends itself to different interpretations, although not as often as the other terms. To be clear, I am not claiming there is only one "correct" definition of those terms that happens to be mine. I will simply provide my definition for those terms so that the rest of my discussion in this chapter will make sense. The alternatives facing a company realizing it does not currently have the capabilities of developing a missing component required for the *whole product* to be attractive are these:[109]

- *Develop internally (*"make"*).* This could be a painful decision with long-lasting consequences. Developing a skill set internally where none exists requires time and significant investment, mostly when the skill set is far from other skill sets the company currently employs, and when it is far from the company's processes, culture, and value. Intel developed software after entering the microprocessor market, but only for a short time. Intel realized that software development was a significant deviation from the company's core competencies, processes, and culture that focused on advanced semiconductor technologies. A company might not have any advantage in developing capabilities otherwise already existing and mature with complementors. There are times, though, when a company must make that significant leap. There is no external communication required with this option.

- **Acquire.** One way to gain the skill set and capabilities, and other advantages such as a patent portfolio, is to acquire a company that already has those. Acquisitions vary in what they are aiming to achieve. When Intel acquired an Israeli company by the name of *Envara*, the company was developing a wireless LAN product and yet after the acquisition they began developing Intel's WiMAX components. The technologies used for the IEEE 802.11a products that *Envara* was developing were related enough to the WiMAX technology to be valuable for Intel. In other cases, companies acquire other companies and keep them working on the same products. When Texas Instruments acquired *Radia* in Sunnyvale, California, it was so that *Radia* would continue to develop exactly the same components it was developing before the acquisition. In rare cases, although it does happen, the acquisition occurs because of the skill sets of the employees, and they are deployed for products completely different from the products they were developing before the acquisition. Sometimes it is easier (and even cheaper) to acquire a company with sixty digital designers than to hire sixty such engineers individually. The fact that the group was working together before is the icing on the cake. The communication between the two companies in this case focuses on the financial transaction associated with the acquisition, after which all the communications between the entities become internal.

- **Partner.** *Partnering* means having a relatively tight and coordinated relationship with another company that will develop the complementary component by itself, but where both components must be sold *together* to constitute the whole product, typically due to a high dependency of the two components on each other. Each company maintains its independence and there are typically no financial or operational transactions between the companies. The partnership may include coordinated development and marketing of the respective products. There is a mutual dependency between the components and the companies, which will require an official relationship.[110] The communications between the two companies in this model will be in the form of a business relationship, including agreement on mutual specifications, bundle pricing, mutual promotions, and confidentiality.

- **Outsource** (*your* people, *my* way). I use the term *outsource* to describe a contractual relationship between *Company A* and *Company B* in which *Company A* needs additional resources (typically human resources) for a specific project, resources that *Company B* has and is willing to "rent." Those resources are required to have certain skill sets and discipline, but the work will be done according to *Company A*'s processes, procedures, and specifications. Those resources will become an extension of *Company A*'s resource pool, and will be managed just like employees. Outsourcing is typically more expensive than hiring the people as internal employees, but benefits a company occasionally as projects require and, therefore, more easily scaled up and down compared to using internal employees. Given the tight linkage between the outsourced resources of *Company B* and *Company A*, managing the project, it is typically important to have geographical closeness between the companies, although sometimes a company will outsource such resources in high-skilled, low-labor-cost countries such as India, China, and Russia. The communications between the two companies will focus on the number of resources that *Company A* will employ for the project, the terms of the transaction, the skill set involved, but no project-specific data will be communicated between the companies as the latter will be communicated once the "outsourced" resources are on board.

- **Contract** (*your* people, *your* way, *my* specifications). There is a relatively small difference between *outsourcing* and *contracting*. The nature of the contract between the companies will be different. When *outsourcing*, Company B will allocate a number of its employees "for hire" to Company A. Company A will retain the responsibility for the overall project deliverables. Company B will not have liability toward the deliverables, but only for the qualifications and performance of its employees. When *contracting*, on the other hand, Company A will transfer the responsibility for the project deliverables to Company B. *Contracting* will typically take place when the company can define part of the project (or component of the *whole product*) well enough to handle it as a stand-alone development effort. While the project will use Company B's *people*, it will also use Company B's *processes*, but according to Company A's *specifications*. When *outsourcing*, specifications do not change hands as the *outsourced* resources become, for the purpose of this project, part of Company A's workforce. When *contracting*, Company A might actually not care much for the number of resources used by Company B in this project, whereas when *outsourcing*, the number of resources is pretty much the only component agreed upon between the parties. At the same time, when *outsourcing*, Company B might not care for the specifications of the project. The communications between the two companies will include specifications of the project, a statement of work (SOW—a document that describes the responsibilities of each party and overall deliverables), a schedule, financial transaction (based on man-hours or a "flat fee"), and other terms and conditions associated with the transaction.

- *Intellectual Property (IP) licensing.* At times, the company will have the resources required to develop certain components, but lacks the man-years required to have the underlying technology, or the underlying technology is protected by patents owned by the company developing this technology first. Whether shortening the time to acquire the technology or to get access to a technology protected by patents, you will need to *license* it from the company that owns that technology. You will get information required to productize this technology, with certain restrictions (your ability to modify it or use it in multiple products, for example). In the late 1990s, the Silicon Valley saw the creation of many IP companies. Those companies developed focused technology, but with no intention of productizing it. They licensed it to other companies that productized it as part of a complete system. This business model was very hard to maintain, as the license fees and royalties had to be low for consideration by the prospective licensees of the technology and, therefore, only a few companies survived. ARM is the main licensor of embedded processor IP, and probably the last pure IP company remaining. Other IP companies focused on specific IP areas, either failed, or went on to complement other companies' IP portfolios through acquisition.

- *Third-party referencing.* In the *reference* model, the company developing the main product provides nothing more than a reference to other companies offering complementary components to the main product. Those components will typically not be critical to the main product. In some applications, though, the access to such components might be important and, therefore, the company might prefer to have those complementary offerings "certified" in some way. One example is Microsoft's WHQL (Windows Hardware Qualification Program). While Microsoft, for the most part, is not in the *hardware* business, they would like to assure that hardware offerings are compatible with the Windows Operating system and do not hurt its performance or stability. While Microsoft does not develop those hardware components by itself or even partner with companies to offer them, as they are not critical to the existence of Windows, Microsoft does *certify* those components and offers references to the different component providers. Texas Instruments, for example, has a third-party network called OTC (OMAP™[111] Technology Center), in which all developers who have components (hardware or software) associated with TI's OMAP family of application processors are referenced (and certified). Those companies offer solutions that can promote the sales of OMAP, but are not necessarily required for a generic application. The transactions between the companies are very loose in this model, and typically focus on communicating generic specifications information, mutual promotion efforts, certification (sometimes), and no financial transactions. This is the loosest type of such relationship.

There is no single factor of the above that will cause a clear selection of any one of the development alternatives offered here. However, there is a correlation between the different factors and those alternatives, and the decision should rest on the cumulative correlation between the specific situation, the factors, and the alternatives. Sometimes more than one alternative emerges for consideration. Figure 34 describes the correlation. That table defines either a positive correlation between the factor and every specific development alternative (marked as +), or as a negative correlation between the factor and every development alternative (market as -). A few, where there was little or no correlation, are marked as "0." For example, if the correlation between the *well-defined boundaries* factor and the *contract* development alternative is positive, then the better defined the project boundaries are, the more it will lead to a choice of *contracting* as a development option. At the same time, a negative correlation between the *confidentiality* factor and the *referencing* development alternative means that the more confidential the overall product development is (as must have been the case when Motorola developed the RAZR phone and when Apple developed the iPod and almost every new product it releases), the less favorable will be the *referencing* model.

		Development Alternatives					
		Develop internally	Acquire	Partner	Outsource	Contract	IP licensing	Reference (3rd party)
Factors affecting choice of alternatives	Central to existence of whole product	+	+	-	+	+	+	-
	Critical to product performance	+	+	-	+	+	+	-
	Competency and bargain power of 3rd party	-	+	+	-	+	+	+
	Ability for independent development	-	0	+	+	+	+	+
	Alignment with internal core competencies	+	-	-	+	-	-	
	High degree of project confidentiality	+	+	-	+	-	+	-
	Multiple different components required	-	-	0	-	-	0	+
	High customer interface and "ownership"	+	+	-	-	-	+	-
	Price sensitivity of overall solution	+	+	-	+	+	-	-

Figure 34—"Make vs. Buy" factors and alternatives

A few examples to show how to use this table follow. The first example was the development of the Apple iPod and its complementor, the iTunes software. The iPod could not exist without iTunes. iTunes had some impact on the performance of the iPod, mostly in the dimension of user experience and convenience. No third-party company offered similar software, and no such company held significant IP rights to such a component. So far, with those three factors alone, both *develop internally* and *outsource* seem to be the leading option, with a positive correlation between *central to existence* and *critical to product performance* and those development options, and a negative correlation between *competency and bargaining power of third party* and those alternatives. There is an ability to develop iTunes and iPod independently, but there is also a high degree of alignment between the requirements of developing iTunes and Apple's core competencies in software development and user interface. Finally, there is a high degree of project confidentiality embedded in Apple "genes" before introducing a new disruptive product, and iTunes does carry a high degree of *customer interface*, which is important for Apple to retain. The latter factors brought the selection between the two alternatives down to an *internal development*, the path that Apple eventually took.

I was more involved with the second example. Texas Instruments' wireless LAN business unit, created through the Alantro acquisition in 2000, had only two of the three main components of a wireless LAN solution: the media access controller (MAC) and the base band processor. It left a third, critical component out—the radio transceiver. The development of the transceiver requires a completely different skill set than the one owned by Alantro. One of my initial tasks when I joined TI in 2002 was to establish partnership relationships with companies that developed radio-integrated circuits usable with the Alantro solution. At the time, TI had a loose partnership with both RFMD and Maxim for that purpose. An analysis of the different factors that affect the development path shows the following: the radio component is critical to the existence of the overall solution, as well as critical to its performance (range, data rate, and power consumption, all used by buyers to compare and select solutions). However, as opposed to the iTunes case, there is significant core competency associated with the development of the radio component, and only a few companies have done it right. The fact that there were only a few companies offering the radio component gave those few a strong bargaining position. To top this off, there was significant price sensitivity to the overall solution, made of the TI components and the partner component. It put TI and its partners in an impossible three-way price negotiation situation, one that was detrimental to the profitability of both. It became obvious, once you consider all the factors mentioned and look at Figure 34, that the best alternative was to *acquire* a company. Sure enough, in September 2003 TI acquired Silicon Valley-based Radio Communications and completed its WLAN product offering.

The last example is the Texas Instruments' OMAP Technology Centers (OTC) program. TI has developed the world's leading mobile application processor, named OMAP. An application processor is a device aimed at running user application software (such as games, Internet connectivity, productivity suites and more). Unlike the PC processor market, the mobile (cell phone, PDA) market is fragmented and the processors offered by TI, Freescale and others are incompatible. The customers (the phone and PDA manufacturers) have to make a choice, knowing that the switching costs are going to be significant after selection. One of the factors when considering the application processor is the availability of software applications that are compatible with that processor. TI understood it had several alternatives in delivering those applications. The applications are not central to the existence of the OMAP product line, nor are they critical to its performance. There are quite a few companies developing such software applications, and while each one of them focuses on certain applications, none carries a significant bargaining power since those applications are not critical to the existence or performance of the OMAP. TI does not have the internal competencies to develop user application software, and there is a relatively low confidentiality level associated with the introduction of those applications. One of the most impactful factors in considering the development alternative is the fact that many such applications need development to offer the variety the customers would want to have. Considering the correlation of the different factors to the different development alternatives for such software applications, as shown in Figure 34, shows that the best approach is *third-party referencing.* TI in fact created the OMAP Technology Center (OTC), allowing referencing of different application software suppliers to customers. The customers work directly with those third-party software suppliers to get any application they choose, thus complementing the OMAP product line offering and creating a wide software base.

Figure 34 is not a scientific table. You will have to use your own judgment to make the final selection of a development path. At times, you may have to consider other factors, and possibly even other alternatives. Occasionally, the factors will change through the life cycle of the technology or product and will cause you to choose other alternatives over time. Some of the factors might be more impactful to the selection in certain scenarios and less impactful in others. You will have to be pragmatic in your use of this table. Its aim is to assist you in the process—not to replace your judgment.

How long will it take?

When considering how long the adoption of new technologies will take, you need to consider several factors:

- Is the adoption required in only one product, in one independent market?
- Is there infrastructure required?
- Is the new technology familiar to consumers?

One product, one market

A significant number of products are independent and represent one market. Any innovation in the digital camera or digital camcorder market (at least an innovation associated with the picture or video capture element of those products, which are the main functionality areas) can disrupt the market and create value by itself. You do not need to wait for something else to happen for this market to change its course. The only thing you need is consumer demand.

On the other hand, there are technologies that require adoption in two (or more) different products, and possibly in several different markets. Connectivity and communications technologies are one example. One specific example is the ultra-wideband technology. While writing these lines, the ultra-wideband (UWB) technology developed by the WiMedia Alliance (of which I am a board member), is being adopted by several markets. UWB is a technology that allows a very fast transfer of data, at rates of 480 Mbps and higher, at relatively short ranges of three meters. The pragmatic use cases of this technology (using the "80/20" or even the "95/5" rule) are:

- Upload of photos from a digital camera, a camera phone, or digital camcorder to a PC, TV or projector.
- Download of audio (music) and video content from a PC or another content-storage device (set-top-box, digital video recorder) to a mobile device such as a MP3 player or a portable media player.

The adoption must take place in more than one product and, therefore, in more than one market. This phenomenon is very typical to many connectivity technologies. Metcalfe's law[112] states, "The value of a telecommunications network is proportional to the square of the number of users of the system." What this means in our case is that there is almost no value in having UWB only in PC's, for example, if none of the other devices that need the UWB connection to transfer content to and from the PC have it. That makes the PC manufacturer wary of embedding UWB in platforms and, more important to the UWB semiconductor manufacturers, paying for it. The value of UWB depends on its adoption in several, independent markets in parallel. Those markets may have different requirements and will sometimes have different opinions in their approach to the adoption of the new technology. This fact slows adoption.

Texas Instruments is the leader in selling FireWire (also known as IEEE 1394, or iLink®[113]) integrated circuits. The IEEE 1394 standard emerged in 1995. Sony, seeing the value of the ability to edit video on the fly using a PC connected to a digital camcorder, included FireWire connectivity in all its digital camcorders, starting in 1995. However, the value of that connectivity did not materialize until 1997, when Microsoft included a native FireWire driver in its Windows 98 operating system.

There is another possibility, though. Adoption of technology can occur in a *primary* market and a *secondary* (or *ancillary*) market. The Bluetooth technology is a perfect example. There are many use cases for Bluetooth connectivity:

- Wireless headsets to cell phones
- Hands-free car operation
- Synchronizing cell phone or PDA data with a PC
- Using a cell phone as a wireless Internet access modem to a laptop

However, the key use case is the wireless headset one. Other than in cell phones (around 350 million in 2006 were Bluetooth enabled), the next market for Bluetooth components is the wireless headsets (close to 55 million in 2006). No other market for Bluetooth components comes even close to those sizes. However, is the Bluetooth wireless headset market a *stand-alone* market? There is a test to apply to answer this question. The first test is the test of the *main functionality* of the main products in this market. The main functionality of the Bluetooth headset is the Bluetooth connectivity. If the main functionality is a technology that depends on something that happens in another market (such as Bluetooth being deployed in the cell phone), then the market is not really an independent market, and the adoption of the technology is similar to the adoption cycle of a new technology in a *single* market. Simply put, the adoption of Bluetooth in headsets and the pervasiveness of the main use case (wireless headsets) did not have to *wait* until Bluetooth headsets adopted the technology. Bluetooth headsets were a creation of the Bluetooth technology. They did not exist by themselves and, therefore, it was the fact that the cell phones adopted Bluetooth technology that gave rise to the ancillary market— the market for Bluetooth headsets, and there was no delay in its creation (unlike the delay in the adoption of FireWire, and now UWB). In fact, with the Bluetooth technology standardized only in 1999, reaching close to a 40% adoption rate in cellular phones in 2006 represents very fast technology adoption.

Applying the same test to the UWB technology will show the *independence* of the target markets for this technology. This adoption of technology will target devices in the PC market, the cell phone market, the digital camera market, the MP3 player market and others. In none of those markets is the main functionality the UWB connectivity. That functionality, while adding value, is *secondary* at best to the main functionality of the products. The development of any of these markets is independent of anything happening in the other markets.

Why does that cause delays? First, the different markets might have slightly (or significantly) different ideas on how the technology should operate. The PC to cell phone market is one example where, for the PC market, the familiar USB is the preferred protocol to use UWB (as defined in the wireless USB specifications, created by the USB Implementers Forum), while for the cell phone market the preferred protocol is the ubiquitous (in this market) Bluetooth protocol. This misalignment causes delay in adoption. The second reason is simply the "chicken and egg" situation caused by Metcalfe's law, where each market waits for another market to adopt the technology first, waiting for the value of the technology to be created, before adopting it itself.

One additional example is Apple's decision to support the Intel-originated USB interface for its iPod and to offer a version of iTunes that runs on Microsoft Windows. Not including those two elements would have eliminated a huge customer base (PC users) for the iPod. It is hard to believe that consumers would have switched from Windows-based PCs to iMac just to enjoy the iPod. The market for iPod might have lost some 85% of its size without USB and Windows support. In fact, while the initial iPods shipped with both a USB and FireWire (Apple's preferred interface) cable, Apple soon realized that the FireWire cable was the one less used and, when it was time to improve profitability and lower cost, this was the first cable to go.

Infrastructure

The product you are about to introduce might require an infrastructure to make it work, or to create the majority of value it will deliver. A perfect example is the cell phone. You can build integrated circuits, write all the software that supports it, but at the end of the day (actually—before the dawn of the day), someone needs to build the infrastructure to support this functionality. Infrastructure, as a rule of thumb, requires significant investment. It is estimated that covering the forty-eight contiguous US states with cellular infrastructure requires 30,000 to 40,000 cell sites, each costing close to $50,000. That translates to costs of $1.5 to $2 billion. Without the infrastructure cost, the value of the cell phones is, well, zero.

An example of products that failed due to the lack of infrastructure is Metricom's Ricochet. Metricom launched the Ricochet service in the Silicon Valley in 1994. It offered the ability to send and receive text messages using a mobile, text-friendly device. However, the infrastructure required for the service needed deployment. Partial deployment meant partial coverage, which hurt the value of the service.

Metricom didn't sign up more than 50,000 subscribers at its peak, and in 2001 filed for bankruptcy. Why then was RIM such a success, offering the same functionality? The answer is simple—RIM used an *existing* infrastructure (the cellular network) for this new service. RIM launched the product with a completely deployed network in place. That made all the difference.

When Apple released the iPod, it had to establish relationships with the record labels to the point that almost every song you might wish to download would be available through iTunes. The value of the iPod/iTunes combination would have diminished if a significant percentage of desired songs had not been available for download. To date, I still can't find some early Led Zeppelin and Beatles songs, but I can find over 95% of the songs I look for. The entire song download infrastructure (including the billing and royalty mechanisms) had to be in place to enable this value chain.

The RFID (Radio Frequency Identification) technology is an example of a great technology that has not met market demand yet, many years after its inception. Initially targeting the replacement of bar codes, the RFID technology, even at a cost of only tens of cents per tracked product, was not economically viable for this application. However, it is finding a new life for contact-less payments. With the market saturation for credit cards, the credit card companies found that allowing such frictionless transactions (contact-less, secure, and requiring no user action) might drive people to use credit cards for small transactions, for which they never used a traditional credit card. However, we are facing deployment delay. There is the "chicken and egg" situation that we see often: what needs to happen first? Do all credit card companies issue RFID-enabled credit cards first, or should there be POS (point of sale) equipment (RFID card readers) deployed first? One cannot go without the other, and this the reason for the delay in the adoption of this technology.

Consumer familiarity

Simply said, the more consumers are familiar with the functionality of the new product, the faster adoption occurs. There is a contradiction here. After all, how can consumers be familiar with a disruptive product they never used before? You would be surprised. First of all, new products typically work like something else we used before. Maybe in a different form factor, but we did use it before. There is no doubt that iPod was disruptive. There was nothing like it before. Or was there? The iPod works like any other content playing device (a Walkman, a CD player, and even a DVD player). It has a "play" button, "forward" and "rewind" buttons, "skip" button, "pause" button, and many other functions that have the same "look and feel" of devices we used before, even though not for the exact same function. This lets consumers know how to operate it quickly, and promotes quick adoption.

Mobile TV (TV on cell phones) is something we never experienced before, but if TV-enabled phones have the standard TV buttons described before, it will be familiar to consumers, and adoption will be rapid. Any other "fancy" operation, while it might add some value to the experience, will delay the market, as consumers will not be familiar with this "new way" of operation.

---

[102] First with Microsoft's "PlayForSure" technology, which was an attempt to build an industry ecosystem around Microsoft's media player and content protection technologies, launched in 2003 and abandoned in 2005, and now (2006) with Zune®, Microsoft's own branded media player.

[103] "The Apple iPod Turns Five," Business Week Online, October 23, 2006.

[104] iMac is a registered trademark of Apple Inc.

[105] "Motorola Ships 50 Millionth MOTORAZR," Motorola Press Release, July 18, 2006.

[106] Assuming $50/month for 24 months.

[107] Michael Porter, "Competitive Strategy: Techniques for Analyzing Industries and Competitors," Free Press, 1980.

[108] Application Programmers' Interface.

[109] Note that the company might choose different relationships for different complementary components to complete the whole product. It doesn't have to choose the same model for all.

[110] When I joined Texas Instruments' wireless LAN group in 2002, I was responsible for the third-party relationship between that group and radio component companies. At the time, WLAN product manufacturers used to negotiate separately with TI and the radio supplier. Those negotiations often did not offer the customer the best price structure. I established a "win-win" agreement with those partner companies such that we eliminated the mistrust between the two companies and allowed them to offer the best-priced overall solution to the customers while assuring optimized profitability for both.

[111] OMAP is a trademark of Texas Instruments

[112] Named after Robert Metcalfe, the co-inventor of Ethernet and co-founder of 3Com.

[113] iLink is a registered trademark of Sony.

Chapter 13
Value-Add Differentiation

First to market

Until this point, this book helped you identify technology trends, and the disruptions they can cause in the disruption-prone electronic product market. At least that was my intention. If you identified a disruption opportunity and seized it, you will be first to go to market with it, by definition.

Why is being first to market so important? The answer should be obvious, but my position is that you need to be first to market simply to improve the return on your investments. There are two ways to look at improving ROI: the *venture* approach and the *market share* approach.[114]

The *venture* approach looks at the investment in a new technology much like venture capital firms view an investment in a new start-up company. There is no doubt that the higher the risk, the higher the potential reward. Investing in low-risk projects will yield low rewards, while investing in riskier projects may potentially yield breakthrough rewards. However, with the higher risk is a lower probability of success. For simplicity, assume that there are ten potential high-risk projects (or start-up companies) to choose from. The investment required for each of those projects will be $100 million. The potential return from a single successful project is $1 billion. The problem is that we do not know which one of those projects will succeed.

Assume the probability of success is 10%.[115] An investor unable to select the one project that will succeed will be investing in all ten projects for a total of $1 billion. The one successful project will yield a return of $1 billion while the other nine projects will fail and yield no return at all. The return on that investment (in all ten projects) is therefore zero.[116]

Now assume that the ability to predict the future will help that investor eliminate the five projects with lower probability of success out of the ten projects. The investment will therefore have to be only $500 million, and the yield of $1 billion from the one successful project will then represent an ROI of 100%. If that investor further improves its ability to predict, it will be able to pick eight projects doomed to fail out of the ten possible projects, and the ROI will skyrocket to 400%. Impressive by all standards.

The *market share* approach looks at market share as the key driver to improve return on investment. Established companies typically use this approach when deciding to address a market and to determine the timing of entering this market. Obviously, the earlier the company enters the market, the riskier it is, and the greater the potential for losing the investment. However, the following shows that the importance of *being first* is critical to achieving the largest market share, and such market share has significant revenue, profitability, and return on investment implications.

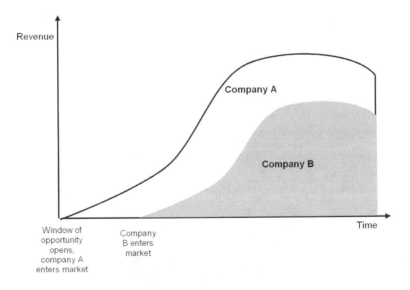

Figure 35—Revenue implications of being first to market

In the diagram above, two companies are entering the same market. Company A enters the market when the *window of opportunity* opens. For the purpose of this discussion, the *window of opportunity* is the time during which a company generates revenue from this market. As shown, the revenue grows initially at the *early adopter* rate, at a relatively moderate rate. After a while, when the new product or technology crosses from the early adoption phase to the mass market phase, the market grows much faster, when the technology is proven and the more conservative buyers/customers in the mainstream market are buying in mass.

For some time, Company A has had no competition and is winning the entire available market with 100% market share. Company B, for some reason, is late to enter the market. When it enters the market, it faces a market that already has a supplier with a competitive product, satisfying 100% of the available market. There must be a good reason for customers to buy from Company B.

At this time, several things might happen, creating an entry barrier to Company B in this market. One is simply the *switching costs* for customers already buying from Company A. For some products, there is a significant cost to switch buying products from Company A to Company B. The switching costs can be training,[117] new infrastructure, testing, redesigning the system in which the product is only one part, and others. Another element of the entry barrier might be interoperability. Company A has established the "industry standard" (or de facto standard) for how the product needs to work. Company B has to meet the same standard and performance that Company A has established in the market with its products. Therefore, Company B finds it is easier to sell products to customers who have not yet bought products from Company A, as they are not facing switching costs. However, Company A has proven itself in the market already, and buying Company B's first products might be a risky proposition.[118] Company B can still sell to customers who already bought the competitive product from Company A, but they would have to give those customers a very good reason to switch. Unless Company B differentiates its product from the product from Company A,[119] this will typically mean offering the product at a lower price, most likely with lower profitability for company B if there is no substantial cost structure advantage to Company B. Company A has established a leading market share position that Company B finds hard to achieve.

The area under the Company B revenue and profitability curve is significantly smaller than the area under Company A curve for several reasons:

- Company B simply misses market opportunity for a period of time after the market window opened and Company A started supplying product, in which there is demand for the product that Company A can fulfill and Company B cannot, as it hasn't launched its product yet;

- Company B faces entry barriers, most of which involves the cost of switching customers away from Company A's products and, therefore, it can address a smaller market share;

- Getting customers to switch to Company B's products has a significant cost, part of which is caused by lower prices leading to lower profitability;

- The market continues to mature, causing prices (for both products) to fall. When Company B reaches production volume, the prices (and, therefore, profitability) are significantly lower.

Do the two companies make different investments? I would expect the investments to be relatively similar as they result in relatively similar products. In fact, I would expect the investment made by Company B to be higher, as it needs to cope with switching costs and interoperability once the products from Company A are already in the market. The marketing investment is also greater. Davidow[120] estimates that the cost of entering a market with an incumbent supplier is 70% of the annual market leader revenue from this market. The main difference is not in the *size* of the investment, but rather in the *risk* that Company A took in order to be first to a market, a market that might not have otherwise evolved.

In summary, the time advantage that Company A has over Company B when introducing the new products into the market leads to a revenue advantage, lower costs, higher prices, and higher profitability. Company A faces a significantly higher return on investment (ROI), which might even make the difference between a profitable business and an unprofitable one.

Defensible competitive advantage

For the last four months before moving from Israel to the Silicon Valley in 1998, I helped a division in the Israeli Ministry of Industry and Trade as the head of high-tech entrepreneurship. The role in the organization was to help entrepreneurs in the earliest stages of their ideas. While we assisted every area of entrepreneurship, my role was to focus on high-tech entrepreneurs. Part of my job was to help find a defensible competitive advantage. Unfortunately, in many cases, the innovation was too obvious, and not defensible. There are three sources of defensible early-stage competitive advantage:

- Cutting-edge technology
- Man-year investment
- Patent protection

Cutting-edge technology is much more than a market disruption. It is not building a better mousetrap. A criterion for *cutting-edge technology* is that it involves the *bleeding edge of knowledge*. Only a handful of people in the world should have this knowledge, typically based on decades of research and experience. Deploying *cutting-edge technology* to create your market disruption is defensible. It is far from being obvious, and competitors will have a very hard time obtaining it. However, you need to be realistic when assuming that the information in your hands is so rare, unique, and essential for the creation of your competitive advantage. When Texas Instruments invented the Digital Light Processing (DLP®) technology, it involved rare knowledge in the ability to move little mirrors over a piece of silicon. Those innovations are rare and far apart. Protected by patents, this competitive advantage is not only defensible, it is highly sustainable, and it is highly unattainable. The advantage you get with cutting-edge technology can vary in length. In most cases, what is considered cutting edge at one time, might be common knowledge ten years (or even less) later. In other cases, if someone maintains the *secret* for a long period, it can give the desired protection for a much longer period than patents can (typically limited up to twenty years). In this case, the cutting-edge technology should be retained as a *trade secret* rather than patented. The Coca-Cola formula is an example of such a trade secret.

Man-year investment advantage is simple. It does not require "rocket science" like the *cutting-edge-technology* source of competitive advantage described above. Achieving the advantage comes through the amount of work already invested in the development of the new product. Assume you have had twenty developers working on the product for over three years so far. This would give you a sixty-man-year advantage over any other competitor starting now. If an established competitor wishes to catch up quickly, it has to apply sixty man-years to the development of a competitive project. If the work could be broken down to 120 pieces, each taking six months, independent of each other, which can be developed in parallel, then a committed competitor will apply 120 people and develop a competing product in six months, which will give you only a six-month advantage. The good news is that the development of a product that otherwise takes three years could not typically be broken down to independent tasks, and applying 120 developers to the competing project might not shorten the development time significantly. Therefore, the time advantage gained through man-year will be defensible. Quite often, this three-year advantage can be very significant to the prospects of a competitive position in a market. Unfortunately, while defensible initially, this type of competitive advantage is not sustainable for long. Once the competitor catches up with you, it may be quick to develop follow-on products. What makes this worse is the fact that your competitive advantage occurs when the market is small, during the early-adoption phase, when volume is small, and your competitor catches up just before the strong growth stage of the market, when revenue is more significant. So, while defensible during an early stage, the man-year advantage is not defensible when it really matters, unless it brings you a defensible first-mover advantage, as described above.

This leaves you with the third early-stage competitive advantage: **Patent Protection**. Patents are a way of assuring that the rights to an invention are yours and yours alone. In America, the US Patent and Trademark Office (USPTO)[121] grants patent rights on a geographical basis (US, Europe, other places) independently. However, with the US being the largest consumer market in the world, US patent protection is the most important one of all. The USPTO grants patent rights for a period of sixteen to twenty years, depending on location and timing. What do patent rights give you? Theoretically, for the protection period, no other company can implement the claims you made in the patent without violating your rights. Compensation, the remedy for violation, can take different shapes and forms:

- You can prevent the other company from manufacturing the infringing product;
- You can claim rights to their profits from selling the infringing product;
- You can charge them a license fee and per-unit royalties for the rights to use the technology protected by your patent;
- You can license your patent-protected technology to the competing company in return for getting a license to use the other company's patent-protected technology (called *cross-licensing*).

Patent rights have special status when associated with standard-based products. Assume you have a technology that you protected with patents, and implementation of a specific standard or industry specification will infringe on your rights (say Bluetooth). There are several answers and possibilities in this case:

- The patent might be *non-essential* to the implementation of the standard. With a non-essential patent, a company does *not* have to infringe on your patent rights in order to build a product that is fully compliant with *mandatory*[122] parts of the standard. Implementing the patented technology will simply add value and competitive advantage to the implementation (lower cost, better performance, lower power consumption, and so on), but a compliant product *can* be implemented otherwise. These are great patents to have, because the standard-developing organization (SDO) typically will *not* enforce licensing terms on its members for such patents, allowing them to differentiate competitively.

- If the patent is *essential* to the implementation of a standard-compliant product, then your membership in the standard-developing organization is key. If you *are* a member of the organization, you might be subject to its intellectual property rights (IPR) policy. Most SDOs today adopt RAND or FRAND (fair, reasonable and non-discriminatory) licensing terms, which means that you will have to license your technology to every other member (some organizations, such as TIA and ECMA will force you to license even to *non-members* and *implementers* of the standard) under reasonable and non-discriminatory terms (everyone gets the same). Note that while members do not consider 50% of the product's selling price reasonable, 0.5% is reasonable in most cases. It is hard to draw a line on what is reasonable, and that leaves some wiggle room. Note also that offering *non-discriminatory* terms does not mean offering the same royalty rate and license fee to everyone, but rather offering the same *under the same circumstances*. Different volume may justify different rates and, therefore, different licensees will pay different rates and still maintain non-discriminatory status. Some organizations are *royalty free* (e.g., RAND-Z, for RAND with *zero royalties*). The Bluetooth SIG is one example. When you are a member of a standard or trade organization with such a policy, you need to consider your patent licensing approach. If you would like to avoid compliance under the IPR policy, you should resign the organization, as otherwise this policy binds you through your membership agreement. You will be free to charge as much in royalties as you would like, but you would most likely force the organization to change the standard to avoid making your IP rights essential to the implementation of a standard-compliant product. This approach is suitable if you do not intend to develop products complying with this standard. However, if you do intend to benefit from the standardization of this product, the IPR policy will compromise your patent rights.

The process of issuing a patent starts with filing it (sometimes you can file a *provisional* patent up to one year ahead of the main filing to get enough time to complete the full patent filing). It then becomes *pending* until review by the patent office. The patent office checks each filing against *prior art* (information known to the public before the invention date), innovation, and other criteria. If approved, the patent rights will protect you for sixteen to twenty years typically from the filing date. If you suspect that someone is infringing on your patent rights, you will claim your rights and demand compensation. The other party (allegedly the *infringing* party) has several options: (1) to settle the dispute and license or cross-license the rights to the protected technology from you, (2) claim in defense that it does not infringe on your rights, or (3) claim that your patent is invalid. Remember that the patent office reviewers are humans and can make mistakes. The allegedly infringing company has the best incentive to show that your patents are invalid and that the USPTO should not have granted them.

The *patent pending* time is important. The patent is pending from the moment you file the patent until you receive approval (assuming you do). Earlier, you did not have access to the pending patent until it was approved, which meant that the patent text would have been a secret until approved and published. During this time, you can claim that you have a patent pending, and that others are infringing on your rights under this patent. Since the rights start at the filing date, the *patent pending* time is included. The allegedly infringing company cannot defend itself, as there is nothing to defend against until the USPTO officially grants and publishes approval. During this very interesting period, you can reach settlements with other companies, and grant rights to technologies that have not yet received formal patent protection. Today, there is greater visibility into the content of the pending, examined patents, allowing companies to evaluate the risks of not licensing this technology from you.

While the patent protection gives a relatively long protection time (sixteen to twenty years), it still is limited. As I write this book, patents issued in 1987 are expiring, and 1987 is not so long ago, even for technology. The cell phone appeared before 1987, as did the personal computer and the Internet. Patents associated with those technologies may have already expired. If the Coca-Cola Company, upon the invention of the popular soft drink in 1885, had patented it, it would have become public domain and unprotected in 1905. Instead, Coca-Cola decided to keep it a *trade secret* and maintained its competitive advantage for more than 120 years. You must be very careful in assessing whether your *secret* technology is one that you should patent or treat as a trade secret to maximize your competitive advantage.

Issuing patents too early, before there is a market for the protected technology, reduces the financial benefit of patent protection resulting from license fees and royalties. Filing for patents too late might mean that (1) a competitor filed a patent before you did, and now the roles (licensee, licensor) switch, or (2) there is enough prior art for your patent not to be granted due to lack of innovation and originality.

Once you are first—differentiate!

So you got to market first. Simply because you were first, you enjoy a period in which you can sustain an advantage over your competitors. As described above, you will get access to the first customers and first programs they launch. Hopefully, you will have created a significant enough entry barrier into this market that will prevent, or at least slow down, your competitors from entering. However, as the life cycle of the new product progresses, the gap will be closing and your competitors will start breathing down your neck. The product, once a major innovation warranting a nice premium, will become a commodity, commanding only the minimal profit margins, if any. Competitors that you perceived as lacking the capabilities of designing and producing such a product, now do. The value chain disintegrates and there are specialized suppliers for the different components of the product, allowing system integrators to build those products quickly and competitively, leveraging economies of scale for their suppliers.

Perhaps one of the best examples to describe the phenomena is the personal computer. Once created by IBM in 1981, attracting nice profit margins,[123] the PC quickly became a commodity. With an open and modular architecture, suppliers started specializing in the individual components. New suppliers emerged that could produce individual components better than anyone else at that time. System integrators could put together those components, lacking the ability (which was not required) to develop those components themselves. They did it for a lower price, without sacrificing performance, quality, or any other value. At some point, IBM retained only three value components that would differentiate its PCs from others: their brand name, the hard disk drives[124] they manufactured, and the new operating system, OS2, competing with Microsoft's Windows operating system. However, throughout the years IBM lost all those advantages. IBM sold its hard disk drives to competitors and did not use them exclusively in its own PCs. It also sold its OS2 to any other PC, and eventually lost the battle against the very focused upstart, Microsoft, whose only focus in life, at that time, was to create a better operating system. System integrator brand names such as Dell, Hewlett-Packard, Compaq, as well as Toshiba, Sony, and others replaced the IBM brand. IBM continued for some time selling laptop computers that users considered more robust and reliable, but finally exited this market after selling the laptop computer division to Lenovo of China in 2005.

Is it time to give up when the market matures? To answer that I would have to examine different markets and see if there are players who continue to mandate leading market shares and command higher-than-average profit margins. Surprisingly, there are companies that succeed in maintaining (and even growing) market shares in mature markets. A few examples are Apple with its iPod and iMac, Nokia and Motorola in cellular phones, Intel with microprocessors, and Texas Instruments with DSP.

In my professional career, I read many books about product strategy, written by authors ranging from Geoffrey Moore to Clayton Christensen, from Michael Porter to Michael McGrath, and many more. I give lectures on strategy at Texas Instruments and I have moderated and facilitated more strategy planning sessions than I can remember. Throughout all those, one message came out very clearly—in order to continue to succeed after the market is maturing, you must be doing something *different* from your competitors, and you must continuously and relentlessly use the same differentiator all the time.

I listened to Prof. Gary Hamel one morning, talking about Avis. Avis, being the second biggest car rental company, tries "harder." That's what they use in their advertisement. Hamel bluntly said, "Don't try *harder*, try *different!*" I will admit, I hate commodities. I don't hate *consuming* them; I hate *building* and *selling* them. Building a commodity is avoiding risk. You build something that everybody else builds, assuming that you will sell it just like everyone else. The only way you can outsell a competitor (assuming no switching costs are involved) is if you can sell it for a lower price. Price leadership is a viable strategy, but only as long as you have a *structural cost advantage*. You must have a cost advantage that your competitors cannot deploy, which will allow you to sell at a lower price and make a profit when your competitors can't.

I believe in taking risk. You have to do something *different*. Do it smart. Do it in a way that brings value. It might be valuable for only a segment of the market, but that segment of the market has to appreciate what you are doing differently. It should also be a big enough market segment to create a favorable return on your investment. This is why I preach that *differentiation* and *segmentation* go hand in hand. You differentiate according to preferences of a specific, sizeable market segment.

The best approach to differentiation I have seen (and followed) is the one offered by Michael McGrath in *Product Strategy for High-Tech Companies*. He offers the concept of *vectors of differentiation*. Simply put, you need to continuously pursue an angle (a *vector*) of differentiation. Whatever it is, I have four rules for successful differentiation:

- It must offer *real* value to the buyers of your product. The cynical example I give at lectures is, "We can be the only company that builds integrated circuits in purple packages, but will our customers care? Will it give us market share?"

- It must be *substantially different* from what your competitors are doing.

- You must *relentlessly* pursue this exact direction and not stray left or right. In other words, you must be committed to this direction. This is equivalent to running in a straight line compared to running in zigzag. Even if you are moving at a speed (innovation, product cycle time) similar to your competitor's, the fact that you are running in a straight line will get you closer to the finish line faster than your competitor, if your competitor is running in zigzag. On the other hand, if you decide to differentiate your product based on appearance and industrial design one year, and the following year with performance, you have not committed yourself to either one and, in fact, did not execute on any of those better than your competitor did, as you cannot achieve leading performance in one year. Running in a straight line, or differentiating along a single vector, will allow you to perfect your ability to differentiate along that vector.

- Your market *must not be disrupted* (other than by you, that is). The following (Other people's money) will discuss that risk in detail.

Other people's money

I should offer a word of caution. Continue to differentiate until substantial disruption occurs in the market for your products (or the markets for the products for which you are a supplier). At that point, the rules of the game change. I gained important insight from a movie titled *Other People's Money* (1991). Danny DeVito plays Lawrence Garfield, "Larry the Liquidator," who comes to a shareholder meeting of a company he is about to take over and most likely break into pieces and then sell. The company produces metallic wires and cables in a world shifting toward fiber-optic communications. As he goes upstage to address the shareholders, he is booed and insulted. Danny DeVito does not have the stage presence of Arnold Schwarzenegger, which is not very helpful in that scene. He swallows his pride and gives one of the top speeches that inspired me in my professional career. He says, "You know, at one time there must've been dozens of companies making buggy whips. And I'll bet the last company around was the one that made the best goddamn buggy whip you ever saw. Now how would you have liked to have been a stockholder in that company? You invested in a business and this business is dead. Let's have the intelligence, let's have the *decency* to sign the death certificate, collect the insurance, and invest in something with a future."

You get it? You do not want to be the last company that builds buggy whips. Your buggy whips will most likely be the best ever built, and will most likely command the highest market share and the best profit margins—but nobody will buy them in a world where people do not ride horses to work anymore.

As a responsible executive in your company, you have to recognize when factors disrupt your market. Andy Grove in *Only the Paranoid Survive* calls *disruption* the "sixth" competitive force, adding to Michael Porter's original five.[125] If your market is disrupted, you need to find a way out, and quickly.

I will use PCTEL as an example once again. Before I do that, let me ask you: do you know if your laptop (or even desktop) computer has a dial-up modem? I wouldn't be as cynical as to ask if you even remember what a dial-up modem is. If you have a dial-up modem, did you ever use it? Do you know if it's working? Do you have a dial-up Internet service provider (ISP) account? Would you know what number to dial if you needed to connect to the Internet using dial-up? I am sure there is a minority of readers who would be offended by those questions as they have, and possibly even recently, used the dial-up modem to connect to the Internet, but let me assure you—they are just that—a minority!

This was not the situation in the year 2000, though. Broadband Internet connection was not as ubiquitous as it is today. In 1995, when PCTEL emerged, less than 100% of computers featured installed dial-up modems because connecting to the Internet was not yet the main reason to own a PC. PCTEL developed a better buggy whip. Maybe even the best buggy whip. PCTEL grew to sales of almost $100 million in five years and commanded a market share of 25%. It did that selling buggy whips, but in a period of time when most people were riding horses. PC users connected to the Internet mostly via dial-up modems. The content in the Internet was such that it could be accessed using a modem with speeds of less than 56 Kbps, the upper limit[126] offered by the V.90 standard used by dial-up modems. When PCTEL initially considered entering the DSL market, it was nascent. Only a small fraction of US households had any kind of broadband Internet connection. PCTEL was certainly looking at the right market, but it was already too late, as PCTEL was entering the market with the *wrong* product. PCTEL did not exit the dial-up modem, then its "cash-cow," fast enough. The company dropped its revenue from almost $100 million in 2000 to just over $40 million in 2001 for three reasons: the transition from dial-up to broadband (maybe not as noticeable in 2001 as it is today), a desperate attempt to achieve market share in 2000 through reducing modem component prices, and the 2001 recession (accompanied by the "dot-com" bubble burst). It took a few years until the company repositioned itself in new markets. In 2003, PCTEL's chief executive sold the dial-up modem unit to Conexant, granting them the greatest market share in this buggy-whip market.

Broadband (cars) at rates measured in Mbps, hundreds of times faster than the dial-up services (horses) have disrupted the market.

After writing about it in this chapter, I just had to check. My laptop (2006) is still equipped with a dial-up modem, and it looks like it is manufactured by Conexant. I wonder if this is a PCTEL "original" modem. As you can probably imagine, I have never used this modem. Since the disruption of the dial-up modem market by the DSL market, a few more disruptions occurred. For frequent travelers like me, Internet connection on the road is very important. Hotels, previously offering only a telephone line to connect to the Internet, started offering the ubiquitous Ethernet connection. While comfortable in my hotel rooms and offices, those *wired* connections are not as comfortable in other public locations such as the hotel lobby, airports, coffee shops, and more. You can see where I am going with this. Another disruption came in the form of Wi-Fi® (based on the IEEE 802.11 family of standards), a local area wireless networking technology, allowing the connection of any portable computer, PDA, or even smart phone to the Internet without wires. While the technology appeared in 1999, it did not cause a major disruption until 2001, or even 2002. When you ordered a laptop computer back then, you had to make sure it had a Wi-Fi® card installed. In fact, my first laptop at Texas Instruments, which I received in May of 2002, did *not* have a Wi-Fi card installed, and I had to install one externally. Today, it is hard to find a laptop that does not have a Wi-Fi adaptor pre-installed as a default. When I bought my wife a laptop in 2006, I forgot to check this. I bought an entry-level laptop, for under $500. When I received it, naturally, it had a Wi-Fi adaptor preinstalled.

Interestingly enough, the Wi-Fi market did not disrupt the DSL market, but actually complemented it in a way that made it grow. Wi-Fi is a *local area networking* technology that builds on the fact that broadband connectivity exists within one hundred feet of where you wish to be connected. That is where to install an *access point* or a *gateway*.

But it does not end there. You should take Andy Grove's advice and always be paranoid. I expect something will disrupt the Wi-Fi market too. Possibly technology such as WiMAX, a *wireless metropolitan area network*, third-generation (3g) or even the fourth generation (also referred to as LTE, or *long-term evolution*) cellular networks, capable of delivering the high-throughput data (and multimedia) connectivity over long distances, without the need for a *wired* broadband connection (as Wi-Fi requires). WiMAX and those other technologies may disrupt not only the market for Wi-Fi products, but also the market for wired broadband connectivity (DSL, cable, and even optical networking).

---

[114] The reason to look at these two different approaches is the different factors that affect start-up companies and those that affect established Fortune 100 companies. Imagine that a $25 million investment is required to launch a technology, over four years, all the way to product release and the first year in which $250 million of revenue generates $50 million of net profit. Would you consider this a successful investment? While you may tend to say yes immediately, keep reading this footnote. If you were a venture capitalist investing those $25m for 50% equity in the start-up company, and assuming the market capitalization-to-sales ratio of the start-up would be 4 to 1 – your investment yielded a market capitalization of $1 billion, of which you own 50%. The same will apply to a price-to-earning ratio of 20 to 1, not unheard of in the technology sector. If you manage to execute an "exit" strategy with this start-up, you increased your invested dollars by a factor of 20. If, on the other hand, you are a Fortune 100 company with annual revenue of $12.5 billion, this increase in revenue represents a mere 2% of the market

capitalization of the company, and a change in the stock price that can be eliminated overnight through stock market trading. Now you have to consider not only the net profit, but you also have to calculate the net present value of that profit. With a cost-of-capital of 20%, the net present value of $50 million in four years is $24 million today. This does not even justify the $25 million investment!

[115] I am sure that many venture capital firms will like those odds any day of the week and twice on Tuesdays. The success rates of start-up companies are much lower than 10%.

[116] $1 billion invested to yield one billion dollars of return. In fact, considering that the alternative risk-free investment opportunity will yield more than 0% - the overall investment underperformed risk-free investment alternatives.

[117] In 1989, I worked for a company called Electronics Line as a designer of alarm systems. We developed a system that addressed the US market, where the incumbent competitors were NAPCO and the Canadian DSC. We developed a very competitive product, with expectations of selling some 10,000 units a month in the US within the first three months since introduction. We sold some 700 units and then the order stream dried up. As a young engineer, I couldn't accept this failure. Interviewing several customers, I realized that the reason for not continuing to buy the system had nothing to do with quality, performance, features, or pricing. The customers liked all those. The problem was that they had to train installers how to program yet another system, once they already knew how to program the NAPCO and DSC. This represented a significant *switching cost* they were not willing to invest.

[118] After all, "nobody ever gets fired for choosing IBM..." You cannot go wrong buying from the market leader, but you are taking a significant personal career risk buying from another supplier.

[119] I claim that if the product is different enough such that some customers will buy it only because it has features important to them – in fact, the products address two different market segments and are not necessarily competing in the same market.

[120] William Davidow, "Marketing High Technology: an insider's view," Free Press, 1986.

[121] www.uspto.gov.

[122] There can be an argument that even if implementing the patented technology to comply with optional components of a standard will make the patented technology essential. Typically, this is not the case.

[123] Initially, there was a significant premium to buy an "original" IBM PC, compared to buying a "clone."

[124] IBM was one of the most innovative hard disk drive manufacturers. Ed Grochowski, whom I interviewed for Chapter 2 of this book, spent a

significant part of his professional career at the IBM Almaden research center in Silicon Valley, California.

[125] Entry barriers, suppliers' bargaining power, buyer bargaining power, substitute products, and intensity of rivalry.

[126] Which typically could not be achieved due to imperfections of telephone lines.

Part 3
Influencing The Future

Chapter 14
Understanding The Ecosystem

The technology ecosystem

The word *ecosystem* is probably one of the most abused words in technology marketing. I have to admit that I abused this word on more than one occasion. However, this word is important in the context of this chapter, so I thought it would be worthwhile to explain it. British ecologist Sir Arthur George Tansley coined the term *ecosystem* in 1935 to describe natural systems in "constant interchange" among their living and nonliving parts.[127] Never officially defined in the technology or business context, the word perfectly describes the *environment* in which people introduce technologies and where products succeed or fail. The equivalent of the *feeding order*, in which organisms feed on each other in a predetermined order, is the *value chain*, in which components integrate into subsystems, which then integrate into complete systems that consumers buy and use. The last link in the *value chain is the consumer*. Sometimes, however, the value chain continues beyond the final consumer. This is true especially where there is a *secondhand* market for the product. Automobiles and homes are perfect examples of an established secondhand market. The product had value when the first consumer bought it, and still had value when the next consumer bought it. However, in this chapter, for simplicity, I will consider only firsthand acquisitions by consumers as the final step in the value chain.

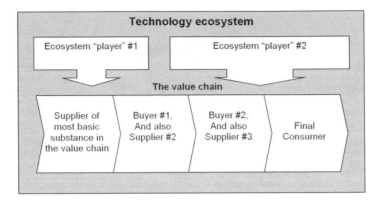

Figure 36—The technology value chain and ecosystem

Figure 36 describes the general technology ecosystem. The value chain is a chain of suppliers and buyers that represents the entire path in which a technology moves from the most basic substance to consumption by the final consumer. The technology, products, and all companies are located somewhere along the value chain. It is important to understand that the players along the value chain are not the only players who have impact on the flow of products and technologies through the value chain. The other, non-value-chain ecosystem players are entities that, while not supplying or consuming along the value chain, have an impact on the value chain, varying from marginal impact to dramatic impact. An ecosystem player has dramatic impact on the value chain if, when removed from the ecosystem, that player might cause the value chain to cease to exist.

One example of an ecosystem is DVD players. The primary suppliers are the suppliers of plastics, metal, and other very basic materials used to build a DVD player. Additional suppliers in the value chain are the semiconductor companies (such as Texas Instruments, Analog Devices, Zoran, and so on) who build the integrated circuits required for the functionality of the DVD player. Following them are the subsystem manufacturers, who build subsystems used in the DVD player (such as the disk loading/unloading mechanism). In some cases, the next step in the value chain is the original design manufacturer (ODM). Those companies are typically designing and manufacturing products as subcontractors for the original equipment manufacturers (OEM), who typically have the brand names. For example, Dell Computers (a very well known and established brand name) is an OEM, while Compal (not as well known as Dell) is the company (in Taiwan) that actually designs and builds the laptops, later sold under the Dell brand name.

At the end of the value chain is the consumer who buys the product from the OEM, possibly through another link in the value chain—the retailer (Best Buy, Circuit City, CompUSA, and others). Can this value chain exist on its own and constitute a complete ecosystem? Although the DVD disks themselves are not part of the DVD player value chain, they are still critical participants in the ecosystem. Is there a purpose in building and selling DVD players if there are no DVDs? Another significant player in this ecosystem is the content owner who produces the movie. Once again, the owner is completely not involved in the value-chain required to deliver a DVD player, but has a dramatic impact on the DVD player value chain. What value will a DVD player have for the consumer if there are no movies to view with it?

Why is it so important to understand the ecosystem? When you introduce a new technology, you focus your attention only on the creation of the value chain. You identify the companies along that value chain that add value all the way to the consumer. You make sure there is a buyer and a supplier in each step of the chain, and that the consumer gets a *whole* product. What you need to assure is that there is an interest from the ecosystem players to support the existence of the value chain. After all, for the DVD player value chain to offer to end consumers there must be incentives for these parts:

- DVD companies to create blank DVDs
- Production DVD burners to build devices that allow burning content on DVDs
- Motion picture companies to create movies and offer them in DVD format
- Distribution companies (such as BlockBuster) to offer them to the same consumers who buy DVD players.

The above description is a simplistic one used for illustration purposes only, whereas the real ecosystems are typically a lot more complex. Sometimes several multiple and different value chains exist in the same ecosystem in parallel. Ecosystems are different geographically, too, and you must consider the changes to the ecosystem and value chain with time.

The cellular phone ecosystem

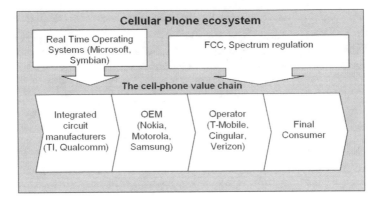

Figure 37—The cellular phone ecosystem

Figure 37 describes the cellular phone ecosystem. Once again, this is a relatively simplistic view of the ecosystem. If a company intends to deliver new products, services, and technologies into the cellular phone ecosystem, a further and much more detailed investigation of the ecosystem is required rather than relying on the brief description provided here. The cellular phone value chain starts with the silicon manufacturers. The leading semiconductor manufacturers in this market in 2006 were Texas Instruments, Qualcomm, and Freescale. The semiconductor manufacturers are selling their components to the ODMs who design the phones as subcontractors to the OEMs, who sell those phones to the service providers. It is important to note that not all OEMs use ODMs as contractors, and that some of them have their own manufacturing facilities, enabling them to design the phones and build them themselves. In some cases the OEMs will design and build some product lines themselves (typically the higher-end, higher-functionality smart phones) while outsourcing other phones (typically the lower-cost, low-end phones with less functionality and complexity) to the ODMs.

There is tension along this value chain. Much like other value chains, different players wish to dominate the chain. By dominating the chain, a company assures its position in that value chain, marginalizes other players in the value-chain, and thus attracts the highest profit margins to itself. Not surprisingly, other players along the value chain wish to do the same. The cellular service providers (Cingular, T-Mobile, Vodafone, Orange, DoCoMo, and others) wish to commoditize the telephones. They do that through several actions:

- In the US, the operators "lock" the telephones to their service. A subscriber cannot buy a telephone that is not associated with that service. Buying a telephone from one service provider and then attempting to use it with service from another service provider will not work. Even with GSM phones, in which the "identity" of the user is stored on a SIM card, transferable from phone to phone, the subscriber cannot transfer the SIM card to a phone purchased from another service provider and expect it to work. It has to be with a phone purchased from the same service provider.

- Some service providers go directly to the ODMs and buy telephones branded with the operator brand. Those typically occur with the lower-end phones, where the operators wish to bypass the profit margins made by the cellular phone OEMs in order to reduce the price and eliminate the dependency on the OEMs.

- Sometimes, operators go to the extreme of getting deeply involved with technological decisions made in the design of the phones, forcing the OEMs to use specific chipsets rather than others. Those operators, taking charge of the performance of the phones they offer their subscribers, further marginalize the OEMs, turning them more into subcontractors.

At the same time, the OEMs are trying to commoditize the ODMs by making semiconductor content decisions themselves. The semiconductor manufacturers are attempting to commoditize the ODMs and OEMs by "selling" the value proposition of their semiconductor content to the operators, trying to influence the operators to make technology decisions, and force them on the OEMs and ODMs. As described above, some of those operators *will* make those decisions.

Never forget there are other players in the ecosystem, players who do not participate directly in the value chain. One example is the real-time operating system manufacturers. The phones today are more programmable and flexible. They have microprocessors and digital signal processors. With increased functionality of the phone and more applications (navigation, games, Internet browsing, SMS, digital camera, mobile TV, and more), those phones need real time operating systems. There are several suppliers of such operating systems. Microsoft offers a "light" version of its Windows operating system, aimed at the cellular phone form-factor and available memory footprint. Symbian offers its own version of the operating system. How can players like this affect the value chain? It is certain that without an operating system the telephone will not work. An operating system needs to be compatible with the instruction set of the processor in the target phone. Those processors, manufactured by different semiconductor suppliers, are not compatible with one another. Texas Instruments OMAP processor is not compatible with Intel s XScale®[128] processor, or with processors from other semiconductor manufacturers. What would happen if Microsoft decides not to have its mobile Windows support the OMAP processor? This will eliminate the value of the OMAP processor in the cellular phone value chain as no OEM or ODM will build a phone based on a processor that cannot run the operating system. This is an example of how a non-value-chain, ecosystem player can affect the value chain without directly being part of it.

The personal computer ecosystem

With more than 200 million personal computers (desktop and laptop) sold in 2006, this is one of the most appealing ecosystems in existence. It is not a very complicated ecosystem either.

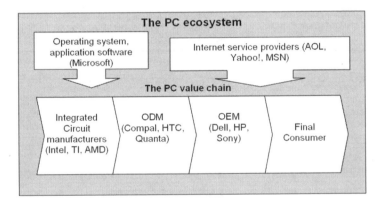

Figure 38—The personal computer ecosystem

The main value chain in the PC ecosystem consists of the semiconductor manufacturers, the original design manufacturers (ODMs), the brand name original equipment manufacturers (OEMs), and the final consumers. There are typically no service providers associated with the PC value chain, as they are not required to utilize a PC. Internet service providers (ISP) used to have a position in the ecosystem, but that was not a position of power similar to that of the operators in the cell phone ecosystem. Why has this value chain developed differently from the cellular phone ecosystem (see following) where the service provider plays a very important role in the value chain? Until the year 2000, the Internet was only a secondary application used with PCs. Around the turn of the century, the Internet took a "front and center" position and became the most important application for the PC. So why are the Internet service providers not significant players in the value chain? To me, there are two main reasons:

- When the personal computer appeared during the late 1970s, the Internet was not publicly available yet. Service was not part of the uses of the PC. The PC value chain developed without service providers. By the time the Internet came along, the PC industry was already a strong one, and adding a player to the value chain was not an option.

- The PC is a highly customized product. Within the first twenty-four hours after receiving a newly purchased PC, the consumer will load it with programs, customized to his own uses, and for the rest of the life of that PC, he will continue to customize that PC for his unique purposes, preferences, interests, and habits. The loyalty to the service provider is limited. A user cannot allow the service provider to have the same control over the PC as the cellular operator has over the cellular phone. The user cannot allow a decision to switch from one service provider to another to mean changing a PC. Replacing a PC is a painful "recovery" act, and requires absolute justification. If you replaced a PC in the past year, you know what I am talking about.

In 2003, I conducted research in cooperation with strategic marketing managers at Dell to address integrating cellular service in mobile computers. With Wi-Fi for local connectivity and "hot-spot" connectivity available in almost every portable computer, cellular data connectivity (GPRS, EDGE, UMTS, or CDMA) would complement that connectivity, and with ubiquitous, "anywhere, anytime" service, the laptop PC will stay connected forever. This never took off in a commercial way. The biggest hurdle was simply the fact that the cellular service providers, those responsible for providing the data connectivity, would not allow the subscribers to switch service providers at will, much like they do with dial-up, DSL, and cable service providers. The cellular operators demanded that the computers be "locked" to a single service. A PC user cannot allow her highly customized machine to be associated with only one service provider, compelling her to replace the PC if she wishes to switch to a different service provider. So is cellular data connectivity not available for laptop PCs? In fact, it is available, but only as an add-on card that one buys from a service provider. If the user then wishes to switch to a different service provider, she must replace that externally plugged card with another one provided by the new service provider. At the same time, Wi-Fi connectivity, Ethernet, USB, Bluetooth, and other types of connectivity are embedded in the laptop PC and ready for use with any available service.

The consumer electronics ecosystem

As you have noticed, the PC and the cellular phone ecosystems are not very different from one another, and neither is the consumer electronic product ecosystem. Perhaps the most consistent ecosystem is the one for the cellular phone. There is a set number of operators, regardless of the type of phone (smart phone, multimedia phone, low-end phone, and so on). There is a set number of manufacturers, and the products look the same in general. The PC ecosystem is relatively similar, in that it can be segmented (desktop vs. laptop, low-end vs. enterprise vs. high-end gaming), but the value chain overall is similar, made by the same players.

The CE market is highly diversified, though. It is hard to define just one ecosystem structure for it.

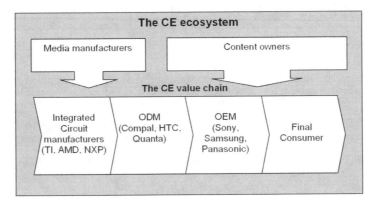

Figure 39—The Consumer electronics ecosystem

There are many different types of consumer electronics products, varying from digital cameras, digital camcorders, DVD players, digital video recorders, set top boxes, television sets, portable music players, automotive entertainment systems and many more. The specialization in each one of those segments does not translate into other segments, and is not a competitive advantage. Specializing in the optical performance of a digital camera might translate into advantage in the digital camcorder segment, but not into the DVD player segment or the television segment. This is true across the value chain, from semiconductor/IC manufacturers to the OEMs. The only common value-chain element throughout the entire CE market is the consumer.

This fact, which I learned firsthand when I was leading the CE connectivity business unit in TI, means that you need to focus on each segment independently. In fact, even the CE companies themselves have different divisions designing and manufacturing different products, completely independent of one another. As a supplier along the value-chain, just because you win business with one CE business unit with Sony does not mean you win business with any other business unit at Sony. Each segment of the CE market deserves a definition of the value-chain and the ecosystem of its own. In general, though, the components are the same (although the players might be different). The value chain is made of a similar set of players like the PC ecosystem, starting with the semiconductor manufacturers, through the ODMs, the OEMs, to the final consumer. In the CE market, the OEMs hold most of the bargaining power, because their brand names are what consumers seek out in retail stores. You will hardly ever see a semiconductor manufacturer that has significant bargaining power in the CE value-chain. Other components of the value chain (changing with different segments) are media manufacturers (cassettes, blank DVDs, and so on) and content owners (movie studios). Some of the market segments have service providers as part of the value chain. For example, in the cable TV, satellite TV, and IPTV (also known as Telco TV), value chains as such, the set top box and digital video recorders are supplied by the service provider, and subsidized by them, rather than users buying them retail. Those ecosystems are the only ones where a service provider actually becomes part of the value chain, rather than being an ecosystem player. The ecosystem players (such as media manufacturers and content creators) have significant impact on the value chain, even when not directly involved. When I try to predict which one of the two high-definition DVD technologies/standards will win (HD-DVD or Blu-ray), the first thing I look for is which major movie studio supports which standard. Once you see that major studios support only one of the two standards, you will know who the winner will be.

PCTEL's Lightspeed DSL modem

It is critical to understand all the participants in the ecosystem and the interests that drive them to participate in that ecosystem. They participate for a reason. Take away the reason for them to participate, and you remove them from the ecosystem. Removing one of them from the ecosystem will remove the value of the value chain and eliminate the need for the product. A perfect example is PCTEL's participation in the DSL market.

In 2000, four months after selling Voyager Technologies to PCTEL, Mark Wilson (my new boss then and the vice president of marketing at PCTEL) asked me to lead the DSL product line. I did not want that position, as I was perfectly happy with the position I held right after the acquisition—director of product marketing for *all* of PCTEL's product lines. For one thing, I didn't know what DSL[129] was. Mark, who is now a close friend of mine, insisted back then that I take the assignment and start digging into the DSL product line. A bit of background on PCTEL is in order. Three partners—Peter Chen, William Hsu, and Han Yeh—founded PCTEL in 1995. The leading PC processor then was the Intel 486, running at 66MHz or 100MHz. The Intel Pentium processor had just emerged, running at 60MHz initially. People bought PCs at that time mainly for off-line applications (such as word processing, finance, presentations, and so on), but the use of the Internet was growing. In 2000, during a meeting with Dan Driscoll, a senior director at Compaq, we realized that the main use of a PC was now becoming Internet connectivity. Back in 1995, most users relied on dial-up modems for Internet connectivity.[130] The dial-up modems' two components were the analog front end (AFE) and the digital signal processor (DSP). The AFE was responsible for a direct connection to the telephone line, converting the analog signals from the telephone lines to digital samples[131] and in the other direction, converting the digital signals from the DSP into analog signals sent to the telephone line.[132] The DSP analyzes the samples received by the AFE and converts them into data. The DSP also converts data sent by the processor into digital signals, which the AFE then converts into analog signals. In the 1980s and 1990s, the most expensive component in the MODEM was the DSP, a very high-performance mathematical processor that only a few companies (Texas Instruments, Rockwell, and a few others) could build.

The three founders of PCTEL had an idea. In fact, it was a *disruptive* idea. They believed that Moore's law would continue its effect on the processing power of PC processors, allowing the main PC processor rather than a DSP to perform the digital processing. This eliminated the need for the expensive DSP, reducing the cost of the MODEM dramatically. Back in 1995, the first Pentium processors struggled with the real-time processing requirements of what PCTEL called a "soft modem" But Chen, Hsu and Yeh didn't give up. They believed in the technology they called host signal processing (HSP[133]) and continued to improve the product for market introduction. They were right—Moore's law kept going, and the Pentium processor (running at 200MHz, 500MHz and beyond) found it a relatively easy task to support the modem signal processing on top of other data processing, performed in parallel, without any noticed performance degradation. In 2000, PCTEL was recognized as the second-fastest-growing company in the Silicon Valley (following Yahoo!), and the seventh-fastest-growing company in North America.[134] PCTEL reported 2000 revenue of $97.2m, only five years after its founding as a start-up. In 2000, "soft modems" constituted 25% of the overall modem market. No doubt, the PCTEL founders understood the behavior of the dial-up modem value chain and ecosystem, and more important, the processing power performance trends.

Then, PCTEL decided to embark on the DSL product line. The premise was "we did it with dial-up modems; we will do it again with DSL." PCTEL started developing a *soft* DSL modem that would be *internal* to PCs. The year 2000 marked the launch of the DSL market. US companies were very excited about the possibility of delivering broadband connectivity at speeds 25 times faster than dial-up to US consumers. There was no doubt that Internet connectivity became a very important function for personal computers. While the telephone companies (*telcos*) moved slowly in building a DSL infrastructure, there was a new breed of telephone companies, moving much faster than the telcos. These were the Competitive Local Exchange Carriers (CLEC). The Telecommunications Act of 1996 made possible the existence of the CLECs by forcing the telcos,[135] who owned the wires going into homes and businesses, to share those lines and lease them to that new breed of telephone companies, thus allowing the CLECs to compete with the telcos. The newly created CLECs were Northpoint, COVAD, and Rythms. Those companies went public at that time, raising billions of dollars in public offerings. Since then, those companies have filed for bankruptcy, with COVAD being the only one of them to go out of bankruptcy and back into business. Another notable DSL company (also bankrupt) was Flashcom, a specialized DSL service provider.

PCTEL's DSL program included a product called "Lightspeed," a PC-internal, soft (host-based) G.Lite[136] DSL modem. In fact, PCTEL made three fatal errors in defining the product: first, by defining an *internal* DSL modem; second, by defining a *G.Lite* modem instead of a *G.DMT* modem; and third, by defining a *soft* modem instead of a DSP-based modem. In the following, I will analyze those three mistakes. The analysis will help understand the value chain and ecosystem.

The first mistake was to build an *internal* DSL modem as opposed to an external one. Dial-up modems started out as *external* modems. They had a serial connection into a PC[137] and used a cable to connect to a PC. The first PCs didn't have internal dial-up modems. First, there was no reason to have a dial-up modem. Second, they were expensive. In fact, in 1995, more than ten years after the introduction of the personal computer, the majority of dial-up modems were still external and most PCs didn't have internal dial-up modems. However, as the Internet became an important use of the personal computers (for both browsing the World Wide Web and for electronic mail), more and more PCs were shipped with already-installed dial-up modems which, in turn, caused most dial-up modems to be internal. The trend was clear, and PCTEL thought the same would happen with the DSL modem. However, interestingly enough, even today broadband modems (DSL and cable) are still external. Why was this different from dial-up modems? There are several reasons for that. One is that more and more households have more than one PC. With PC prices falling[138] and with newer-model PCs operating while the older ones are still in use, the percentage of households having more than one operational PC was growing. With the Internet becoming the main usage of a PC, they all had to be connected. How can you connect several computers to the Internet at the same time? You cannot connect computers in parallel to the telephone line for DSL connectivity (or even for dial-up connectivity). With DSL connectivity costing some $40 a month, consumers want to connect several computers in parallel. Another thing to remember is that DSL is an "always on" connectivity. The DSL-connected computer is connected twenty-four hours a day and not "at will" as with a dial-up connection. How can you connect several computers in parallel to the single DSL connection? Through a *router* or a *switch*. An *external* DSL (or cable) modem has a *router* bundled with it in the same case. The router allows routing the DSL connection to and from several computers. The most common DSL modems have four ports, thus allowing users to connect four computers in parallel.[139] Having an *internal* DSL modem in one PC does not allow the user to share the DSL connection with other computers.

Another reason why the DSL modem could not have been an internal modem had to do with the *point of demarcation*. That is the point of transferring liability for the DSL service from the service provider (the telephone company, the CLEC, or the DSL service provider) to the PC manufacturer. It was close to impossible for the DSL service providers to maintain profitability as is. With $40 a month (of which the CLEC had to pay $20 to the ILEC for leasing the lines owned by the ILEC) and an installation cost of $800 per subscriber,[140] the breakeven point would occur only after forty months (more than three years!). Add to that support calls to resolve service disruptions, and they could never become profitable.[141] Supporting an external modem was relatively simple. If the green light on the modem was blinking, there was no service interruption, and if you still couldn't get an Internet connection, you must have a problem with your computer, which would not be handled by the service provider. However, if the modem was internal to the PC, there could be many reasons why service interruptions would occur, and finding the source of the problem would require a highly skilled technician, at a cost that the DSL service providers could not afford.

This leads to the third reason why *internal* DSL modems were not acceptable. If you subscribed to a DSL service, you knew that you were asked for your telephone number to verify that you qualified for service. The telephone companies hold a data base that includes information about the copper wires used for your telephone service. A DSL connection requires the line between the central office (CO) and the customer premises (CPE) to be less than 18,000 feet. Typically, service providers limited the number to 12,000 feet, to assure better quality of service (and, more important, service that would be less susceptible to interruptions). The database held that information. If the database showed that the customer premises were more than 12,000 feet away from the CO, the company would not offer service. However,[142] we found out that even if the database showed that the customer's premises were within 12,000 feet of the CO, there was still a 30% probability that the company could not provide DSL service. There were several reasons for that. One was that the database was not completely accurate. Sometimes technicians would change the routing of telephone lines at the premises and forget to update the database. Another reason was that sometimes there were other physical limitations to the telephone lines that nobody described in the database and, while allowing voice telephone service, prevented DSL service over those lines. Now you need to understand how consumers buy computers. While you can easily install *external* PC accessories (printer, external modem, CD burner, and other devices) with a cable without having to open the computer case, consumers typically order all internal accessories (internal modems, graphic accelerator cards, and other items) bundled with the computer. Opening the computer case to add those is a task requiring a highly skilled technician, and might void the computer warranty if done by the consumer. An *internal* DSL modem had to be ordered with the computer. This is the time to mention that the gross profit margins for PC manufacturers are in the 10% to 25% range. So for a $400 computer,[143] a PC manufacturer would make $40 to $100 gross profit. A DSL modem would increase the computer price by approximately $100. Assume a consumer buys a computer for $500 instead of $400, since it appears (based on database check) that the consumer's home is eligible for DSL service. Upon arriving home and attempting to connect to DSL service, the consumer discovers that he is among the 30% who, while initially qualified for DSL service (based only on database data and not a physical line check), cannot get that service. What would that consumer do? Return the PC and get a $400 PC without an internal DSL modem. This just wiped out the PC manufacturer's gross margin. Shipping computers with a bundled internal DSL modem is not a good idea for PC manufacturers.

The second mistake PCTEL made when defining the product was to define a G.Lite modem. PCTEL was correct in assuming that DSL service would not be available at a speed higher than 1.5Mbps, and that users would not need speeds higher than that. However, the price difference between a 1.5Mbps G.Lite modem and an 8Mbps G.DMT modem was relatively small. The DSP that handled 1.5Mbps could handle 8Mbps. The DSP was strong enough. The Pentium processor, on the other hand, was a different story. PCTEL estimated that it would take approximately 150MHz off the Pentium processor[144] to process a G.Lite signal, whereas it would take more than 400MHz to process a G.DMT signal. Due to the relatively small price difference, the DSL service providers were offering only G.DMT external DSL modems. It is somewhat similar to the introduction of Ethernet routers capable of 100Mbps. Consumers, needing Ethernet routers, noticed that the price difference between the 10Mbps routers and the new 100Mbps routers was only 10% and opted to buy the more expensive ones, regardless of whether they really needed 100Mbps connectivity rates. In fact, to date consumers hardly even get to utilize the 100Mbps capabilities. A more recent similar situation occurred with the Wi-Fi wireless routers implementing the IEEE 802.11g standard, offering 54Mbps (compared to the previous Wi-Fi routers, implementing the IEEE 802.11b standard, only offering 11Mbps). While the consumers did not really need the five times speed improvement, the 20% price difference was small enough for consumers to buy the higher speed wireless routers. If PCTEL had realized that the small price difference between G.Lite modems and G.DMT (also known as "full speed") DSL modems would cause the service providers to choose only full speed modems, it would have never considered G.Lite modems. In fact, the G.Lite modem market never took off, and DSL modems continue to reach higher speeds.

The third mistake PCTEL made was attempting to implement the signal processing by the host Pentium processor. Why was that a mistake this time while a great success with dial-up modems? The answer lies in the fact that DSL modems are *always on*. Dial-up modems operate only a small fraction of the time, when the user needs to connect to the telephone line. The fact that users typically shared the same telephone line between voice calls and Internet connectivity helped. People used dial-up modems the most when Internet was still not the main use cause for the PC. Assuming that the modem was used 10% of the time, and the host signal processing required some 10% of the overall available Pentium processing power, it was bearable. Overall, one might argue that using the host signal processing reduced the value of the processor by only a mere 1%.[145] However, since a DSL modem is "always on" (connected to the Internet 100% of the time and not only when the user needs to connect) the signal processor (be it DSP or the Pentium "host") was required to analyze incoming signals 100% of the time. To make it worse, analyzing incoming DSL signals requires a higher processor "cycle" on a different order of magnitude. PCTEL estimated that it would require approximately 150MHz of processing power to analyze a G.Lite signal. This would depreciate the value of the processor dramatically. Even today, with a 1.5GHz Pentium IV processor, 150MHz would drop the available performance of this processor for other applications to the equivalent of a 1.35GHz processor. The price difference between a 1.5GHz processor and a 1.35GHz processor was, in fact, much higher than the savings in modem cost due to the switch from DSP-based DSL modems to host-based modems. There was simply no justification to develop a "soft" DSL modem.

So why did PCTEL develop an internal "soft" G.Lite DSL modem? There were two reasons. I mentioned the first one: PCTEL assumed, erroneously, that the great success in soft dial-up modems was repeatable with "soft" DSL modems. In fact, PCTEL became a brand name in "soft" modems, and if the "soft" DSL modem market had ever emerged, PCTEL would definitely have been a winner in such a market. The second reason, though, was simple: PCTEL *listened to its customers.* I caught you off guard now, didn't I? It's true. At the time, Compaq and Dell, being the two leaders in the PC market, had outstanding RFQs[146] collectively for close to 700,000 internal DSL modems. PCTEL developed a product the customers asked for. So why did PCTEL get "punished" for simply doing what the customers asked for? If you ever held a sales position, you know that "the customer is always right." With time, and many scars to show for it, I learned that "the customer is *not* always right." In fact, I live my life under this modified phrase. It also goes to the distinction between what the customer *wants* and what the customer *needs.* The DSL market was in its infancy in the US and around the world. There was no experience to draw on. Dell and Compaq simply made an innocent mistake thinking that *internal* DSL modems were what they needed. They might not have been aware of the "30% rule," or thought they could handle it in a financially viable way. PCTEL's mistake here was to focus on what Dell and Compaq *wanted* rather than analyze what they really *needed.* In my marketing lectures, I always emphasize the importance of understanding the entire value chain and the entire ecosystem in which the product or technology in development will exist. Focusing only on the *immediate* customer[147] is a mistake, and not even necessarily the best thing for your immediate customer. I teach that as a supplier you are responsible for your customer's *success*, and not only to fulfill their orders. You need to assure that there will be a market for their products. It's simple: if there is no market for their products, they will not need to buy your product. Only if you apply yourself to understand the entire value chain and the ecosystem surrounding it will you be able to supply your customers' *needs*.

PCTEL completed the development of its "Lightspeed" internal, G.Lite, DSL product and sold approximately 100 units as engineering samples. The product never went into mass production, as there was no need for such a product. Unfortunately, I joined the DSL team at PCTEL only six months before they completed the project, and, less than one month before the completion of the development, I managed to convince the executive management team that there would not be a market for the product. I didn't manage to save the company money. PCTEL went on to enter the Wi-Fi market, but a little too late at that time.

Qualcomm and CDMA

Qualcomm is a company with a brilliant strategy. In 2003, 25% of Qualcomm's revenue came from royalties and license fees. In 2005, this number grew to 34%. The importance of revenue from royalty is, it has no direct costs associated with it. When a semiconductor company sells an integrated circuit, there are direct costs associated with it: the cost of the silicon wafer, the production process, the testing process, packaging, storing, shipping, and other costs. Integrated circuits often sell with a gross profit margin of 40% and below. Qualcomm's financial data reflects the very significant (and growing) share of their revenue resulting from royalties and license fees. In 2003, Qualcomm's overall gross profit margin was 67%, which grew to 71% in 2005. The company's net profit also grew, quite significantly, from 21.5% of revenue in 2003 to 37.8% in 2005.

What is it that allows Qualcomm to generate such a significant and admirable percentage of revenue from royalties and license fees and create such great financial results?

Qualcomm understood that "going with the flow" would not result in such impressive financial results. To generate such results, a company must take a path different from anyone else. For Qualcomm in the late 1980s the "road less traveled" was CDMA. Qualcomm pushed its own cellular standard against the leading worldwide GSM standard and today the CDMA technology generates a significant part of its $2 billion royalties and license fees.

It is important to notice that Qualcomm, being a (fabless) semiconductor company, understood that while it intended to generate revenue from CDMA integrated circuits and royalties on this technology, it needed to guarantee the existence of an ecosystem supporting this technology. As described in Figure 37, certain elements must be in place for the cellular phone ecosystem. Qualcomm covered the semiconductor element, but what about the rest? Someone needed to build the phones, someone needed to deliver an operating system and a platform for applications, and someone had to build out the network infrastructure. Against all odds, Qualcomm started building phones, and even infrastructure to support its CDMA technology. Today, Qualcomm is repeating this strategy by investing $800 million in building a US infrastructure for its FLO® technology for mobile TV, against the industry-supported DVB-H standard. At the time of writing this book, two major US operators (Verizon and AT&T-Cingular) announced the adoption of the MediaFLO® network built by Qualcomm, and Qualcomm is guaranteeing a new royalty stream for the use of this technology.[148] Building your own infrastructure to enable an ecosystem is a major commitment, but one that leads to a significant value chain position.

Dominating the ecosystem

Almost every ecosystem has a *dominating* entity. The control may shift from one entity to another over time, but there is typically only one controlling entity at any point in time. The controlling entity is the one that has the strongest bargaining power along the value chain. Michael Porter[149] defined the five forces of competition in a market. I will categorize them in a slightly different way than he has:

- *Rivalry*—This will include competition between competitors offering the *same* products in the same market. *Entry barriers* describes the competition with sellers who are planning to enter the market, and *intensity of rivalry* describes the competition with other competitors who are already inside the market.

- *External*—*Substitute products* are external products that might, if they serve the same job that the products in this market serve, increase the intensity of competition through an external force.

- *Value chain*—These forces intensify the competition along the value chain. According to Porter, they include *buyer bargaining power* and *supplier bargaining power.* In the following paragraphs, I will focus on those *value chain* competitive forces.

In general, we tend to consider only our *classic* competitors as competitors. We focus on only one of the five competitive forces brought by Porter—*intensity of rivalry.* Sometimes, we consider competitors who can *potentially* enter the market as competitors, thus addressing a second competitive force—*barriers to entry.* However, we typically neglect to address the competition we get along the value chain from our suppliers and, worst of all, from our *customers.*

Every value chain needs a *dominating* force. (Somehow, including the words "chain" and "domination" in the same sentence does not feel right...) There is a constant power struggle up and down the value chain. In each of the links in the value chain there is a company that wishes to dominate that link and, once it succeeds in doing so, it starts dominating the rest of the value chain simply by not giving any other company in any other link in the value chain an alternative.

An example is appropriate here. The personal computing industry started with the Apple, Commodore, Radio Shack computers, and even computers by Texas Instruments. There were many computers fighting over the consumer, there were many microprocessor companies fighting over market share with those personal computers (Intel, Zilog, Motorola, and others), and there was no standard operating system. When IBM introduced the IBM PC in August 1981, it immediately dominated the value chain with a new architecture that promised to be flexible, user friendly, and most important, standard.

IBM chose a microprocessor made by Intel (the 8088), and an operating system made by Microsoft (DOS). IBM probably did not expect to dominate the value chain for long, as it pursued an *open-architecture* platform, allowing other competitors to offer competing products. IBM's vision might have been different from what happened. IBM might have pursued an open architecture to commoditize the components from which an IBM PC arose, so there would be multiple sources for every such component, and IBM would drive those costs down. Sure enough, competitors to IBM came into the market. It was that exact open architecture and multiple component sources that IBM created that allowed no-name companies to build PCs competitive with IBM. Initially, it was in the form of Asian "white box" (or "PC-compatible") manufacturers, but then it was companies such as Dell, Compaq, HP, Sony, Toshiba, and others. IBM lost its position as a *dominator* in that value chain. But did Dell or the other PC manufacturers assume that role? Not really. It was the Santa Clara-based Intel that made sure the x86 platform would *dominate* the value chain. While there were quite a few alternatives in the PC manufacturer link in the value chain, soon there was only one alternative in the processor market—Intel. Microsoft took a *dominator* position in the ecosystem, but not in the value chain. What IBM neglected to do was to prevent multiple competitors from using the Intel x86 processors. Not completely without competition (AMD, Transmeta, and even Texas Instruments, at some point), Intel's focus on delivering an ever-improving x86 processor roadmap kept it in a dominating position in the PC value chain.

What does *dominating the value chain* mean for a company? In the PC example, while the PC manufacturers are "enjoying" 10% to 25% gross margins, Intel enjoys gross margins closer to 60%. Porter's rules work— if you have higher bargaining power, the intensity of competition you face is lower, you get a premium for your product, and you increase your revenue, profit, and return on investment.

Here is another example. A similar struggle is taking place in the cell phone market. There are at least three entities wishing to dominate the value chain: the semiconductor manufacturers (e.g., Texas Instruments, Qualcomm), the phone manufacturers (e.g., Nokia, Motorola, Samsung), and the operators (e.g., Cingular, Sprint, Vodafone). With more than a billion phones shipped in a year to close to 3 billion subscribers worldwide, this is a very significant market, and any percentage point of profit translates into a critical improvement in return on investment. What can the different entities do to achieve domination of this value chain?

- The semiconductor companies can build proprietary solutions that add significant value to the operators. Note that the focus is on the operators and not the handset manufacturers. Why so? Because the handset manufacturers are the immediate customers, and the semiconductor suppliers should not give them too much bargaining power. Qualcomm's BREW® technology is a perfect example, where the semiconductor company wishes to offer value directly to the operator by creating an application platform for revenue-generating applications downloaded from the operator. Qualcomm also went the extra mile to build the MediaFLO® network, offering the operators a "shrink-wrapped" infrastructure to deliver mobile TV to handsets, as long as they are using Qualcomm's proprietary FLO® specification. Those actions may lead to commoditizing the role of the handset manufacturers, as the operator will be in a position to demand support for specific features and even specific integrated circuits to be included in new handsets. The endgame may be very similar to the PC market where the balance of power shifted from the PC manufacturer (IBM) to the microprocessor manufacturer (Intel).

- The handset manufacturers, feeling the risk of semiconductor manufacturers commoditizing them are, in turn, trying to commoditize the semiconductor content of a phone. They do that by creating their own specifications with which the semiconductor suppliers need to comply, demanding *pin-to-pin* compatibility,[150] and often even software reuse.

- The operators, trying not to let the handset manufacturers hold them hostage, are opting to have phones designed for them by ODMs and not by OEMs. This will eliminate the possibility of the OEM (Nokia, Motorola, Sony-Ericsson, Samsung) promoting specific phones directly to consumers, and allow the operators to specify phone functionality even to the OEMs.

Throughout all those examples, there are two important messages. Be careful from repeating these messages aloud in your company. They are not going to help your career. First, *the customer is not always right*. You should move away from fulfilling customers' requirements and toward understanding what the customer really needs. If you see yourself as responsible for customer success, you will look yourself for what is better for the customer, and not allow the customer to blind you with specific requests. Second, your immediate customer is also your *competitor* in the value chain. Just like your customer wishes to achieve a competitive position within its position in the value chain, it also wishes to make its position in the value chain the one that attracts the highest profitability, at the expense of other links in the value chain, including yours. This is where you and your customer are at odds. Your customer wishes to commoditize you, allowing your competitors to compete better with you, granting your customer a stronger bargaining position in the value chain.

---

[127] Source: MSN Encarta® encyclopedia.

[128] XScale is a registered trademark of Intel Corporation.

[129] Digital Subscriber Line.

[130] I just realized that, although included in the last five computers I bought, I haven't used a dial-up modem to connect to the Internet in any of those last five computers. For clarification – a dial-up modem allows the computer to connect to an Internet service provider (ISP) through regular telephone lines and using a telephone number provided by the ISP. The ISP, in turn, connects the subscriber to the Internet "back bone." The speeds of dial-up modems reached 56Kbps with the last standard created, known as V.90. Those modems hardly ever reached that top speed of 56Kbps due to imperfections of the telephone lines. In comparison, a DSL or cable Internet connectivity (also referred to as *broadband* connectivity) offers speeds of 1.5Mbps (25 times faster than dial-up modems). Wi-Fi connectivity (wireless "hot spots" like the ones available in airports, hotels, Starbucks® stores and at home) offers connectivity speeds of 11Mbps to 54Mbps, and is moving on to 300Mbps and beyond.

[131] A function called *demodulating*.

[132] A function called *modulating*. The combination of *Modulating* and *Demodulating* created the name MODEM.

[133] As opposed to Digital Signal Processing, or DSP.

[134] Based on growth in revenue over a period of five years (1995-2000).

[135] Also known as ILEC – Incumbent Local Exchange Carrier, as they owned the copper wires and infrastructure.

[136] G.Lite was a name for an ITU standard called ITU-G992.2. It offered a lower-speed DSL service (up to 1.5 Mbps) compared with the G.DMT (ITU-G992.1) standard, offering speeds up to 8 Mbps.

[137] That connection was called RS232.

[138] As an example – I bought a 120MHz laptop in 1997 and paid $2,700. That was a non-recognized brand. In 2006 I bough a 1.8GHz Dell laptop for $499.

[139] A more common connection method today includes a Wi-Fi router, which shares the DSL (or cable) connectivity wirelessly to a much larger number of computers, typically 256.

[140] The major components of the installation cost were the cost of the subscriber modem (also known as the subscriber premise equipment [CPE]) and the central office (CO) modem, as well as the "truck roll," which was the term used to describe the dispatching of a technician to install the modem at the customer premises.

[141] In fact, that was the reason the CLECs went bankrupt. Some claim that the huge write-offs that took place when the CLECs invested billions of dollars raised in public offerings in infrastructure later

acquired for cents-on-the-dollar by the ILECs, enabled the DSL market we have today, which might not have emerged without those write-offs.
[142] As I discovered in a meeting with Flashcom in Huntington Beach, California, in 2000, in which five minutes after the meeting started we were told that Flashcom is recommending to PC manufacturers *not* to bundle internal DSL modems.
[143] Even in 2000, $400 computers were available from "white box" manufacturers (another name for "no-name" manufacturers, typically in Taiwan).
[144] Which, at that time had approximately 450MHz.
[145] 10% of the processing power for 10% of the overall usage time.
[146] Request for Quotation. When a buyer intends to buy a product or component, often it issues an RFQ to several suppliers with requirements, seeking responses (the "Quotation") from the suppliers. Based on the quotations – the buyer decides which supplier to choose.
[147] The immediate customer is the buyer who buys directly from you, to whom you are the immediate supplier.
[148] According to Qualcomm, royalties will be charged for non-CDMA phones implementing the FLO technology.
[149] Porter, Michael E. "Competitive Strategy: Techniques for Analyzing Industries and Competitors," Free Press Publishing, 1998.
[150] Pin-to-pin compatibility means that two different integrated circuits, manufactured typically by two different suppliers, will be able to be replaced on the same board without any further changes (except, possibly, software changes), thus reducing switching costs.

Chapter 15
Industry Standards

Standard-based products

I will start by defining standards, standard-based products, and who needs standards anyway. To start with, I will define *open systems* with *closed systems*. For the sake of discussion, a *closed system* is a system that does not require any component outside of that system to operate and deliver its complete functionality. An *open system*, in contrast, is a system that requires other components, not included within the system, in order to operate. Most products are, in fact, parts of *open systems*. As an example, a telephone requires the network for operation. The telephone by itself will not deliver its functionality without that network. When you buy a telephone (wired or wireless)—you do not buy the network. A DVD player requires a DVD with content. The DVD and the content (the movie) do not come with the DVD player you buy.

A *standard* is a common, predefined way by which those different components, purchased at different times and often from different suppliers, interact with each other. Both components (the system and the external component) need to adhere to this standard in order to produce the value that prompted the purchase. A few examples follow:

- Consumers get the cellular phone independently from the cellular network. In fact, consumers never buy the cellular network and rather buy service from that network.[151] The phones are required to interact with the service provider. There is a wide range of standards defined for this purpose. One of them is the GSM standard. Another is the TIA[152] IS-

95 standard. The network's structure supports this standard; independently, so do the cellular phones. When both the network and cellular phone support the same standard, they can communicate and deliver the value expected when they were purchased.

- Consumers buy DVD players through retail chains from consumer electronics manufacturers such as Sony, Panasonic, Samsung, and others. Independently, they buy or rent DVD content that movie studios create. Standard digital rights management (DRM) standards protect the content. Once compressed, the content fits the capacity of a DVD. A standard called MPEG2 compresses that content. If compressed in any way other than the decoding mechanism included in the DVD player, the user would be unable to view the content. Furthermore, even the size of the DVD and the hole in its center are standardized. Otherwise—the DVD player would not have been able to load the disk.

- Users typically buy personal computers and their peripherals (printers, scanners, cameras, and so on) separately, and most likely from different vendors. When content needs to move from one product to another, communication must occur over a standard connection. The Universal Serial Bus (USB) is a standard developed by the USB promoters group to define such a connection. It assures that personal computers, PC peripherals, and even the USB cables connecting them will assure delivering the expected value (you can move pictures from your digital camera to the PC, download music from the PC to a portable MP3 player, print documents, and more). Without a standard way for connecting all those devices, this value could never have been delivered.

- The entire Internet operation uses standards developed by the Internet Engineering Task Force (IETF). One of those standards is the Internet protocol (IP) itself. Computers that are not compliant with this standard will not be able to communicate with other computers or servers on the Internet.

I could go on and on with many examples that will illustrate the importance of standards, but the bottom line is that when you buy products you expect them to interact with other products, systems, networks, or services purchased at a different time and from a different manufacturer. Without standards, those individual purchases will not deliver the expected value that will come only when all those products, networks, and services are compatible with the same standards. In the next part of this chapter, I will introduce the concept of *product interoperability* distinctly from *standard compliance* and show the importance, advantages, and disadvantages of both.

Having read the above, you must ask, "When should I care about standards?" The answer to this question depends on the answer to two other questions:

- *Is the standard-based part of the proposed product a key function or feature of your product and can it differentiate your offering and possibly give you an "unfair advantage" if implemented in a certain way?* The two parts of the question intertwine. I would claim that the fact that the standard function is capable of giving you an "unfair" competitive advantage is exactly what makes that function so important. If I go back to the DVD player example, the format of the DVD can certainly give a competitor an unfair advantage. Take, for example, the HD-DVD vs. Blu-ray Disc competition happening right now. Both standards provide high-definition movie storage. Their characteristics are relatively similar. Blu-ray, supported by Apple, Dell, HP, Hitachi, Mitsubishi, Panasonic, Philips, Samsung, Sharp, Sony, and others competes head to head with the HD-DVD format, supported by Toshiba, NEC, Sanyo, Microsoft, and Intel. As we have seen in the past, during the Betamax vs. VHS competition, only one standard will prevail in the market. At some point, the consumers will make the choice. The companies that support the winning standard will have a time-to-market advantage (as they have already invested in developing products based on the "right" standard) as well as an intellectual property advantage (having patents for which they can claim royalties) that can be translated to cost-structure advantage. On the other hand, the high-speed serial connection in the back of that DVD player, be it USB, FireWire, or any other serial interface standard, will not be able to differentiate the product as it is *not key* to the functionality or performance of the product.

- *Are there standards that cover exactly what the standard-based component intends to perform and if so, are those standards still developing?* Where standards already exist, you will be fighting an uphill battle to get your competing version market share. There can be several stages in the life of an existing standard. It can still be in the development phase. If the standard development process is still before a confirmation of the proposal, and is, therefore, still open to receive new proposals, your technology has a fighting chance *within* the standard development organization and process just like any other proposal being considered. If, on the other hand, the standard development process has already passed this stage and someone is editing a final proposal into a standard, you will need to compete from outside the standard development organization. This will then become a game of getting industry support for your standard against a more mature, industry-supported standard. If the standard is already complete and the first products are in the market supporting this standard and establishing the basis for product interoperability, your chances of winning with a competing standard are slim to none. The only responsible decision that you can make is to adopt the existing standard.

In summary, there are four scenarios to consider, as seen in Figure 40, depending on whether the standard is a key feature in the product or not, and whether the standard is established or not. If the standard is a key feature for the product but not developed, it offers a unique opportunity to develop and drive your own standard. You need to deploy all your skills in driving a new standard. The other extreme will be a standard that, while not constituting a key feature of the product, is already established. This will be simply a case of adopting the established standard as is. You should not differentiate with this standard.

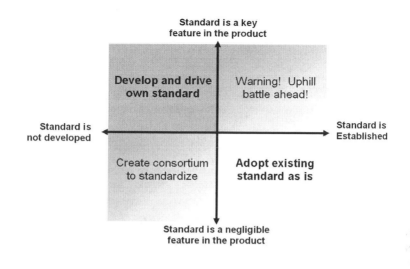

Figure 40—When should you care about standards?

Another relatively easy scenario to address arises when the standard is not a key feature of the product, but it is undeveloped. If the standard is, in fact, required to complete the whole product, you should form a coalition in the right venue to create an industry standard. The politics of developing this standard should not be too adversarial, as it does not constitute a key feature with differentiation potential for your product. The worst scenario exists when the standard is already established, and it does constitute a key feature and is, therefore, a significant differentiation opportunity for your product. Here you are facing a few possible alternatives:

- You can decide to adopt the existing standard. You will not be a market leader, and can decide to deploy a fast-follower strategy. You will face significant costs in switching existing customers[153] from the market leader products to your products and for positioning your product against the market leader.

- There is a wide range from a *nonexistent* standard to a *fully established* standard. If the standard falls short of being fully established, you may want to fight *within* the standard-development process to promote your own version of the standard that differentiates and proves advantageous to your product.

- You may want to drive a competing standard. This is definitely an uphill battle, and top political skills will be required to win it.

If, after reviewing the above, you realize you need to get very involved in the development of a standard—go ahead and read the rest of this chapter. It will give you the tools you need to establish standard leadership. If, on the other hand, you determine that no significant standard-development involvement is required, skip to the next chapter.

Interoperability vs. standard compliance

As stated above, in order for two components made by different suppliers to work together, there must be a standard, and they must both comply with that standard. That is a prerequisite. However, is it enough? It really depends on several factors: (1) the standard's complexity, (2) the level at which one can interpret it in different incompatible ways, (3) how comprehensive and complete the standard is, and (4) whether or not it has alternative options built in.

- If one can interpret the standard in several *incompatible* ways, the manufacturer of one component might interpret it one way, and the manufacturer of the other component might interpret it in a different way. Both will claim standard compliance, but the two parts will not work as a whole system. Imagine if the DVD disk dimensions were open to interpretation. Different DVD manufacturers would build DVDs in different sizes, and the DVD player manufacturers would build DVD players capable of accepting different, but not all, DVD sizes. Not every DVD player could play every DVD, and the value of the DVD market would diminish.

- If the standard is not comprehensive and complete enough, and for the full functional operation of the components manufactured by different manufacturers there are other elements that need to be compatible, it is equivalent to leaving the standard open for interpretation. To take the DVD player example again, imagine a well-defined DVD size, but a DVD recording format that is undefined. One studio will record its movies using MPEG2 content format, while another will record its movies using Windows Media format. If the DVD player supported only MPEG2 format, it would be limited in the content it could play, once again reducing significantly the value of this market.

- If the standard has several alternative options built into it, even if those are well defined and specified, it will allow one manufacturer to support one alternative, while another supports another alternative. In the early days of wireless local area networking (WLAN), based on the IEEE 802.11 standard, there were several air-interface alternatives defined in it, none of which was mandatory. One was Direct Sequence Spread Spectrum (DSSS), another was Frequency Hopping Spread Spectrum (FHSS), and the third was optical infrared-based. Those alternative air-interface options were completely *incompatible,* and while suppliers of components of wireless LAN systems claimed compatibility with the IEEE 802.11 standard, their products were not interoperable with one another.

If any one or more of those conditions exist in the standard, it significantly reduces the value of standard-compliance, as it does not guarantee that components made by one supplier will work with components made by another supplier to deliver the value for which the consumer bought both components. After all, this is exactly what prompted standards creation initially. The answer is in another term: *interoperability.*

Standard compliance simply means that each product (in Figure 41, Product A or Product B) is *independently* compliant with the standard.

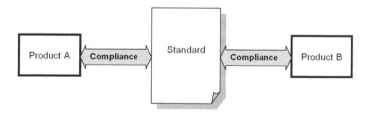

Figure 41—Standard compliance

As long as the standard is simple enough, well enough defined, does not have any alternative implementation options, and is comprehensive enough, and assuming both products are fully compliant with that standard, both products will work with one another without further action or tests. However, if the standard is too complicated, can be interpreted in several incompatible ways, or if the standard is not comprehensive enough, requiring the manufacturers to "fill in the blanks" to deliver the *whole* product, or if the standard has several incompatible alternative options, standard compliance cannot assure that Product A will work with Product B, as the different manufacturers will implement the standard differently, while still claiming standard compatibility.

Due to this fact, several organizations and laboratories emerged in different industries to assure and even certify *interoperability*. Interoperability starts by assuring that the products comply with the same standard. However, testing the operation of the two products (Product A and Product B) occurs to assure that they work together as a whole system as intended and deliver the expected value to the consumer.

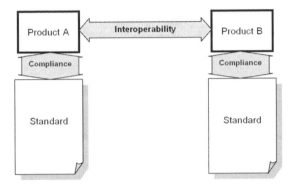

Figure 42—Product interoperability

Although there are many examples, I will use one I was deeply involved with—the Wi-Fi example. As stated before, the IEEE standard for wireless networking, 802.11, met some of the criteria for which mere standard compliance was not enough. It was too complicated not to generate different interpretations by different manufacturers; it had options that were not interoperable, although it was comprehensive. In wireless local area networking, there are two main components that communicate to create a complete system that delivers the value to the consumer: the network interface card (NIC), also called the "client" card, or the "station," and the access point. The access point is the device that connects to the Internet through an Ethernet wire, while wirelessly sharing this connection with "clients" equipped with the same type of networking capabilities. Laptop computers[154] are equipped with the NIC "client," and behave as if wired to the Internet.

In the early days, the interoperability problem was unnoticed. Not because it didn't exist, but for a different reason. Wireless networking was simply not available anywhere, and the first adopters of this technology had to buy all the components at one time—the access point as well as the client card to install in the PC—sold together as a "kit." A "kit" typically included one access point and one or more client cards, manufactured by the same firm (Lucent, Motorola, Cisco, or others), and offered in a single package. Even when they were offered as individual packages (access point sold separately from client card), consumers preferred to buy all components from the same manufacturer. It seemed intuitive that an access point from a certain manufacturer was bound to work with client card made by the same manufacturer. However, when it was time to buy another client card, and for some reason the customer bought a card made by another manufacturer, interoperability problems started. Suddenly the "IEEE 802.11 compliant" label on the box meant nothing. If you bought an access point from Cisco and a client card from Lucent, they didn't necessarily work together. The industry was at a risk of stalling.

And then, in 1999, right after the higher-speed version of the IEEE 802.11 standard was released called 802.11b,[155] a small team of people from 3Com, including David Cohen, then a product manager for wireless networking products, and Jeff Abramowitz, a marketing manager there, decided to form the Wireless Ethernet Compatibility Alliance (WECA). The purpose was to test and certify products for interoperability rather than certify standard compliance. Later, in 2001, the Alliance changed its name to the more familiar name—the Wi-Fi Alliance.[156] The mission of the Wi-Fi Alliance is to certify the interoperability of Wi-Fi products manufactured by different vendors, to assure consumers who buy those products—labeled with the Wi-Fi CERTIFIED logo—that they will work with any other such product, even if another manufacturer makes them. The Alliance planned to achieve its goal by developing test plans based on a test *suite*, made with "gold standard products." Initially, it tested compliance of those products with the IEEE 802.11 standard, but then it made a test suite out of a few products, and every new product that wished to be certified had to be interoperable with this test suite and to achieve a certain performance level. Note that the discussion about being *first to market* (Chapter 13) just added a new dimension of value for being first to market. When your product is one of the first ones built in compliance with a new standard, and you want to certify interoperability, your product will likely become part of this "gold standard" test suite, and certifiers will test other products against *your* product, rather than the other way around. Standards tend to have room for interpretation. It will be *your* interpretation that others will test against. This gives you an advantage over your later competitors, who will need to interoperate with your interpretation.

Other organizations materialized to certify interoperability of multiple products. Some of those organizations, like the Wi-Fi Alliance, certify interoperability based on standards created by another organization (the 1394 Trade Association certifies based on the IEEE 1394 standard, and so on). Some organizations combine the creation of the standards with the interoperability certification (the USB Implementers Forum, developing the USB specifications and certifying accordingly; the Bluetooth SIG, developing the Bluetooth specifications and certifying accordingly; the HDMI Forum, and others).

The process of developing a standard

Standards develop in a Standard Development Organization (SDO). In order to be effective, efficient, and fair, those SDOs have rules and processes to develop standards. Those rules vary from SDO to SDO but, in general, they perform the following steps:

- Developing a charter for the standard. Why is there a need for this standard? How is it different than or competing with any other existing standard? Is there really a need for this standard? Is it feasible to build?[157]

- Determining the requirements, criteria, and metrics for selection of proposals. Since the following stage will be the submission of proposals, this stage is extremely important in that it will help the working group determine which of the proposals will best meet the criteria and should therefore be chosen.

- Calling for proposals. This is an official and administrative step, in which the proposal submission period officially opens. It includes the criteria developed in the previous step as guidance. It includes a deadline for the submission of proposals. It is typically open to all.

- Submitting proposals. Various entities are submitting proposals. Those entities vary from companies that intend to build products,[158] to research institutes, universities, and individuals. The proposals are supposed to be complete, descriptive, and typically include a part that states the compliance of this proposal with the criteria set forth above.

- Selecting proposals. To respond appropriately to submitted proposals, there needs to be a down selection process. The down selection process will reduce the number of proposals to just one, to base the final standard on. The process of down selection can take many shapes. It can include merger of proposals, combining the "good" from each proposal. It can include combining proposals as different options[159] of a single standard, or simply the voting down of proposals that are less attractive or less compliant with the set criteria. This step can be highly adversarial, as companies stand to gain or lose a lot if their technology is (or is not) selected for the standard baseline.[160]

- Confirming the decision. Once the down-selection process is complete, and there is only one proposal left for consideration, there is a requirement for a confirmation. This is typically a vote of confidence by the organization membership body, showing a willingness to take this "last standing" proposal down the path of creating a complete standard.

- Editing the standard. As the proposal is typically in the form of a presentation, not in the final format for a published standard, it goes into a phase of *technical editing*. During this period, there will be much technical discussion on different aspects of the standards, as more details surface. The result of this step is a draft standard, complete with all its components, and in a format appropriate for publication by this organization.

- Voting on the draft standard. At this time, voting on the draft standard occurs. The vote can take place in a meeting, or using a letter ballot, which is more typical. Every eligible voter in this working group will have the right to approve the standard draft, reject it, or abstain from voting. This would be a good time to submit comments[161] to improve the standard. The comments can be editorial or technical.[162]

- Meeting for comment resolution. Once the comment period ends, the entire group enters a process known as comment resolution. The entire group must address every single comment. If the group accepts comments as they are, the draft will change to reflect such acceptance. Rejected comments must include an explanation for the rejection.[163] The group can debate comments and develop other modifications to the draft. Once all comments are resolved, the group generates a new draft for a new ballot.

- Achieving consensus. If the number of approval votes the draft receives meets or exceeds the required level for standard approval,[164] the group will approve the standard, even though there are outstanding comments that might not have been resolved. SDOs typically attempt to resolve as many comments as possible to achieve the highest level of consensus possible, within a reasonable time.

- Voting a second time. Some organizations require a second level of voting or balloting. Some organizations have task groups developing standards as subsidiaries of larger working groups with a wider scope of interests, and the publication of the standard requires the approval of the appropriate majority of the "parent" working group.[165]

- Publishing the standard. Eventually—once all approvals are achieved—the standard is published by the SDO, and becomes publicly available.

Once the standard is published, products should either be standard compliant, or interoperable with each other, according to the standard, as described above.

CDMA, again

The following example describes a situation in which a company had to decide on whether to build essential (complementary) parts of the ecosystem and value chain itself, or if it should partner to create the ecosystem.

In 1988, Qualcomm conceived a technology called CDMA. It was an innovative cellular technology, different from any other cellular technology available at the time. One can argue the advantages and disadvantages of that technology compared to the competing GSM technology, but it did gain market share. Qualcomm targeted the US market initially. Qualcomm, for those of you who do not know the company, is a technology company and a fabless semiconductor manufacturer, producing integrated circuits for cell phones. I see them foremost as a technology company. As described above, Qualcomm's revenue share derived from royalties and licenses grew from 25% in 2003 to 34% in 2005. To me, this fact demonstrates Qualcomm's focus on delivering new technologies. When Qualcomm tried to promote its CDMA technology, it faced major skepticism. To whom was Qualcomm trying to sell this technology? Qualcomm's immediate customers in the cell phone value chain were the cell phone manufacturers (Motorola,

Nokia, and others). However, they did not make the decisions about selecting the technologies. The consumers did not decide which technology to choose either. After all, could you tell the difference between a CDMA phone and a GSM phone? I bet you couldn't. You will not be able to tell the difference between a Motorola RAZR® phone working in the Cingular GSM network vs. the same phone working in the Verizon CDMA network, even though they use completely different technologies. They look the same, perform the same functions, and offer the same performance. One difference will be that a GSM phone can be used in most of the world outside the US while a CDMA phone has very limited coverage outside the US, but most users will neither know this fact, nor care. So who makes the technology decision? The cellular operators. Qualcomm had to convince the operators to choose CDMA. Appealing to their technology-savvy people did not help. Qualcomm understood that there was no way the operators would choose the CDMA technology if there was no phone supporting it. Knowing that the cell phone giants (Motorola, Nokia, Samsung, LG, and others) would not build CDMA phones without demand from the operators, Qualcomm built its own phone. In fact, I used to own a Qualcomm phone when I was a Verizon customer. Building the phone was not enough; Qualcomm had to build the infrastructure (a cellular network) and offer service. In 1992, US West became the first operator to order CDMA phones, and in 1993, commercial service appeared for the first time in South Korea. So, while Qualcomm was focused on generating revenue from its CDMA *technology*, it had to offer a *phone*, *infrastructure*, and *service*. Did this strategy succeed? In 2005, Qualcomm generated revenue of $5.7 billion, most of it from its CDMA technology, of which $1.9 billion came from licensing and royalties of its CDMA technology.

So is the only way to create a *whole product* to build it yourself? Not necessarily. The alternative to CDMA is a technology called GSM. More than 80% of the cell phones sold in 2005 were GSM phones, and less than 20% of the phones were CDMA ones. The GSM story is different from the CDMA one.

In 1982, the Conference of European Posts and Telegraphs (CEPT), an organization that combines cellular operators in Europe, created a group called Groupe Special Mobile (GSM) to develop a pan-European cellular technology. No doubt, a *committee* developed GSM, not a single company. In 1990, the European Telecommunication Standards Institute (ETSI) published the GSM specifications, which led to a commercial service launch in 1991. Many companies contributed to the development of the standard that, with 8,000 pages and many options, accommodated many of them. The main advantage of GSM (today the acronym stands for Global System for Mobile telecommunications, used globally by more than 2 billion subscribers) is in its wide industry support, allowing equal footing for all GSM supporters. In opposition, the CDMA ecosystem is an unbalanced one, with one technology provider (Qualcomm) "controlling" that ecosystem.

While it took GSM nine years to go from inception to commercial service launch, it took CDMA only four years to do the same. No doubt, developing the ecosystem and value-chain by committee and consensus of multiple companies takes significantly longer. It is also worth noting that Qualcomm has achieved an undisputed lion's share in the CDMA market, whereas there is a split *distribution of power, which is* much more even in the GSM market. When you consider creating a new industry standard vs. adopting one, you should keep in mind that achieving industry consensus takes longer and distributes power more evenly.

---

[151] In the US, consumers buy the phone from the cellular operator (Cingular, T-Mobile, Verizon, Sprint, and other) so we tend to think that the service is provided together with the phone. In Europe and many other places in the world, though, the consumer can actually buy the phone through a retail chain, completely independent from the service, and then subscribe to service through any operator of choice.

[152] Telecommunications Industry Association, a US-based telecommunications standards organization.

[153] Typically, when the standard already exists, it indicates that there is a market for products based on this standard already.

[154] Or desktop computers, or other devices that may use wireless networking as the way to connect to the Internet without wires. Today, even certain cellular phones have wireless networking capabilities using Wi-Fi technology.

[155] The original IEEE 802.11 standard, released in 1991, supported a data rate of up to 2Mbps. The 802.11b derivative, released in 1999, supported up to 11Mbps. In 2003, the IEEE released the next standard called 802.11g, capable of delivering up to 54Mbps. In 2007 it is expected that IEEE will release yet another generation called 802.11n, capable of speeds up to 300Mbps.

[156] Wi-Fi stands for Wireless Fidelity.

[157] The IEEE 802.1 Working Group is notorious in this requirement. It usually asks to see a final implementation in order to determine its feasibility, somehow bypassing the entire process of development of a standard.

[158] When the standard is expected to be released in a relatively short

period, and where a standard is a natural evolution of another standard, therefore addressing an existing market – most proposals are submitted by companies. When the standard addresses a market that does not exist or is expected to emerge within more than just a few years – research institutes, universities, and individuals will submit most proposals.

[159] Different options are typically not interoperable, and in time, only one option will prevail. One example is the 802.11 standard, the first wireless LAN standard (known today as Wi-Fi). It had three non-interoperable options: Direct Sequence Spread Spectrum (DSSS), Frequency Hopping Spread Spectrum (FHSS), and Infra-Red. Eventually, the DSSS prevailed and the 802.11b standard that launched this industry included only DSSS. A similar thing happened with the next generation, 802.11g standard, which had one mandatory interface (OFDM) and two other optional interfaces called PBCC and CCK-OFDM, much less known as they are not implemented.

[160] Two examples are the ultra-wideband (UWB) standard that has been in development in IEEE, and the next-generation, high-speed wireless networking 802.11n standard, also in IEEE. The UWB standard was an extreme example where not only was there a lot of vested commercial interest in the adoption of two competing standards, but there were two camps that were approximately even in support, to the point of not being able to down select to one proposal. In January 2006, three and a half years after the development of the UWB standard in IEEE (in task group 802.15.3a) started – the group was disbanded without creating a standard. The work continued outside of IEEE in two parallel Industry Trade Associations: The WiMedia Alliance (led by Intel, Texas Instruments and others) and the ultra-wideband Forum, led by Freescale.

[161] Submitting comments is typically possible regardless of whether the voter votes to approve or reject the draft. There are organizations, though, that require comments in case of a no-vote.

[162] Typically, the definition of a technical comment is that accepting it will require a change of the implementation, whereas an editorial comment will not.

[163] One reason, for example, is that the comment is incorrect.

[164] Different organizations and different standards have different requirements for the level of approval. IEEE, for example, requires 75% of all eligible voters who returned a vote (either "yes" or "no," but not an abstention) in order to approve a standard.

[165] ECMA (www.ecma-international.org), for example, requires the approval of the *general assembly* to publish a standard created by any of its task groups.

Chapter 16
Influencing Industry

Steering a freight ship

With a growing pace of technology changes, a shortening product development cycle and product life cycle, high-tech companies show a growing impatience to see quick results. Companies focus more on short-term results rather than long-term ones. Results of your *industry participation* are almost never short-term. Often company management has no understanding or appreciation of the significant long-term results of that industry participation. However, I expect that you do.

Impacting industry standards

The process of developing the standard is different among the various organizations, and requires skill to understand and analyze. There are companies that see the standard development process as a "necessary evil." They participate in this process reluctantly. They (especially the engineers among them) despise the politics involved. Their involvement is typically passive and reactive, instead of proactive. Other companies have experts who know how to extract the benefits of actively participating in this process. As this section describes, there are significant benefits resulting from such participation. However, the benefits of being involved in this process are common, and the top seven follow.

Value 1: Getting early insight into emerging standards

Being involved in the standard development process means the ability to "see where the wind is blowing" long before there is a standard. This ability allows the development team to start developing (even if only to start designing) the products long before the standard is complete. One example was Broadcom's ability to be the first to market with their 802.11g high-rate Wi-Fi products. The IEEE was struggling for some time in achieving consensus[166] around a draft of the 802.11g standard. In a meeting in Austin in November of 2001, at the risk that not achieving a consensus in that meeting would mean termination of this standard, they finally reached a consensus. Broadcom was wise to identify what the standard would look like long before they finalized it in IEEE. In November 2001, it started the development, assuming the risk that there would still be changes to the standard. It released prototypes to customers in February of 2003, four months before the IEEE finalized the standard in June of that year, long before any competitor managed to have a prototype supporting the new standard. Depending on the standard, sometimes more than a year passes from the moment the standard draft has *stabilized* until the *finalized version*. This is time well spent in development. Any final changes are typically small ones, and a company is wise to create a prototype based on the preliminary standard and implement minor modifications once the standard is finalized rather than not even starting the development until the standard is finalized. The real value here is time-to-market and the advantages of time-to-market, especially in standard-based products, which I discussed earlier.

Value 2: Ability to influence standards

Many companies and individuals take a passive approach to the standard development process and use the process in one direction: report progress from the SDO to their company. They "feed" their development teams with information about the standard development progress. If they do a good job, they will maximize the first value, described above. However, the standard development process offers value in the opposite direction, too. The company can drive information and direction *into* the standard development process. Doing so is a very important skill, which involves the ability to influence others in many ways and to use the standard development process to the company's benefit. We will discuss these skills later in this chapter. However, the value of driving information into the standard has many advantages to the company. Companies typically have specific intellectual property (IP) that, if entered into the standard, gives them a competitive advantage mostly in the form of cost advantage compared to other companies that will have to license and even pay royalties to companies that own such IP. Companies also have core competencies which, when driven into the standards as requirements, will give them a competitive advantage. For example, let's assume that Company A has a core competency in analog IC design. If Company A manages to drive requirements into the standard so that they will require implementers of products based on this standard to develop analog IC design competencies, Company A will have a competitive advantage in the market based on those products.

Value 3: Gathering competitive intelligence

The process of standard creation teaches us a great deal. Companies trying to maximize the second value will try to inject requirements into the standard. Observing those behaviors will provide competitive intelligence in those companies. We can observe the dynamics between companies too (alignment, misalignment, cooperation, competition). The directions that market-makers take with the standard can also be learned, and the requirements that potential customers dive into the standards will give you an advanced warning on the requirements they will have for the final product. Overall, the participation in the standards development process can provide a significant amount of intelligence on your competitors, customers, and other ecosystem players.

Value 4: Achieving alignment with market-makers

My definition for market-makers is "those ecosystem companies whose actions and selections can make or break a specific market." Those are the biggest among the ecosystem players, typically not part of the value chain. The most important thing is to identify those market-makers. They typically see the importance of the standard being developed to a market they play a "market-maker" role in. Intel, while not an initial Wi-Fi IC manufacturer or customer, was a market-maker in this market. With the PC market segment being so important to the Wi-Fi market, Intel's actions and selections were critical to the success or failure of the Wi-Fi market. Microsoft played a similar role in this market. You should never ignore the behavior of market-makers who participate in the standard development process. You must always keep them within your sight. Create a good relationship with them. Understand why certain things are important to them in the standard and why other things are not important. Understanding that will make your decisions and options in your own product definition appropriate to what the market will eventually require. Participating in the standard development process is an excellent opportunity to achieve such alignment with the market-makers.

Value 5: Get exposure to early adopters

When a new standard emerges, there are just a few companies willing to bet on this new standard or technology. These are the early adopter customers. Comments abound about these early adopter customers, about them being visionaries, about them taking risks, but the fact remains, you need to win the early adopters to stand a chance in a new market. They are the customers who will drive this new market. Those customers typically participate in the standard creation process even though they are not developing technology for the market. They will be *customers* for this newly developed technology and, as such, want to assure it will meet their needs in the products they will build using this technology. Your interaction with them will give you insight into their requirements so that your company will develop the right products. That interaction will build the relationship with them and provide a higher probability for you to be able to sell your products to them in the future. Interacting with them will help you influence their requirements through technical (and non-technical) discussions in a way that will leverage your competitive advantages. Your participation in the standard creation process gives you that exposure.

Value 6: Establishing interoperability

We discussed standard compliance vs. interoperability in Chapter 15. In a perfect world, if two products comply with the same standard, they will interoperate. In a real world, the standard leaves much to interpretation and people don't address the many "corner cases." Furthermore, products have bugs in them. It's a fact of life. It does not matter how simple the standards and the products are—there is always the possibility of bugs. Interoperability is typically associated with certification. The Bluetooth Special Interest Group certifies products that comply with the Bluetooth standard and provide a certification logo. The Wi-Fi Alliance does the same for "Wi-Fi Certified" products, and so does the USB Implementers Forum, and many more. The interoperability certification process takes the first products that claim to be compliant with the new standard and makes them "the gold standard." To achieve certification for interoperability, any new product has to interoperate with those first products. Those first products have bugs, naturally. If you manage to have your products as the "gold standard" products, every new product manufacturer will have to "live with your bugs," whereas if you let a competitor establish their products as the "gold standard," you will have to live with their bugs. Living with someone else's bugs is a lot more difficult and expensive than having them live with yours. Participating in the standard creation process, and especially the interoperability test plan and test suite creation, helps dramatically in establishing your products as the "gold standard."

Value 7: Position your company as a leader

Perception plays a very important role in buying decisions made by customers. Especially when betting on a new technology or a new standard, a customer wants to know that her vendor of choice is a leader, has a thorough understanding of this new standard, and will offer products that are standard-compliant, interoperable, and superior in many other ways that only a market leader can achieve. Your company's participation in the standard creation process, the impact it has on the standard outcome, as well as the ability of your company to create the "gold standard" products for purposes of interoperability creates the perception of your company as a leader in this new market.

Creating an industry alliance

In my professional life, I used three different ways to drive industry consensus and create the desired ecosystem around an offering. Those include creating an *informal industry alliance,* adopting an existing *industry trade association (ITA)* or *standard development organization (SDO)* venue, or creating a *formal new industry association.*

Adopting an existing SDO/ITA

Advantages of adopting an existing SDO/ITA
- The costs associated with an already-existing organization are minimal, and typically involve only paying membership fees.

- The organization already has established processes, structure, and mechanisms to deliver the desired results, saving a lot of time in reaching them.

- There is a possibility of "economies of scale" and "economies of scope" in leveraging similar processes and tools to achieve the goals of the new initiative, if it is similar enough to the existing ones and previous work done by the existing organization.

- Using the existing infrastructure and processes may allow achieving the goals quicker and allows focusing on the subject matter (or "substance") rather than procedural issues (such as the setup of the organization, membership recruitment, and so on).

- The organization may already be credible and have market and industry visibility, and therefore "lends" that visibility and credibility to the new initiative. The IEEE 802 project is one example of an existing organization with established credibility and visibility. This organization delivered successful technologies such as Ethernet (802.3), Wireless Local Area Networking (802.11, or Wi-Fi), short range technologies (the Bluetooth specification was adopted by IEEE 802 as 802.15), and Wireless Metropolitan Area Networking (802.16, and WiMAX). Even fourth-generation cellular technologies are trying to leverage the IEEE 802 project credibility in forming 802.20.

- The organization may already have the target membership list (or as close to it as possible) as members, which will make new member recruitment unnecessary. It may offer a very valuable industry representation available to the new initiative from the get go.

- The organization most likely already has an established intellectual property rights (IPR) policy that protects any intellectual property (IP) introduced into the organization by members or created by the organization.

Disadvantages of adopting an existing SDO/ITA
- An existing organization comes with an existing set of members. Some of those members might be uninterested in the new initiatives, and some might oppose the new technology seeking industry support. This may cause delay in achieving the desired objectives, or even prevent reaching them at all. The "battle over ultra-wideband" is a perfect example. Using the IEEE as a venue to standardize the technology (as IEEE 802.15.3a), two opposing camps emerged. Texas Instruments and Intel led one and Freescale led the other. Over a period of three years, while using the IEEE process, the standardization efforts reached an impasse, eventually leading to the disbandment of the task group and the IEEE as a venue.[167]

- The existing organization might not be perfectly suited to the new technology. There might not be a fit between the deliverables required for the new alliance and the processes in place by the existing organization.

- The existing processes of the organization might, at times, be cumbersome and cause unnecessary delays in delivering the desired results. Those processes might be rigid and not easily changed (or at all) to support the required agility of the new technology. A significant number of existing members may require processes be more complex and accommodate a large number of members, whereas only a small number of members will be interested in the new organization, to which simpler and faster processes might be more appropriate.

- There might not be a *founder* or *sponsor* membership class in existence or available to the founding members of the new initiative. Therefore, even though the "founders" of the new initiative may want to be driving industry consensus, they will have less ability to do so. Furthermore, the existing organization might already have a *sponsor* membership class that is not available to the founders of the new initiative, which will place the "old" sponsors in the driver's seat of the new technology, and put the "new" sponsors of the new technology in the passenger seat, with much less control than if they could attain *sponsorship* status.

- Sometimes, the founders of the new initiative might have a different view of the IPR protection sought for the new initiative compared with those offered by the existing organization. Changing the IPR policy is one of the hardest actions to take within an existing organization; it might cause significant membership attrition.

<u>When best to adopt an existing SDO/ITA</u>
- When an organization (be it a standard development organization or an industry trade association) exists, such that it addresses relatively *similar objectives* as the ones sought by the new initiative. This is why almost all networking technologies adopted the IEEE 802 project, as those new technologies have many similarities with existing technologies, and, therefore, require similar processes and structure to deliver relatively similar deliverables to the ones already delivered by this organization.

- When the existing organization is *scalable* to support new initiatives. The existing organization might be limited in official scope (through bylaws or an unchangeable mission statement), in its ability to support new membership, in its processes and structure that might not allow new initiative support, or by the focus of the existing membership, unable to take on a new initiative.

- When there is a relatively high level of *correlation* between the target *membership* of the new initiative and the current membership of the existing organization. This correlation will assure swift progress due to alignment of interests.

- When the IPR policy is in line with the IP protection sought by the founders of the new initiative.

Forming a formal industry alliance

Advantages of forming a formal industry alliance
- The organization is tailor-made to the specific mission that led to its founding. No tradeoffs occur in order to achieve the exact goals of the new initiative. Membership recruitment begins from scratch, offering a precise representation of member companies interested in the new initiative.

- A *formal* industry alliance (as opposed to an *informal* one) offers the protection that a legal entity offers its members. It offers a degree of separation between the organization and its members, and offers some antitrust liability exposure reduction by having antitrust policies in place.

- A new organization will *focus* on the new initiative, without any "legacy" work items that might distract from that new focus. It does not suffer from existing "baggage" associated with previous initiatives that require ongoing support and maintenance. That focus allows the delivery of results in a faster manner.

- With the new organization focused on a very specific initiative, the visibility to industry and media is dedicated. The organization will avoid confusing the media with existing activities, and will deliver a clear message.

- Not having an existing membership structure, or even potentially an existing *sponsor* membership class to which the founders of the new initiative may not have access, allows the founders of the new technology to be in control of the direction of the organization. Even the new *members at large* will have more control over this organization when existing members with less interest in the new initiative do not mitigate or delay their actions.

- The exact IPR protection and policy sought by the founders of the new technology will take effect, without the need for a compromise with an existing IPR policy, or the lack of an IPR policy that characterizes an informal organization.

Disadvantages of forming a formal industry alliance
- The expenses associated with creating a new industry organization are the highest of all three alternatives. The setup fee is considerable. There is no existing management and infrastructure to leverage to support the new initiative and it all has to start from scratch.

- With no infrastructure in place, you will spend a significant amount of effort, resources, and time establishing the organization, rather than going straight to work on the deliverables for which the organization is to be established. Even once the organization is past the formation phase (which might last longer than envisioned), a significant part of the founders' time and efforts must be dedicated to procedural items rather than the deliverables for which the organization was established. Things like membership meetings, member recruitment, press coverage, policy creation, and other procedural activities take the place of creating substantive deliverables.

- The organization does not have an already established credibility and industry and media visibility. Those items take a long time to establish. In spite of significant efforts to establish them, the organization might never achieve that goal. Many organizations never reached the credibility and visibility required for industry success, and they fell into oblivion. An alternative to *organization-based* credibility is *founder-based* credibility. Start an organization with a few small start-up companies and you will find it extremely hard to achieve industry credibility. Start an organization with Intel, Microsoft, Dell, Texas Instruments, Nokia, Motorola, Sony,

Cisco, Hewlett-Packard and the like, and your organization gets immediate credibility, visibility, and coverage due to the players involved.

When to form a formal industry alliance

- When a large number of members plan to participate in this initiative and take an active role in creating the deliverables, creating an alliance with a large number of active players without formalizing it with processes, policies, legal, and operational structure would be insane.

- The higher the level of member interaction required, the more formal the organization structure needs to be. High levels of interaction require parliamentary procedures to be in place, mailing lists and associated logistics to exist, and membership meetings (face to face, videoconferences, teleconferences, and others) will have to take place in a formal manner.

- The longer the list of deliverables for this new initiative, the more formal you will need to make the creation process. You will need to set priorities, create the organizational structure (committees, working groups, task groups, tiger teams) that can support creating a wide range of deliverables. You will also need formal processes and policies in place to achieve the deliverables as envisioned.

- If the objectives are such that they will take more than a year to achieve, it is better to formalize the creation process. The longer it takes to reach the objectives and create the deliverables, the higher is the probability that an informal organization will go sideways and uncertainties and lack of clarity will set in. Over a long period, membership changes, company interests change, the marketplace changes along with the overall business environment, and only a formal organization structure can maintain consistency.

- Driving the direction of an organization works best when organized by a small group of *sponsor* members, often serving on the board of directors of the organization. The more different the new initiative is from other initiatives already handled by existing organizations, the better it is to create a new organization with a *sponsor* member core group and board of directors driving it in the desired direction. An informal organization will not have such a core group.

- When the founding company list includes brand names that provide "instant credibility" to the new organization, a new organization will be appropriate. If, on the other hand, small, unknown companies promote the new initiative or technology, they will not add credibility or visibility to the organization and will have to fight long until such credibility and visibility occur.

- When IPR protection is important, a formal organization (whether existing or new) is required, one that has an IPR policy that addresses the desired level and type of protection. IPR protection will not be available through an informal organization. If an existing organization is considered, but the IPR terms are not favorable or preferred by the founding members of the new initiative, then the existing organization will not be an appropriate venue for this initiative, and only a brand new *formal* organization will be appropriate.

Creating an informal industry alliance

Advantages of creating an informal industry alliance
- Much like the *formal* alliance, the *informal* alliance targets specific goals and objectives as defined, and does not suffer from incompatibilities with existing organizations.

- The *informal* alliance achieves better focus on the specific deliverables than even the *formal* alliance, as no attention is required to procedures, logistics, and operations of the organization, simply because the *informal* alliance is not an official organization or a legal entity. This increased focus allows creating the deliverables in a faster manner without distractions.

- The *informal* organization is the most inexpensive to operate. No management services are required, and no external services (legal, accounting) are needed. All expenses come out of member companies' pockets, but no funding is required to maintain a legal entity. Keep in mind that approximately 25%-30% of the organization's budget (and therefore membership fees) will support management expenses.

Disadvantages of creating an informal industry alliance

- An *informal* alliance does not provide the legal separation between the organization entity and the membership entity. If any legal actions arise against this *collaboration of members*, they will involve the members themselves, without the protection of an official legal entity, which is typically (to some extent) separate from its members.

- One of the biggest challenges is the potential antitrust liability exposure of such an informal organization. Lacking an official antitrust policy, non-members can claim *collusion* and *anticompetitive behavior* by the participants of this association.

- An informal alliance might not have the desired structure and tools in place to support complex missions. Developing specifications, for example, is a very complex mission that requires putting tools, structure, discipline, and processes into place, and an informal alliance finds it very hard to establish those. It is not impossible, but typically, one company will have to be the provider of those services on a voluntary basis. Intel is famous for driving such activities and providing the infrastructure for initiatives such as USB, PCI, S-ATA and a few others. Lacking such a champion member will prevent the informal organization from completing complex tasks.

- The control and workload might be unevenly distributed since it lacks formal processes, policies, and structure. In the examples above, Intel carries the majority of the workload associated with driving the new initiative, but also enjoys a disproportionate (large) influence over the direction.

- An informal organization lacks the credibility of a formal organization or a well-established one. There is no doubt that adding "instant credibility" brand names as members would enhance credibility but, overall, the perceived lack of commitment by not formalizing the effort into a formal entity will hurt.

- Where IPR protection is important, the informal organization will suffer significantly from its inability to protect those rights. Not being a formal, legally binding organization will take away that protection. Multiparty agreements between companies can address IPR protection, but they will not be as enforceable as an IPR policy that is part of an official formal and legally binding organization.

When to create an informal industry alliance

- When only a small number of members plan to participate in driving the new initiative to the completion of its objectives, an informal industry alliance, governed by multiparty agreements might be enough.

- A low level of member interaction will not require the infrastructure, policies, and processes that an informal organization might not be able to provide.

- A short and limited scope of objectives can be manageable by an informal organization without special structures in place. Sometimes organizations develop to promote a technology in the marketplace through promotional activities only. An informal alliance will suffice to achieve such goals. However, when it comes to creating specification, the scope is large enough that it will not be manageable by an informal alliance. The same applies to time-bound (typically less than one year) activities. Such activities do not require the consistency and stability of a formal organization, whereas activities that will last longer will require one.

- When no one expects that *members will contribute* intellectual property or the organization itself will not develop intellectual property, IPR protection is not required, and an informal alliance will suffice. However, one must be very careful making this assumption, as companies may realize that IP was inadvertently contributed or developed and will seek protection of such IP. The founding members must be certain that no one will contribute IP and the organization will not develop IP. This will preclude the need for developing an IPR policy.

Summary of forms of alliances

Type of venue	Advantages	Disadvantages	When to use
Using an existing SDO/ITA	• Less costly (if any) • Established processes and structure • Possible "economies of scale" • May expedite creation of international standards • Allows focus on substance rather than procedure • Access to wide membership base and industry representation • Known, credible, and visible organization • Established IPR policy	• Might allow non-interested members to slow down process • Might not be perfectly suited for the specific objectives • Process might be too cumbersome to achieve goals in a timely manner • No "founder" or "sponsor" member status • Less "control" over process and results • Potentially undesired IPR policy	• Organization exists that addresses relatively similar objectives • Organization is scalable • Relatively similar "player set" • IPR policy in line with objectives
Formal industry alliance	• Customized and optimized to the specific mission • Provides legal entity protection • Creates industry focus and better visibility • Relatively quick to deliver desired results • More "control" by *sponsor* members and members at large • IPR protection	• Costly • Time consuming (with procedural activities) • Lack of existing credibility or visibility	• Large number of members expected • High level of member interaction • Long list of objectives • Objectives are non-time-bound, or expected to last more than one year • "Founder" or "sponsor" member status is required • IPR protection is important and not offered by existing organizations • Founder list include "instant credibility" companies and market-makers
Informal industry alliance	• Customized to specific mission • Allows best focus on objectives • The fastest in delivering desired results • Relatively inexpensive	• Does not provide legal entity protection • Lacking structure to achieve complex objectives • Higher potential antitrust exposure • Lack of credibility or visibility • Lack of IPR protection • Control and workload might be unevenly distributed	• Small/finite number of members expected • Low level of member interaction • Short/limited scope of objectives • Time-bound objectives, less than one year • IPR protection is not important

Figure 43—Comparison of alliances alternatives

Intellectual Property Rights (IPR)

There is nothing like a good disclaimer to kick off this section. Do not rely on the advice I will give you in this part. You must consult with an IP attorney or legal counsel to decide what IPR protection you need and should pursue in the alliance you are seeking to create.

Companies are seeing more and more value in intellectual property (IP) they develop in-house. In fact, some companies make this a strategy to develop IP. In the late 1990s, a whole industry for IP developed (mostly in the Silicon Valley in California) around the trading of IP. IP equaled a revenue stream made of licensing fees and royalties. A significant group of companies established as their sole business model licensing IP. The vast majority of them did not manage to turn this into a sustainable business and disappeared into the history pages. Companies like BOPS, who developed DSP IP, did not make it. A few did. ARM, a UK processor IP company is a successful example. In 2005, its revenue was in excess of 230 million pounds (of which 45% originated in licensing fees and 38% in royalties), posted a profit of more than 40 million pounds, after its customers shipped almost 1.7 billion products based on ARM IP.[168] No doubt that ARM's dominance in licensing IP into the cellular phone market was a dramatic contributing factor to that success.

In comparison, their key competitor, MIPS Technologies (Mountain View, California), generated revenue in 2005 of just under $30 million, less than 10% of ARM's revenue. There is no doubt that in the IP industry there is a "gorilla" player (ARM), a far second (MIPS), and a long list of failures.

Another example of a company that has IP as a key part of its strategy is Qualcomm, with $1.9 billion in revenue from licensing and royalties of its CDMA technology, representing 32% of its overall revenue in 2005, and by far the largest revenue generated from IP licensing by a single company.

For most companies, or at least most large companies, the IP strategy is a *defensive* one. Semiconductor companies develop IP only to incorporate it into their integrated circuits. Product companies develop IP to integrate it into their products. They do not develop the IP so they can license it to other companies and generate a revenue stream from licensing fees or royalties. A *defensive* IP strategy aims to maintain the rights to that IP so that if another company holds IP it can incorporate into the products the first company is developing; the IP held by both companies will be *cross-licensed* rather than used offensively.

IPR policies are not very complicated. Of course, that is not what the IP attorneys will tell you. They do get contentious, though, and there is a lot of vested interest in protecting company IP, be it for *defensive* purposes or *offensive* ones. There are several degrees of freedom in IPR agreements:

- What are the licensing terms of the Intellectual Property Rights? The most common term is *reasonable and non-discriminatory* (RAND). The IP contributed will be licensed to the licensees on a reasonable basis as well as a non-discriminatory basis. *Reasonable* basis means that the licensing fees and royalties will be reasonable. This is a somewhat vague term, and different companies will interpret *reasonable* differently. Some will consider *reasonable* royalties as 5% of the cost of the integrated circuit in which the IP was included. If the IC sells for $5, this will represent 25 cents. Others might consider *reasonable* royalties as 5% of the selling price of the end product in which the technology is embedded. For a $100 cell phone, 5% is $5, or twenty times higher than the previous definition of *reasonable. Non-discriminatory* means that companies will experience no discrimination when licensing the same technology from the same company under the *same circumstances.* However, defining *same circumstances* is tricky. Asking different levels of royalties for the same technology from two different licensees (say 5% from one and 10% from the other) sounds *discriminatory.* However, if there are *different circumstances* for both licensees, licensing the same technology (such as different volume or multiple licensing deals with the same licensor) that lead to different licensing fees and royalty rates will not suggest *discriminatory* licensing policy.

- What is the scope of licensing? Is it global? Is it geographically limited? Who gets the license? Is it only to other member companies of the same organization, or is it to the whole wide world? In organizations such as the Wi-Fi Alliance, the WiMedia Alliance, and the Mobile DTV Alliance, just to name a few, IP owners license their technology only to other member companies who, in turn, license their own IP to all members. In organizations such as ECMA, IEEE, ETSI, and TIA, member companies license their IP to the whole wide world, whether the licensee is a member of the organization or not. Furthermore, will you grant the license to your IP to a single implementation of it, or will you allow many? Will you allow *modifications* to the IP by the licensee?

- When will companies be entitled to become licensees? In some organizations, member (or non-member) companies become licensees of the protected technology simply by being members (or not even by being members). In some organizations, in an effort to enforce interoperability certification of products according to the specifications, the license is granted upon interoperability certification of the products. The Wi-Fi Alliance and the Bluetooth organizations are two examples.

Is it important to note that IPR policies typically cover *essential* IP? The definition of *essential IP* is typically "IP that is essential to the implementation of any of the mandatory parts of the specifications created by the organization." Let us assume that Company A holds all the IP rights to a specific technology. Let us further assume that the company is a member of the organization and bound by its IPR policy. The specifications call for the use of this technology as a mandatory feature. Any company that implements this mandatory feature violates the IP rights of Company A. However, under the IPR policy the company will receive a license to this IP. Another possibility is that the technology owned by Company A is essential to the implementation of an *optional* part of the specifications. In this case, companies implementing this optional feature will not enjoy the licensing terms of the IPR policy. Yet another possibility is that the technology owned by Company A is not essential to the implementation of any part of the specifications created by the organization (*mandatory* or *optional*). The technology might offer a more competitive way to make products according to the specifications, but there can be other ways to make such products, albeit not as competitive. Since the specifications do not call for the use of this technology in the implementation of the specification-based products, other members will not receive licenses for the technology.

Antitrust

Once again, I offer the same disclaimer. Do not treat the following text as legal antitrust advice. You should seek formal legal advice on antitrust behavior. Treat the following, at best, as a warning.

When I started looking for founding partners to create the Mobile DTV Alliance, I was "invited" to Ted McGehee's office. Ted is a Texas Instruments lawyer. He is not what you would expect from a lawyer. He drives a black Corvette and sometimes reminds me of Jack Nicholson in "A Few Good Men." In a three-hour conversation (although, at the time, it felt more like a colonoscopy), he gave me the "lay of the land" from an antitrust perspective. He told me what I should do and not do when forming an organization. I have to admit I learned a lot from that conversation—and what I learned I implemented.

One thing to keep in mind is that you can really get into trouble for taking anticompetitive steps or violating antitrust laws. The more potential there is for the technology you are introducing and to the market that it addresses, the more sensitive companies are to not having "equal footing" with all other companies. Anticompetitive claims can result from many actions, but essentially are driven by companies (outside or even inside the organization) feeling disenfranchised by the cooperation of the other companies. A company might claim that the organization did not invite it to join and, therefore, the other companies formed a "coalition" that was anticompetitive.

You should always remember that you are forming an industry alliance as a "pre-competitive cooperation" venue, and not as a tool to gain advantage over your competitors. That's how you might get into trouble.

Creating the organization

How do you create a formal industry alliance? I have witnessed the creation of several formal industry alliances/organizations, and even formed one myself, the Mobile DTV Alliance. I will use it as a way to convey the process details.

The first step was to decide on the type of alliance I needed to create. It started with defining the preliminary mission and objectives of the organization. While the mission and objectives often changed several times until the organization was officially and formally created, I had to start with something. Learning from other industries (WiMAX, Wi-Fi, GSM and others), I knew I would have three major objectives:

- Promoting the technology and the cooperation of a multitude of companies around an open standard
- Developing *recommended practices* in the deployment of this technology
- Creating an interoperability program that assured that all components of an end-to-end system would work together, even if each part was made by a different company.

As described above, there were three alternatives: using an existing organization, creating an informal alliance, or creating a formal one. The first step was to choose the right alternative. Considering the criteria listed in Figure 43, I thought the best thing would be to form a *formal alliance*. I expected a significant number of members to participate, as more than one hundred companies supported the standard (DVB-H) that was the underlying basis for this alliance. Given the need to develop recommended practices and an interoperability program, I expected the level of interaction to be relatively high. I did not believe I could accomplish this work in less than one year.

The second step in creating the alliance was to identify the *core* companies that would constitute the *founder group*, sometimes called the *sponsor* companies, and typically constituting the initial *board of directors*. In selecting this group, I would recommend selecting five to eight companies. This group needs to represent a critical mass of well-diversified players in the ecosystem in which your product needs to participate. You must keep in mind that there is a possibility that no additional companies will participate, and that the selected participants constitute a strong enough body of support for the ecosystem. I recommend that at the same time you make sure you do not leave out a critical mass of companies that might create an opposing organization simply because you did not include them. When you look at the HD-DVD vs. Blu-Ray initiatives, you can't help but wonder why none of these groups ensured they reached a critical mass of support that would allow only one of those standards to exist. At the same time, if you are in a fragmented market and ecosystem, you may not be able to achieve such critical mass. Why five to eight founding companies? With fewer than five companies, you run the risk of an ecosystem representation that is not robust enough. With more than eight companies, you run the risk of not being able to move forward due to "analysis paralysis." It is hard to achieve consensus with more than eight members. Another consideration for me was choosing a group of market-makers that would provide "instant credibility" to the newly formed organization. Since we built this organization from the ground up, that credibility was important. The companies I identified for the *core group* were Texas Instruments, Nokia, Motorola, Intel, Microsoft, and Modeo. I initially had individual meetings with each company to share the idea and understand its goals. To me, this group represented the critical mass of the required ecosystem. Nokia and Motorola represented almost 60% of the cell phones sold worldwide. Intel and Texas Instruments represented a significant share of cell phone, PDA, and PC integrated circuit manufacturers. Microsoft represented an operating system giant as well as media transport provider. Modeo, a spin off from Crown Castle International, represented an infrastructure player who owned spectrum committed for DVB-H deployment.

Throughout those individual meetings, I concluded that all six companies shared a vision and the objectives and would, therefore, be a good, representative, robust *core founder group.*

This is the time to address the fact that the group includes competitors. While writing this book, the Alliance is made of almost forty companies, many of which are competitors. Why would competitors be cooperating in such an industry alliance? The answer is similar to the reason that semiconductor manufacturers cooperate in solving the hurdles in maintaining the Moore's law curve and the reason that hard disk drive manufacturers cooperate in solving barriers in the hard disk drive industry. If this cooperation did not exist, there would be no market to compete over. Fierce competitors cooperate in the *pre-competition* phase to create a market in which they will later compete.

The following step was to get all six companies to meet in one place and openly discuss the creation of the Alliance. Intel hosted that meeting in its offices in Santa Clara, California. There was a lot of tension in the meeting while each participant tried to "feel out" the other participants, to assure that this alliance was really the right thing to do, and that the objectives of all participants were truly in alignment. By the end of the meeting, we managed to draft a letter of intentions, and we set out to create the Alliance as an official and legal entity. The process of creating the entity and operating it was quite complex, and unless you intend to use a full-time experienced person to conduct it, you should use professionals. There are companies with the experience in setting up and operating such organizations. I turned to a company I knew fairly well, Global Inventures,[169] in San Ramon, California. These experts were handling other industry alliances too. There is no doubt, they represented an excellent example of *economies of scale*. With a team of close to forty people, they operated fifteen industry organizations, giving each organization services equal to several full-time employees. The services included legal and accounting services (typically using external legal counsel), account management, assigned executive director, event management, membership services, Web site presence, and much, much more. You would be amazed at the level of small details associated with every move the organization makes, and a company like Global Inventures makes it happen for a nominal fee. In the early days of every organization, hiring such a firm makes a lot of sense, and you want to hire a firm that has the experience with the type of technology and markets you are addressing. Global Inventures, for example, had previous experience with organizations such as WiMedia, the SD-Card Association, the ZigBee Alliance, and quite a few more. The Bluetooth SIG and the Wi-Fi Alliances started in the same way, using management companies. As they turned into much larger organizations with significantly higher budgets, as well as greater need for additional, more customized and market-specific services, they hired staff and moved away from management companies. In the early stages, though, a management company takes a lot of the logistical "headache" from the founders and lets them focus on the mission of the alliance.

After agreeing on the initial set of principles for the new Mobile DTV Alliance, the six founders went on to establish the foundation for the organization. We agreed on a mission, sponsor member agreements,[170] management agreement with Global Inventures, and all the legal documents required to officially and legally form this entity. On January 17, 2006, we held a formation board meeting to officially launch this Alliance, for the directors to take their official positions on the board, and for the officers (president, vice president, treasurer, secretary) to assume their statutory duties. The first two goals were to announce the formation of the organization, and to start the recruitment of new members. A week later, on January 23, during the National Association of Television Program Executives (NATPE) conference in Las Vegas, we announced the organization to the world. By March 1, we started accepting new member applications.

Impact on industry through participation

In general, a participant in the industry will have an impact on this industry and the market for the products and technologies in it. In my years of experience in industry participation, I have seen different people make different types of impact on the industry. Figure 44 describes graphically four types of possible impact.

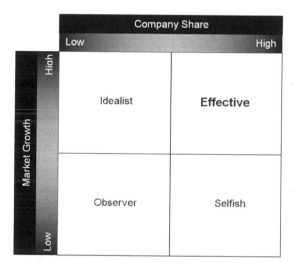

Figure 44—Impact on the industry through participation

A participant's impact on the industry is a transitional one. Before that participation, or impact, the industry is at a certain size and growth trajectory. The participant represents a company and its interests in this industry, and before the *participation effect*, it has a certain market share and position within this market. The participant's participation will affect both—the market growth and the growth of its company's share in that market.

Figure 44 shows two dimensions of impact: market growth and company share. The four types of industry participants (people, not companies) appear in positions in this chart according to the impact they have on both dimensions.

The least effective participation (and thus impact) on the market is achieved by the participant I call *observer*. That participant does not affect the growth of the market, nor does he affect the market share of his own company in this market. This is attributable to several possible reasons: lack of interest in revenue from this market, lack of reciprocal impact of this market on the company, or simply lack of effectiveness in affecting the total market or the company's market share. Assuming that all participants in this market/industry behave in a similar way, this market will not grow and the distribution of wealth in this market will not change, making this market unattractive.

I call the second type of participant *selfish*. This participant cares only for and affects his own company's share in the market. He will not participate in activities that grow the overall market. He will be effective in growing his company's share in this market, but only as a *zero-sum game*.[171] Without growing the total available market, such behavior and impact will cause the market to be much more competitive. If the market does not grow, the only way to grow revenue in the market will be at the expense of other competitors, which leads to fierce competition.

Often you find the third type, the *idealist*, representing the company in industry organizations. They "suffer" from a syndrome known as S4, or the *System Standards Stockholm Syndrome*. It describes the behavior of participants in standard development organizations that become "hostages" to the technology, the market, the organization itself. In the process, they lose sight of their company's interests in their participation. Such a participant will do everything in her power to assure growth of the total available market, without growing her company's share in the process. These participants become very friendly with their competitors, and create a very positive market development atmosphere. In the early stages of the technology and market development, such behavior is acceptable. The market has to grow to make it attractive, and only once the market is attractive will it become competitive as different companies seek to gain market share at the expense of their competitors. Once the market becomes competitive, however, those *idealist* participants will discover that they have not secured a competitive foothold in this market for their company and will essentially let their competition win this market. Intel, in several markets, sent participants as *idealists* in different industry organizations as a strategy. For Intel, the growth of these markets could have had an indirect impact on their business. Take Intel's participation in the Wi-Fi Alliance (promoting wireless local area networking), for example. When Intel started participating in promoting this market, I was puzzled. Intel is in the business of selling processors for hundreds of dollars each, making some 60% gross profit on them. Why would they all of a sudden be so interested in growing a market for $10 components with 40% gross profit? To further my surprise, Intel launched a $300 million market-development program called

Centrino, aimed at promoting technologies such as Wi-Fi and others. Then it dawned on me: Intel was not interested in the Wi-Fi market as a market. It was interested in this market as a reason for people to buy more laptop and mobile computers rather than desktop computers. There is no doubt, with Internet becoming the major use of a computer, that wireless networking will be a major enabler for mobile computers. Assuring that the wireless networking (Wi-Fi included in it, along with other technologies such as WiMAX) market grows would mean that consumers (and companies) would buy more laptop computers and be able to connect them wirelessly to the Internet. In fact, if you saw the Centrino commercials, they do not focus on a specific type of technology, but rather on the fact that the laptop computer can be portable and still be connected to the Internet. In early 2003, when Intel launched the Centrino program, the price of a mobile Pentium processor was close to $700. At the same time, the price of a desktop Pentium was just about $200. Assuming 60% gross profit, any computer purchase that will be a laptop computer rather than a desktop computer will mean $300 profit more for Intel. Manage to switch one million computer users[172] from buying a desktop to buying a laptop computer, and you will have recovered the $300m invested in the Centrino program. Any additional computer buyer beyond the first one million will create pure profit. Intel was not interested in the revenue it could generate from the Wi-Fi market. What drove Intel's commitment to grow this market was a benefit external to this market—the shift in demand from desktop to laptop computers due to the increased mobility provided by the new wireless technology. Intel's participants in the Wi-Fi market played the *idealist*, focusing only on the market growth.

If there is one bit of advice I would like you to take when you are about to participate in a market and affect it, it would be, "be *effective*." Being effective means assuring two things simultaneously: grow the market and grow your company's share in the market. From an overall revenue growth perspective, there is nothing that compares to double growth. Assume there is a market with a total size (in revenue dollars) of $1 billion. Further, assume that your company's share is 25% of this market, thus generating $250m in revenue. If this market grew 20% the following year while your company maintained the same market share, your company's revenue will grow 20% to $300m. That will be the result of playing the *idealist* strategy. If you focused only on growing your company's share, at the expense of efforts to grow the overall market, and assuming you grew share from 25% to 30%, theoretically, your company's revenue will grow to $300m. However, when a market stops growing, the intensity of rivalry within the market grows. This typically leads to price pressures, often so that price erosion takes away from incremental revenue due to market share growth. The market share growth might have been accompanied by a 10% price decline overall in the market, and thus revenue growth would go only to $270m rather than $300m. This would be the result of implementing the *selfish* strategy. However, if you play the *effective* strategy, and assuming you will help the overall market grow 20% and your company's share grows from 25% to 30%, your company's revenue will grow from the original $250m to $360m. Most likely, price erosion will not compensate for this, as it is less common in growing markets compared to stagnant markets.

It is worth mentioning that the different types of participation have different impacts in the various stages of the market development. In Figure 45, I reviewed the impact that the different strategies will have on the market growth and company share, depending on the two main market stages, infancy and maturity:

Market Stage	Observer	Selfish	Idealist	Effective
Infancy	No impact on the market. In fact, during the infancy stage, observers might lead to the market never developing. Markets in their infancy stage require a lot of nurturing.	The company will win share in early market, but without growing the market, or delaying its growth. It might turn to be futile as the market might never leave infancy.	The market will grow to exit its infancy stage, but with the company not establishing a foothold in the market. It will be hard for this company to gain market share later, although the competitors will be grateful for the efforts.	The market will grow while the company will establish a significant foothold that will translate into a major market share and revenue when the market reaches maturity.
Maturity	There is not impact on the market, although the market does exist. If the market stops growing – the company may loose share due to intensifying competition and decrease revenue due to eroding prices.	If the market does not grow – the competition will intensify, most likely causing price declines. The company may win market share, but revenue and profitability may be impacted by price declines	You might be the only one helping the market to grow, while all other participants (competitors) are eying your market share, which will erode. Market maturity is time of intensifying competition, even if the market grows moderately.	While the market is growing in a moderate rate, you may be addressing new and adjacent markets, in which you may want to establish foothold for your company. As long as the market keeps growing, prices will only moderately erode. You enjoy share growth and market growth.

Figure 45—Impact on the industry in different maturity phases

---

[166] IEEE rules require 75% of all voters to vote in support of a standard draft before it can become a standard.

[167] The Texas Instruments and Intel camp adopted another existing ITA, the WiMedia Alliance, where this technology reached maturity. The Freescale camp created a competing ITA, called the "UWB Forum,"

to promote the competing technology. In early 2006, Freescale finally abandoned the technology and the organization.

[168] From ARM PLC 2005 Annual Report.

[169] www.inventures.com.

[170] The six founders held a "sponsor" membership level, higher than the "contributor" and "associate" levels, and had the right to place a board member.

[171] The term *zero-sum game* comes from *game theory*, and represents a strategic result in which the overall "good" is not growing, and only the distribution of such "good" changes. For someone to win (in this example – for the participant's company's share to grow) someone has to lose (in this example – the market share of all other companies).

[172] It is estimated that in 2005 there were 128m desktop computers purchased, and 50m laptop computers. Converting 1m desktop buyers represents less than 1% of desktop computer buyers. The potential in 2005 was to convert 128m desktop computer purchasers to laptops, generating a potential incremental profit of $38 billion.

Chapter 17
Passion, Persuasion, Perception, And Hype

Passion and conviction

You've heard the phrase "If it's worth doing, it's worth doing it right." Well, I modified it a little to, "If it's worth doing, it's worth doing it right, *and with passion.*"

During the early days of a new disruptive technology, you need to be a believer, and you need to make believers out of everyone who may touch this technology. The easiest approach is to start your own company and fund it yourself. You don't have to convince anyone of the value of the new technology or disruptive implementation until you have a product or a service you can show, and preferably sell. However, in today's high-tech world, the investment required is beyond the means of almost everyone but a few billionaires who can afford to make such investments, and even *they* won't. The other alternative is to start a company and raise money from investors. You will have to convince them that their investment will multiply itself by an order of magnitude within the next four years. Be careful; they have seen many great ideas crash and burn—some because they were not such great ideas. Some were great ideas, but for a small market. Some were great ideas for a large market, but did not get the industry support to make them happen, while competing technologies emerged and "stole" the market from underneath them. It is not going to be easy to convince the venture capital industry to invest in your venture. The more disruptive it is, the harder it gets.

Finally, you can try to convince the *Fortune 500* company you work at right now to invest in this idea. You may be facing the greatest challenge here. In those companies, the term *seniority* still matters. People want to keep their jobs until retirement. Retirement benefits are great if you work for such a company. You do not want to "rock the boat" (and believe me, pushing disruptive technologies *will* rock the boat) when you work there. You want smooth sailing. You do not mind entering the market late and missing the great opportunities associated with being first. You can be risk-averse and still make it to your company's *top 10* list,[173] and you can be driving risky new ventures, and even when those are successful, you might find yourself in the *bottom 10* list, and out of the company. I walked that line many times at Texas Instruments and at PCTEL.

Either way, you have a very tall tree to climb. You have to make believers out of people who simply do not share your vision, or are simply afraid of rocking the boat. You need to find "partners" in this company who are willing to rock the boat with you. Sometimes it is simply that the company (or business unit) cannot afford to invest in new ventures while maintaining the profitability goals set by higher management.

You can't begin to convince others until you are convinced yourself. This would be a perfect time for you to stop and ask if you believe in your idea. Ask yourself if you are pragmatic enough in analyzing the opportunity, and how it will materialize. Then, do the right thing for the company. Even if the company doesn't believe in it. Yet.

Persuasion

Once you are convinced, it is time to convince others. One evening I attended a meeting of the Dallas chapter of the Association for Strategic Planning.[174] The meeting was interesting and exciting and discussed the accountability of the strategic planner for the success of the idea he was pushing. The 1980s strategic planner was someone who had performed the situational analysis, assessed the market, proposed the technology, typed a nicely formatted report, and his accountability ended there. "You can lead a horse to water, but you can't make it drink." I don't agree with this statement. You can make it impossible for the horse to do anything else. If you think that drinking is important to this horse—*make it drink!* I expect this kind of accountability from the modern twenty-first century strategic planner.

In that meeting, one of the strategic planners, very respected, suggested that you can convince your investors (internal or external) only by using facts and figures. Others argued with her. Perhaps the strongest argument against her position was that in such an early stage of a new technology, a new market, or a new product, there are not too many facts to use. There can be analysis, there can be assumptions, but there are not a lot of facts. The market can skyrocket, or it can stall.

One thing for sure, it is non-existent at this point, so anyone's guess is valid. The argument quickly shifted toward whether the persuasion skills of the strategic planner had any value. I believed they had *all* the value. I don't believe you can convince anyone of the *huge* potential of the new technology if you are not passionate.

However, being passionate will not be a substitute for facts, solid data, and a strong plausible theory of success. You should base a theory of success on previous successes with obvious parallels. When you analyze the potential growth, adoption, and timing of a market, I recommend you use other markets with similar characteristics. Make sure you observe what is *similar* and what is *different* between the market and technology you are predicting, and the empirical model you are using.

Remember one thing—the people you are trying to convince consider you reckless, irresponsible, and as completely disregarding risks. Sometimes your passion comes across as avoiding the facts and those risks. The more detailed your plan is and the closer your theory of success is to an undisputable historical success of another technology, the more credible and convincing it will be to your audience.

While this chapter focused thus far on the investors, inside and outside your company, you need to remember that you will need to convince others. These people do not need to make investments as great as those you need from your investors, but they are still essential for the success of the new product. They are the future customers, suppliers, and other ecosystem players. You will need to have those in place, as the new product or technology cannot exist in a vacuum. You will need to convince others that they need to help you.

Hype vs. reality

Gartner, a leading industry analysis firm, coined the term *The Hype Cycle* in 1995.[175] Ever since, it has mapped different technologies according to their position within that hype cycle.

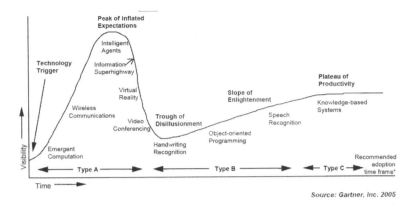

Source: Gartner, Inc. 2005

Figure 46—The Gartner Hype Cycle for Emerging Technologies, 1995

The hype cycle, simply put, represents the level of visibility and expectations that an emerging technology receives. An emerging technology always starts with a very low level of visibility. During the *introduction* phase, it receives great visibility, and expectations are inflated. A company positions the new technology to perform miracles and address many needs of many markets. It can be everything for everyone. Once the company puts the new technology into practice, the reality sinks in, and the decline in expectations sometimes undershoots the real value of the technology. Following the *trough of disillusionment*, expectations rise again to the real expected performance and value of the new technology, through the *slope of enlightenment* to the *plateau of productivity*.

The higher the *peak of inflated expectations* is, the harder the fall to the *trough of disillusionment* is, possibly even to the point of no return, when the new technology will sink into oblivion. In my early days with the Wi-Fi Alliance, I distinctly remember a presentation made by a vice president of CompUSA®, describing the high return rate of Wi-Fi gear in retail.[176] He cited one of the main reasons as *poor coverage*. Buyers, reading the package label clearly stating a range of 300 feet, expected that range in their home installations. Much to their surprise (and disappointment), the range was closer to 100 feet, and sometimes even less. Furthermore, at that range, the "guaranteed" 11Mbps connection speed was not achievable, and lower speeds occurred. While the lower data speed was not an issue,[177] the incomplete coverage range was.

As the following figure shows, all connectivity technologies (wired and wireless) exercise the same tradeoff: the longer the range is, the lower the connection speed can be. I will not discuss in detail the reason for this phenomenon and, for now, we will take this for granted.

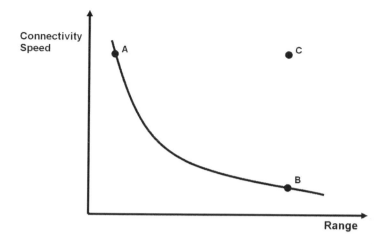

Figure 47—Connectivity technology speed vs. range

I remember hearing consumers disappointed with Wi-Fi products, claiming "they don't work" and complaining about the "lies" printed on the product packages. Were those lies? Not really. The *theoretical* range of those products, achievable in perfect conditions, could have been 300 feet. That is what the engineering department in those product companies claimed. The marketing department went ahead and printed those numbers on the packages and data sheets. However, the home environment is far from perfect or theoretical. There are *path losses* due to wall penetration of radio waves, and *multipath* reflections of signals, not to mention interference due to other radio products working in the same area (wireless video monitoring systems and baby monitors, for example). The worst part is that the consumers had to find that out for themselves, taking the technology into the *trough of disillusionment,* but such that the industry did recover from and reached a very productive plateau.

During my involvement with the ultra-wideband technology, a technology capable of delivering ultra-high-speed connectivity at short ranges, I encountered another case of unmet expectations. During a meeting with a leading Korean consumer electronics manufacturer, the engineers we met described an application in which a set top box would be connected to multiple TVs using an ultra-wideband link. They knew that the expected connection speed of this technology would be 480Mbps, and that the expected range of this technology was thirty feet. What escaped them (not due to their fault, but due to unclear messaging from the ultra-wideband technology companies) was that there was an "either/or" in there. Figure 47 shows that as the range goes up, the connectivity speed goes down, and to maintain a higher connectivity speed, the range must be shorter. While the ultra-wideband technology could (and will) deliver up to 480Mbps, it will do it at ranges of ten feet or less (as depicted by *Point A* on the graph). While the technology can deliver a signal to a range of thirty feet, it will do so at a speed of 100Mbps or less (as depicted by *Point B* on the graph). That certainly did not address the application and scenario sought by the engineers we met. Furthermore, they did not consider the interference and frequency-sharing issue. While in my home town of Plano, Texas, the homes are large and the distance between them is great, that is not the case in Korea or Japan, just to name two. There, in large apartment buildings, you might expect that four inches behind your TV, facing the opposite direction, will be your neighbor's TV. If both use the same ultra-wideband (or any other wireless) technology, they will interfere with one another. One of my colleagues at Texas Instruments referred to that meeting as the "scorched earth" meeting, in which I broke many myths they might have had. Does that mean that the ultra-wideband technology is no good? No, it doesn't. The ultra-wideband technology is great for quite a few applications. It is just not good for the one envisioned by those engineers. They came to believe there was a performance *Point C* on the graph, a point that does not exist. In order to determine the applications that connectivity technology *can* enable, we must choose a point that is *on* the graph, such as *A* or *B*. Choosing *Point A* for the ultra-wideband technology represents speeds up to 480Mbps at a range of ten feet. Not surprisingly, in early 2004, the USB Implementers Forum chose to adopt ultra-wideband as the underlying technology for the *wireless* version of their highly successful USB standard, naming it Wireless USB™.

The conclusion from these stories is simple. You must be *pragmatic* in describing the capabilities of the emerging technology. You must understand the scenarios, environments, and applications in which people will use the new product or technology, and be realistic about its capabilities and expected performance in those scenarios. Over hyping the product or technology will only lead to a much stronger fall to disillusionment, possibly one that will not be recovered from.

Don't get me wrong—I am not proposing to *under hype* the emerging technology or new product. Under hyping it may cause it not to be adopted at all, but over hyping it—while it will allow you to sell to the few initial early adopters—will not get it to the main market. After all, as Abraham Lincoln said: "You can fool all the people some of the time, and some of the people all the time, but you cannot fool all the people all the time." Not that I am suggesting you are trying to fool them, but if I translate that into product marketing words: if you over-promise and under-deliver product performance, you will not be able to sell the product beyond the initial early adopter market.

---

[173] The term *top 10* came from General Electric, which decided every year to rank all employees into the top 10% performers (top 10), the bottom 10% performers (bottom 10), and the "other 80." Other companies emulated this annual ranking process, differentiating the *top 10* performers by higher pay increases, higher bonuses, and more stock options, while the *bottom 10* performers faced *performance improvement plans*, or even termination.

[174] www.strategyplus.org.

[175] Jackie Fenn, Alexander Linden, "Gartner Hype Cycle Special Report for 2005," Gartner Inc.

[176] He described it as 40%, compared to an average of 25% for general networking equipment.

[177] After all, the bottleneck of home Internet connectivity was, back in the early 2000s, the broadband connection, DSL or cable, that were at best capable of delivering up to 1.5Mbps.

Chapter 18
Conclusion—Bowling With A Crystal Ball

"Two roads diverged in the wood, and I—
I took the one less traveled by,
And that has made all the difference."
Robert Frost, "The Road not Taken," 1920

I consider myself an innovator. Maybe it's because of the adrenaline rush we get when we innovate something that will potentially change the *rules of the game*. Maybe it's because I lose my attention in mature markets with commodity products. I am guessing that if you reached this part of the book—unless you started with reading the conclusion—that you are the same.

Innovation can be a random act, but it can also be an intentional and deliberate process. In fact, I submit to you that people like to think of market disruption as a random act, because it takes away the responsibility of innovating and disrupting and lets them act like victims, rather than doing it to others.

The innovation process relies on people and the human factor: the ability to believe in the future, despite how inconceivable it might appear; the ability to find opportunities in this future; and the ability to influence the creation of a supporting ecosystem to make it happen. This book includes the process to create the right environment to have strategists innovate.

The takeaways I would like you to take from *Bowling with a Crystal Ball* are these:

- There are reasons, psychological and others, why technology trends will continue along the same trend line they have for many years. Those technologies will reach levels of performance, compactness, and cost that are hard to imagine today. You have to overcome this *disbelief* and embrace your findings. Instead of asking *whether* the technologies will reach those characteristics, ask yourself, *what will they enable?*

- High technologies emerged, initially fueled by markets for products that needed them. However, once the initial investment in a technology has occurred, the companies that focus on those technologies continue to improve along very steep trend lines, causing those technologies to go beyond the maximum required performance for the markets that gave them their initial investments. At that point, those technologies will potentially disrupt the markets that gave birth to them, or move on to disrupt other markets.

- If you observe the development and disruptions of markets, you will notice consistencies in how those disruptions occur. They will occur by adding mobility, moving from mechanical to solid state, and adding other dimensions of value. To find the opportunities for disruptions, you need to find a market that has those opportunities, and find the technological trend that will make it happen. Put the two together and you will cause a disruption.

- In the $1.3 trillion electronic product market, every tiny opportunity can cause a billion-dollar disruption. With some 20% of that market represented by semiconductor content, every tiny semiconductor opportunity translates into new, hundreds-of millions-of-dollars markets.

- Every *major* disruption creates opportunities for many *derivative* disruptions. While innovators typically target the main disruptions, you can target the derivative disruptions and still create hundreds of millions of dollars worth of markets. In this book, I intended to give you the tools to be able to identify those derivative opportunities as well, and not only the main ones.

- Even once the innovation occurs, the probability of it creating a major market is tiny. So many pieces of a puzzle need to fall into place to create an industry, an ecosystem, a value chain capable of consuming the product, service, or technology invented to create billion-dollar revenue. Many forces work against the disruption. Your responsibility does not end with creating the invention. That was the easy part. The hard part is navigating it through the creation of an industry and an ecosystem that supports it. To achieve that, you need passion, conviction, and persuasion. You need to identify the visionaries in other companies, required to support this market disruption, and get them on your side.

- One key trait you need to adopt is pragmatism. Do not confuse pragmatism with conservatism, a force that works against innovation. Pragmatism means having a realistic view of how users will adopt a technology and how consumers will use it. This would be the time to realize that you are *not* the average consumer, and that the future market for your product, service, or technology is made of average consumers, and not you.

Do you have what it takes?

"…You've got to ask yourself a question: Do I feel lucky? Well, do you, punk?" (Clint Eastwood as *Dirty Harry*, 1971). I hope this book taught you that luck has almost nothing to do with creating disruption. You do not need to be lucky (well, you shouldn't be *unlucky* either). You need to have the right "stuff" to be a *disruptor*. What is this "stuff"? Read on.

Technical and business savvy

Being a technologist is not enough if you cannot think about the business aspects of a technical disruption. Being a businessperson is not enough if you do not understand the technology enough to know what it can, and cannot do. You have to be savvy at both. You do not need to have a PhD in electronic engineering, computer sciences, mathematics, physics, marketing, or business, but you need to know enough.

The technical background must be as multidisciplinary as possible. The more you know about other things that are related—and even not directly related—the more you can harness the success of the proposed disruption. You do not need to have a deep understanding of everything. Nobody does. Nevertheless, the more you know about different things, the more you can find disruption implementations. My understanding of how disk drives work led me to know that as they increase in capacity, they increase in speed. This led me to innovations at Texas Instruments. You must understand how an electrical motor works. How radar works.

How the Internet works. You must be extremely curious to learn all of this, and it takes a long time to get to know all of this. If you have not done it thus far, chances are it is too late to start now. It also indicates that you do not have the required curiosity, which is not something you can simply turn on. Your knowledge must be only "knee-deep." You do not need to be an expert in any of those fields. You will need to tap into the experts, and probably get them involved in the disruption process. You need to know enough to *know what is possible.*

Most of all, you need to have scars. Whenever I interview a person in a position from which I expect to see disruptive innovation, I ask about his or her scars. Failures are as important as successes. Successes without failures are less valuable. The more experience, the better.

Ability to dive into details

Although your knowledge must be very wide and multidisciplinary as well as only knee-deep, you need to have the ability to learn instantly and dive into the details. There are several reasons for that. One is that you need to understand what is possible and what is not, with every piece of the technology. You do not need to be able to develop different components of the whole product, but you need to be able to have a very detailed conversation with the people who will be developing those components. The second reason is that to convince others, you need to have a credible amount of information. The more you know, the more credibility you will have.

"Big Picture" view

When you sit in a commercial jetliner, getting ready to take off, look through the window and try to situate yourself at the airport. It is hard. When you are on the ground, your eyes are less than thirty feet higher than the ground; you cannot see the structure of the airport. The airplane is on the taxiway, but you cannot see where the taxiway will lead. It is hard to see how to get to the runway. Pilots get very specific instructions from the ground controller, and follow signs on the sides of the taxiways and runways to get to the right place. Once the plane takes off, look outside the window again and see the airport. All of a sudden, it makes much more sense. You can see how the taxiways lead to the runways, and how runway positions keep airplanes from colliding right after takeoff. When you fly higher, say at 10,000 feet, you will notice where the airport is located in the city, and how far it is from different landmarks. At 30,000 feet, you might actually lose important details of the overall picture.

In a similar way, it is hard to see "the big picture" of the market you are in. You tend to focus on the details closer to you, and miss the details that cannot be easily seen, yet which have a dramatic impact on your success or failure. Your ability to be "outside" of your company and view the market, value chain, and ecosystem from 10,000 feet (the altitude from which bombers drop their bombs), dramatically affects your ability to successfully disrupt a market and competitively position a product or service there.

Visionary

What does the word *visionary* mean to you? I checked with a few dictionaries and got definitions such as "a person given to fanciful speculations and enthusiasms with little regard for what is possible,"[178] or "One who is given to impractical or speculative ideas; a dreamer,"[179] or "Having the nature of fantasies or dreams; illusory."[180] I've been called all of those. They're not very complimentary, are they? To me, though, the definition of *visionary* is different. It is the ability to visualize the future to the point of envisioning yourself living in it. Sometimes I am jealous of my eight- and 6-year-old daughters. They have imaginary friends, but the vividness and detail with which they can describe them is what I need today. This may be a skill you lose if you do not use it as often as *they* do. If you cannot leave the present to visualize the future, you will miss the opportunities that lie there. You need to be able to "time shift" or transport yourself into the future, four to eight years out, and be able to see the details. If you can do that, you will be able to create disruptions. If not, the present will hold you back. Remaining entrenched in the present means you will not be ready to accept that in 2008-2009 the average PC hard disk drive will have 2.8 terabytes of capacity, and that there will be an application that will require it. Being a visionary will not only help you accept this fact, but actually to find opportunities around it.

Understanding how people use products

So many products fell into the abyss of history because they did not work the way people expected them to. Christensen, in *The Innovator's Solution*, described how Sony was so successful in developing innovative products (such as the Walkman and others), due to its CEO's ability to understand how people use products. I described this ability in detail in this book, but you need to know if you have this ability or not. It really is part of being a visionary—being able to close your eyes and visualize the product or service and how people will use it in different day-to-day scenarios. Furthermore, you need to have the ability to describe this usage to potential consumers, reporters, analysts, and people in your own company. The more disruptive it is, the harder it is to convince people of this new usage.

Pragmatic and methodic

Being a visionary does not mean that you should accept things without question. Things need to make sense. People need to have a reason to use the product or service you are envisioning, for the price you think they should pay. Though it is easy to consider the entire world population as your target market, do six billion consumers really need your product? Segmentation is a key activity in determining the target market size. It will be extremely important to understand who would really use your product and why. You cannot leave any stone unturned. You need to understand the price people are willing to pay. You need to understand the relationship between the new product or service and existing ones. You cannot fool all the people all the time. For your disruption to achieve the goals you have set, it has to be right for all the people in your target market. Solram Electronics did sell a few hundreds of its InterHome product, but it did not reach the entire target market. It is easy to sell to the early adopters, but you must pragmatically tailor your value proposition to the mainstream market to achieve your goals. At the end, the entire consumption of the product or service must make sense. If you don't pursue a full understanding of how it will (or will not) make sense, your probability of success is lower. To me, this pursuit is the true meaning of the word *pragmatism.*

Optimistic

Just as being a visionary does *not* mean you cannot be a pragmatic one, being pragmatic does *not* mean you should not be optimistic. When I joined as the head of the consumer electronics connectivity group at Texas Instruments in 2003, there was a project that was highly risky, very complicated, and required us to step into unknown territories. In other words—everybody wanted to kill it. Except me. While everyone was pointing out the (obvious) risks, I suggested we kick off the project and list all the risks, with mitigation programs for them. The group was accustomed to ranking risks by color. *Green* indicated a manageable risk, one that has little impact on the overall success of the program; *yellow* meant a risk that could be mitigated but had a higher level of impact on overall success; and *red* meant a risk that did not have a clear mitigation plan or had a significant impact on the success of the program. Most programs launched had three or four *green* risks, one or two *yellow* ones, and no *red* risks. When we met to review the risk assessment, the team identified more than ten risks. One of them was *yellow.* The others were *red.* To their surprise, I was supportive in that meeting. Instead of challenging them criticality, trying to turn *red* risks into *yellow* or *green* ones, I appreciated them for recognizing the risks.

If the team did not recognize the risks, the risks would surprise the team. If they did recognize them upfront, they would not be surprised. Then I asked them if there was any chance, even the remotest one, that we could navigate through this minefield of risks. As long as there was a way to navigate, we simply needed to mitigate those risks as we went, and keep our eyes and ears open to any change in those risks. Visionaries need to see the *possibilities* and not the *impossibilities*.

Passionate, persuasive, and persistent

The bigger the disruption is, the more resistance it faces from consumers, the market, the value chain, ecosystem players, and worst of all—your own company. People are risk-averse and change-resistant beings. You need to know that you start by having no friends, but it should not deter you. The three P's you need to overcome resistance are passion, persuasiveness, and persistence. You need to convince people of the value of the new product or service. You cannot do it if you are not convinced yourself. A key element of your ability to convince them is the passion with which you talk about the new product. You need to be able to walk on water and make it seem easy. People will initially see you are a dreamer, completely disconnected from reality but, with time, your passion will rub off on them. This is how you will create your initial "believer" core group. The group will continue to spread the word further. Passion is only one component of persuasion. You'll need to use other components too. One thing to keep in mind—keep your integrity. Do not stretch the *truth*. Stretch the *possibilities*. Finally, you need to be persistent. You cannot let setbacks and resistance discourage you. Your attitude must be such that as long is it makes sense to you, it will eventually make sense to others, and it is just a matter of time and continuous "pounding" of the gospel that will turn the resistors around. The late US Navy Admiral Hyman Rickover, considered "The Father of the Nuclear Navy," said, "Good ideas are not adopted automatically. They must be driven into practice with courageous patience."

Ability to take bullets, even in your back

In late 2001, Marty Singer took over the role of the chief executive of PCTEL, after serving a few years as a board member, and later as the chairman of the board. We talked about discovering that the DSL modem we had been developing was the wrong product to develop. He asked me if I knew how to spot a pioneer, and before I answered, he said, "By the arrows in his back." Visionaries face resistance from customers, from competitors, from other competing products, and from other players in the ecosystem. But the worst resistance comes from their own company. Fearing change, not believing in it, preferring the "evil we know," the companies turn on their visionaries. To create disruptions, you must be able to face that resistance and crash it. You will do it one person at a time. You will face countless internal meetings where they will ridicule you, they will de-prioritize your projects, and they will assign the least-skilled engineers to it, at minimum budget. You will win this battle one person at a time. You will have to be persistent.

Risk-taker

Disruptions are risky. They are also very rewarding (assuming, of course, they succeed). It might be obvious, but you *must* be willing to accept the risk of failure. More disruptions fail than succeed. It is a fact of life. You might have missed something in visualizing the use of the product that will lead to its demise before it ever takes off. Most disruptive products actually end up put to use in ways developers of the technology didn't consider. As long as there is a use case that the product can fill, economically, it will succeed. But it might fail. If you are concerned about your job security to the point that it prevents you from accepting the risks associated with disruptions, this is not for you. It is obviously easier to assume risks if you are already independently wealthy, and losing your job will only mean you can embark on that long-needed vacation. If you need your job so you and your family can survive in the next year, to the point it immobilizes you—you are not a risk-taker. I believe you cannot do your job right (any job, not only a disruptive job) if you are consistently concerned about your job security. Only if you are not afraid to do the right thing for your company, even if it does not seem to be the popular or favorite thing to do at the time, will you truly serve your company right. There were countless times in my professional career when I did what I thought was right for the company, "whether it liked it or not." You should not confuse this with not listening to others, who might have different opinions than yours, but you must consider them and then do what you think is right. If people perceive you as a "lone rider," you will not get the company support you need. The answer is somewhere in between.

Politician

I call myself a politician. People's reaction to this word is not necessarily favorable, given government's partisan political history. Dictionary definitions for the word *politics* vary from "the science or art of political government" to "use of intrigue or strategy in obtaining any position of power or control." Industry politics is the science (and art) of garnering support among different companies with different business agendas for cooperating toward a joint industry goal. Every company might get something else out of it. Industry politics might include cooperation of competitors in creating a market to compete over, as well as outmaneuvering your competitors to achieve a favorable competitive position for your company in this market. It is a tricky science. You must own those skills; otherwise, your disruptive ideas will be lost in history.

It takes other people too

I talked about the "stuff" *you* need to have to turn your ideas into successful market disruptions, but I need to emphasize that you cannot do it all by yourself. It will take a high-performance team of people dedicated to make it happen. Most of them will be specialists in specific aspects of the overall solution. You will need to win them over with your idea to the point they will be willing to go the extra mile for this idea. You will need each person to (i) focus on his or her area of expertise and do the impossible; and (ii) be an agent of this disruption, spreading the word, and convincing other people, whether inside the company or outside it, of the greatness of the new technology, product, or service.

When is it time to move on?

The product (or technology) life cycle diagram is all too familiar. We tend to focus on the early adoption and fast growth stages, and sometimes on the maturity stage. However, it is the back end of it that interests me at this time—the *decline* of the new technology.

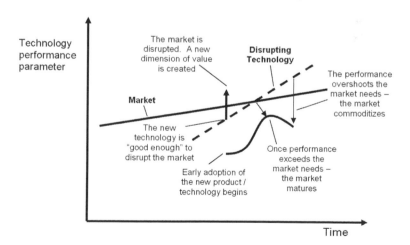

Figure 48—The life cycle of a disrupting technology

In Figure 48 I attempted to combine the market disruption by a new technology and the product life cycle in that market. The number of units consumed, revenue in dollars, or other similar parameters measure the product life cycle. Regardless of the parameter you use to describe the size of the market, there is no market for the new product *before* the disruption occurs, simply because there is no product before then. Once the disruption occurs and the new product enters the market, you can say that the market begins its life cycle. Following Christensen's disruption theory, the disruption actually occurs when the performance of the new technology does not meet the required performance in the market. As you see in Figure 48, the product life cycle begins with the early adoption when the technology is only "good enough" for the market needs.

Two things then happen in parallel: the performance improves to meet the market requirements, and the market matures. When the performance starts to exceed the market needs, the market starts commoditizing. There is nothing to improve anymore, and the only available dimension of competition is price (and cost). Companies then focus on cost cutting (whether *variable*, or *production* costs, or *fixed* costs). Any further improvements in the technology that once disrupted this market are irrelevant, while this technology goes on to disrupt other markets or, as suggested before, may even disrupt the same market again, causing the beginning of a completely new product life cycle for the same market. Companies refer to the latter phenomena as the "S-curves" theory. The beginning of a new S-curve is only a result of a new disruption of the same market. Figure 49 demonstrates it.

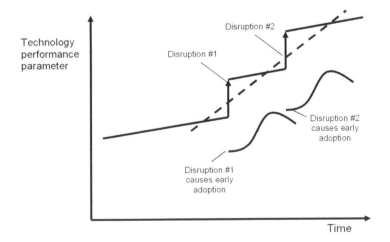

Figure 49—Market disruption and S-Curves

So what do you do when the market matures once the disrupting technology overshoots the market performance needs? There is no doubt that there is a lot of profit in a commodity market. In fact, there are companies and business units within companies that turn in very nice profits from commodities. However, it is a completely different type of company or business compared with the market during the early days of the disruption and the fast growth of the market. Don't get me wrong—I admire those companies and those businesses, but I find it personally very hard to get excited over selling a commodity. If you are in the business of selling commodities, I apologize for my comments. I am what Dr. Gary Hamel calls a "grey haired revolutionary." I get my energy from revolutionizing industries, and not squeezing costs out of them.

So when the market reaches maturity, commoditization, or even the decline phase, and you are a revolutionary like me, you have two options: find the next technology to disrupt the same market, or seek the next market to be disrupted by the technology that by now overshot the current market.

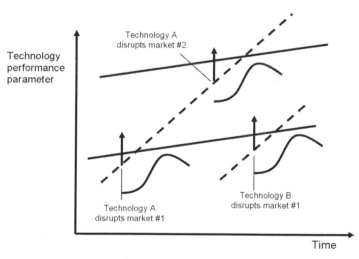

Figure 50—The next disruption

In his work, Christensen focused mostly on finding the next technology that would disrupt the same market. I, on the other hand (not out of compassion to the already-disrupted market), am taking the other route. I continue to follow the technology that disrupted one market, to see which market it is capable of disrupting next. I am probably taking an easier route here, but there is nothing wrong with that. Why is it an easier route? Once market disruption occurs, it introduces a new dimension of value to this market. Consumers will take a few years to realize the new value. It takes a long time to realize the newly created value, and appreciate the opportunities from it. It will also take a relatively long time to settle on usage habits of the new products, and sometimes the usage habits during the maturity of the market and products are different from the ones envisioned when the disruption occurred and the market was in its early adoption phase. It is the same human factor that causes our performance needs to be much slower than technology improvements. This enables market disruption, and makes it hard for us to see how market disruption could occur again. Furthermore, once we disrupt the market, even if we would prefer not to follow the development of this market through maturity and decline, we are more interested in exploiting the financial potential of the market before disrupting it again.

For all those reasons, it is easier for us to envision how technology A will disrupt market #2 than to identify technology B, which will disrupt the same market #1, the disruption of which we just witnessed (if not *caused*). Market #1 is still in turmoil from the previous disruption, while market #2 is in a mature, commodity phase, and, therefore, ripe for disruption.

This brings me to the question, "*When* is it time to move on?" You can move on when you realize there is an opportunity for disruption and you initiated the first moves to capitalize on it. This, however, would most likely be too early. The people who need to drive this all the way to market disruption are still missing the "lunatic" visionary that you are. At Texas Instruments, in 2004, I envisioned a new market disruption. Since that disruption has not occurred yet, I cannot discuss it in detail. Driving a market disruption within a conservative, multi-business, profit-oriented company such as Texas Instruments was an uphill battle. However, this is where persistence and persuasion pay off. After a while, I managed to convince the top management and the operational management that this disruption is inevitable, that we are seeing it before everyone else, and that we are in a position to become a market leader once the disruption occurs and for some time after that. I could feel the level of "buy in" from people involved growing as the level of engineering resources allocated to the new project increased, and the top engineers were allocated for the research. But then, in 2005, I found myself in the middle of a major organizational change at Texas Instruments, and I opted to move to TI's biggest business unit, the mobile phone one. While keeping in touch with the people who were involved with the project until the organizational change, I saw the decline in the momentum. Don't get me wrong—I am still convinced the disruption will occur. It is just that I don't believe it will start in Dallas, Texas. The lack of passion and conviction is what led to the loss of momentum.

The second alternative is to move on once the market disruption occurs, and the new products hit the market. In my opinion, even this might be a bit too early, for several reasons. In the early adopter stage, usage habits of the new products will still change. It takes a visionary to be able to adapt the new product to the new usage habits to turn it into a success. The visionary is you. If you leave now, you may be leaving the product in the hands of people who will *stay on target* and miss the fact that the product still needs some changes to become a success. In that stage, even though the team created a product, they are still somewhat skeptical of its market success and its ability to disrupt a market in a significant way. Without your continuous passion, conviction, and persuasion skills, they will find it too easy to accept initial market rejection (and believe me, there *will* be initial market rejection!) and kill the product in its infancy, missing the market opportunity. Last, but not least, the early adoption phase is a tricky one. The market itself is not convinced. Players in the market may fear cannibalization of their business models. There is an overall resistance to adopting the new product and the new technology. After all, it does not perform as well as the old technology, and who really cares for the new value-add? When cellular phones appeared, nobody believed there would be a market for more than one million subscribers worldwide. Today, cell phone markers are eying the *fourth* billion. Your conviction is still required to flush out the early adopters and put those products in their hands. It is further required to *cross the chasm* (using Geoffrey Moore's terminology[181]) and get this product into the mainstream market.

However, when the product enters the mainstream market and enters the *tornado* (to use Moore's terminology once again), when it is performing "good enough," the business becomes an operationally oriented one. The product matures to its near-commodity form, and the market acknowledges its disruption. There will always be those who still believe this is a temporary thing, and common sense will prevail while the market returns to the previous products, but market players who embrace the new products outnumber those who do not. Neither the market nor your company needs your passion, conviction, or persuasion anymore. The disruption finally took on a life of its own. It is time to move on. For me, anyway. I find it hard to believe that the same person can have the creativity, innovation, passion, and conviction to lead a market in its early adoption phase, and yet be disciplined and structured enough to continue and make the right operational decisions when the market is *inside the tornado*, or in its maturity. I am wrong, of course, as there are quite a few examples of leaders who took a start-up company from day one to billion-dollar revenues in a mature business. I am not one of them. While I did run a $100 million business unit at Texas Instruments, playing in a mature (and mostly *commoditized*) market, improving its growth and profitability, I didn't find it exciting.

Bowling with a Crystal Ball mostly talked about the $1.3 trillion electronic product market, although it focused on the $155 billion *consumer electronics* market,[182] the $120 billion *personal computing* market, the $180 billion *mobile telecommunications* market, and other consumer-related markets. However, the concepts in this book are applicable to many other markets, for products and services, consumer-related or not, technology-related or not. Do not let the focus and examples of this book lead you to think the concepts are limited in any way. All you have to do is apply them to your market of interest.

With this last thought, I bid you farewell. I hope you enjoyed reading this book as much as I enjoyed writing it. Please check www. bowlingwithacrystalball.com for additional information that might be available in the future to support this book, and to keep up to date with my latest thoughts and articles on the topic. Good luck!

---

[178] WordNet® 2.1, Princeton University.
[179] The American Heritage® Dictionary of the English Language, Fourth Edition.
[180] Same.
[181] Geoffrey Moore, "Crossing the Chasm," Harper Business, 1991.
[182] According to the Consumer Electronics Association (CEA), www. ce.org, the revenue in 2006 was $145 billion, and in 2007 is expected to be $155 billion.

Index